Touring with Legends

A comic's tale of opening for Rodney Dangerfield, Joan Rivers, George Carlin, Tom Jones and many more...

By Dennis Blair

Touring with Legends

Touring with Legends
By Dennis Blair
Copyright © 2021 Dennis Blair
No part of this book may be reproduced in any form or by any means, electronic, mechanical, digital, photocopying, or recording, except for inclusion of a review, without permission in writing from the publisher or Author. No copyright is claimed for the photos within this book. They are used for the purposes of publicity only.

Published in the USA by:
BearManor Media
1317 Edgewater Dr #110
Orlando, FL 32804
www.bearmanormedia.com

Perfect ISBN 978-1-62933-672-5
Case ISBN 978-1-62933-673-2

BearManor Media, Orlando, Florida
Printed in the United States of America
Book design by Robbie Adkins, www.adkinsconsult.com
Cover photo by Ed Foster

Table of Contents

CHAPTER 1: "GET OFF THE STAGE!" 1

CHAPTER 2: DANGERFIELD'S 9

CHAPTER 3: JACKIE MASON 12

CHAPTER 4: SEINFELD ET AL (featuring Rich Hall, ... 19
    Paul Reiser and Carol Leifer)

CHAPTER 5 : RODNEY: THE EARLY YEARS 24
    (featuring David Frye, The Unknown Comic and Paul Newman)

CHAPTER 6: JAMES BROWN 34

CHAPTER 7: PAUL ANKA 36
    (also Dionne Warwick and Marvin Hamlisch)

CHAPTER 8: THE BEACH BOYS 41

CHAPTER 9: RODNEY'S NEW PROTEGE 44
    (featuring George Carlin)

CHAPTER 10: THE MAGIC BUS 52

CHAPTER 11: SAM KINISON and other stories 54

CHAPTER 12: EASY MONEY 63
    (featuring Joe Pesci and the Playmate of the Year)

CHAPTER 13: TV LAND AND OTHER RODNEY ADVENTURES ... 70
    (with Bill Murray and the Atlantic City Gypsies)

CHAPTER 14: THE RESCUE COMIC (rescues the Pointer 78
    Sisters, Eddie Rabbit and Ben Vereen)

CHAPTER 15: BEST-SELLING AUTHOR ROBERT LUDLUM 81

CHAPTER 16: THE BIG KISS OFF (or "How I Lost my Gig") 84

CHAPTER 17: HOWARD STERN 91

CHAPTER 18: TREADING WATER 94
    (featuring Shirley Bassey)

CHAPTER 19: GILBERT GOTTFRIED 102

CHAPTER 20: ENTER JOAN RIVERS (AND GARRY SHANDLING) .. 107

CHAPTER 21: ELVIS PRESLEY (SORT OF)..........................115
CHAPTER 22: JOAN RIVERS PART TWO 120
(with Linda Hopkins and Father Guido Sarducci)
PHOTO GALLERY..124
CHAPTER 23: MORE GARRY SHANDLING 134
CHAPTER 24: THE TONIGHT SHOW..............................139
CHAPTER 25: UH...I'VE MADE IT?.................................142
CHAPTER 26: BACK TO THE DRAWING BOARD.............148
CHAPTER 27: THE FOUR TOPS 151
CHAPTER 28: GLADYS KNIGHT AND THE PIPS..............155
CHAPTER 29: JULIE BUDD, THREE DOG NIGHT, ...158
 GLORIA ESTEFAN AND ELAYNE BOOSLER
CHAPTER 30 : TOM JONES..167
CHAPTER 31: GEORGE CARLIN...................................172
CHAPTER 32: A STEADY GIG IN SHOW BUSINESS?............189
CHAPTER 33: RODNEY RETURNS 201
CHAPTER 34: "THE GEORGE CARLIN SHOW" AND MY 205
 OWN PERSONAL HELL
CHAPTER 35: JACKIE MASON SAVES VAUDEVILLE 215
CHAPTER 36: TROUBLE..223
CHAPTER 37: JOAN RIVERS ONE MORE TIME 236
CHAPTER 38: SKIPPING AHEAD (Billy Davis and Marilyn 238
 McCoo, Melissa Manchester, Charo, and Norm MacDonald)
AFTERWORD..243

Chapter 1.
"Get Off the Stage!"

THE SCENE: A thousand-seat theater somewhere in America. The show that the enthusiastic, rabid audience is there to see this evening is sold out.

The lights slowly dim as the crowd erupts in cheers and applause. They can hardly contain their excitement.

ANNOUNCER: "Ladies and Gentlemen, welcome to the Starlight Theater. Are you ready to rock and roll!??"

CROWD: Yyyyyyeeeeeeeeeeeaaaaaahhhh!!!"

ANNOUNCER: "Oh come on, you can do better than that, ARE YOU READY TO ROCK AND ROOOOLLLL!!"

CROWD: "YYYEEEEEEEUUUUUUUUOOOOOOOAAAAAAMMMM!!!"

ANNOUNCER: Okay. But before we get to our main attraction, please welcome to the stage our special guest this evening....

CROWD: "YYYYEEEEEAAA...HUH???????

ANNOUNCER: "DENNIS BLAIR!!!!"

CROWD: "NNNNNNOOOOOOOOOOOOOO!!!!!!!"

    My name is Dennis Blair. I realize that may mean little or nothing to most of you who are reading these pages, so let me explain. I'm a comedian who hasn't made the big time, and yet I've had a satisfying and interesting career and have made a very good living for the most part. I guess you could say I made the medium time.

    But since that means I am a virtual unknown to the populace at large, and since the fact that you're reading this means you probably have an interest in show business and in the subject at hand, please allow me to fill you in briefly on who I am and how I came to be associated with a whole bunch of famous people.

Touring with Legends

As of this writing I have been a professional entertainer for over 40 years, and a comedian for most of them, performing at clubs and theaters and banquet halls and casinos and state fairs and clam bakes and everywhere else where there's an audience and a paycheck. But for most of those years, for the bulk of my career, I have specialized in one particular area of the comedy business...I have been what is commonly referred to as the opening act.

You know what I mean. I'm the guy that goes on before the big-time headliner. I'm the guy who's "in the way." The minor annoyance whose entrance onstage makes you groan a little, then look at your watch, then turn to your spouse and say, "Let's go to the lobby and buy M&M's until Tony Orlando comes on." The person who's often referred to on the ticket or the program as "Special Guest," which of course registers in your mind as "Now I've gotta pay the babysitter for an extra half-hour."

The opening act. Even if he or she is talented and (surprise surprise) entertaining, you still didn't pay $77.50 to see this bozo. And if he's not talented and (horror of horrors) boring, you might fidget in your seat, mumble an obscenity, let out a raspberry, then finally yell, "Get off! Where's Carrot Top?"

And if you're a bit more even-tempered than that, the opener is still the person who you always try to get to the theatre just in time to miss. And if you do accidentally happen to catch him, he's the person you hate for at least the first four minutes of the show even if he's good. If he's not so good, you hate him the entire time he's onstage, right up until when he says, "Thank you, you've been a great audience." to people who've been fantasizing what they'd like to do to his nostrils with a serving fork.

I'm exaggerating a bit here. It's not always that bad. In fact, most audiences are fairly accepting of the opening act, some even going so far as to enjoy him. But it is also true that opening for an established star can be difficult at times. Basically, as an opening act, you're delaying the audience from seeing the person they paid to see. So they're pissed off at you already, even before they've heard your first joke. When I opened for Rodney Dangerfield during the height of his fame in the eighties, the predominantly male, beer-drinking college-age audiences would tell me I sucked before I even got to the microphone. That's a real confidence-booster. You haven't even told your first joke, and yet you suck.

"Hey Dennis, how'd your show go?"

"I'm not sure. It was hard to tell over all the booing."

Let me point out that I'm not being judgmental here. I've been guilty of the same thing as an audience member myself. Once I took my eight-year-old son to see the Beach Boys. The lights went down, and instead of the Beach Boys, out came this comedian who wasn't even on the bill. The reaction from the adrenaline-fueled audience was: "YAAAAAYY (then, after seeing him) OOOOOH." And I was right there with them. I found myself thinking things like, "Damn, I wonder how long he's gonna do. I wasn't expecting an opening act."

And then I thought, "Hey, wait a minute. I'm an opening act."

Most audiences were not as brutal to the opener as Rodney's concert crowds were, but some could make you feel just as uncomfortable in more subtle ways. I remember opening for singer/songwriter Melissa Manchester at the Concord hotel in the Catskill Mountains to a predominantly older audience, who seemed to have been instructed to ignore me and my little comedy skit at all costs. For the twenty minutes I was sentenced to be onstage, the biggest laughs I got were from the band members behind the curtain. As far as the audience was concerned, I was a plasma screen TV that they couldn't turn off. (One guy kept clicking a remote and saying, "Damn, he's on every channel.") I left the stage to an ovation that lasted, at most, an eighth of a second. I had come off stage so quickly that Melissa wasn't ready to come out yet. The stage hands were running around in a panic yelling "Where's Melissa?" I turned to them and said, "She's probably waiting for my applause to die down."

Fortunately though, the audiences have usually been won over, and it's a great feeling. Just don't expect me to go rushing back to the Catskills.

If truth be told, I'm not strictly or exclusively an opening act. No one goes into show business saying, "Screw the money, screw the fame, I want to miss headlining by inches and be an opening act forever." It just seems to have worked out that way for me over the bulk of my career.

In the eighties, during the so-called "comedy boom," I was an up-and-coming comedian who would often headline at the comedy clubs that had sprung up on every corner of every city in the country. (In New York City alone in 1982 there were about a hundred comedy clubs per square mile. Nationwide, comedy clubs outnumbered McDonalds, Starbucks and ATM's. And they all had those annoying, cutesy-poo names, too, like "Giggles," "Yuk Yuks," "Funnybone," etc. (I seem to remember playing a club called "Fucking Hilarious," or maybe that was just a dream I had.)

During that "comedy boom" I did a bunch of TV shows, including the Tonight Show and the Phil Donahue Show and Live at Five in New York. I also appeared on the shows that proliferated on every channel such as "Evening at the Improv" and "Comic Strip Live," the ones that featured brick walls and goofy MC's and showcased so many comics so often that people got sick of watching comedians on TV and started the backlash which eventually became known as the "comedy bust." But times were good for comedians back then, and work was plentiful. I headlined many comedy clubs, but even so, the nature of my act was such that I was most often, for a major portion of my career, hired to open for celebrities.

My stage persona is that of a goofy guy who uses a guitar to do song parodies and musical takeoffs along with my standup material. This presentation has gotten me a lot of work on my own over the years. It has also made me a natural choice for established comedians who want an opening act who can get the audience in a comedy frame of mind without conflicting with their own comedic style.

The reason I became a "musical comedian" is simple. My first love was not comedy. It was music. I had played in bands and as a solo act since I was in my teens, and I was pretty good at the craft. I had always thought I would forge a career as a singer-songwriter, in the mold of a Paul Simon or a James Taylor, but without that pesky heroin addiction. As it turned out, my dreams of being a rock star were shared by approximately fifty-seven million other teenage kids, so my chances of making it were right up there with winning the lottery or climbing Mount Everest or running into Rush Limbaugh at a PETA rally.

While I was waiting for my rock star dreams to come to fruition, I started playing in "club date" bands to earn money. Club dates were bookings for bands that played at wedding and bar-mitzvahs, and I was a valuable asset in these bands because I could play pop songs by ear and was also a good singer, so I could sing a lot of the songs as well. That was the good news.

The bad news was that the band members were forced by the circumstances to play those cheesy versions of songs you all remember from Aunt Gretta's anniversary party. You know: "Feelings." "Color My World." "You Light Up My Life." I'm getting nauseous just remembering them. And even when we did do the occasional "hip" tune (i.e., "Jeremiah Was A Bullfrog"), it was either played at a ridiculous tempo or phrased in such a way that even deaf people could tell we were...well....a bunch of white guys.

To break up the monotony (and the agony) of doing these shows, I would often go out on my own and perform the popular songs of the day in "wine and cheese" clubs on Long Island. These were not the greatest of gigs. The clubs were dark and smelly (I still have some residual "Au De Incense" stench caught in my lungs), and the people were usually too engrossed in either conversation or the effects of cheap Sangria to pay much attention to me. But at least I got to perform the way I wanted to. I also got to meet my future wife, Peggy, who worked as a waitress in one wine and cheese club in particular called, for some reason, "Fern's Harness Shop" (that name always puzzled me. I never really understood the connection between harnesses and cheese). Peggy would often jeopardize her own livelihood by going up to people who were talking through my set and telling them, as politely as possible, to shut the fuck up.

(Interesting aside: At one of these Long Island bars, I first met Billy Joel. This was during his "52nd Street" days, when he was nearing the height of his fame. I had always been a huge fan of his, and to see him sitting at the bar was one of the most exciting things that had happened in my young life so far. I actually summoned the nerve to go up to him and slobber, like a typical star-struck idiot, "I'm such a fan of yours, I can't believe you're here in this bar, this is such an honor, please lick me!"...or words to that effect. Billy turned to me and, obviously impressed with my enthusiasm, said, "Hey, ya wanna come into the bathroom and watch me take a shit?"

Years later, when I was opening for Rodney Dangerfield at Westbury Music Fair, I came offstage and ran into Billy in the backstage hallway. Billy was a big Rodney fan, and had watched my show, completely sober by the way. He stuck out his hand and said, 'Dennis! Good show!" He obviously didn't remember me from our fateful meeting at that Long Island bar. I briefly considered asking him if he wanted to watch me take a shit, but decided against it.

Later on that evening I lived through a kind of shoe-on-the-other-foot moment. Billy was as big a fan of Rodney as I was of Billy, and was as nervous hanging out with Rodney in his dressing room as I had been running in to him all those years ago. Peggy and I sat on the sofa in Rodney's room and watched as Billy attempted, like many people do, to be funny when hanging out with a comedian.

BILLY: "Hey Rodney, on my next tour, I'm gonna have a TV onstage that'll be turned on to the Beverly Hillbillies or something while we play. Whaddya think?"

Rodney laughed politely at the thought, and then changed the subject. As they talked, Billy sensed another opportunity to put in a word about his tour...

BILLY: "Yeah, and like I said, we're gonna have a TV onstage for my next tour."

Rodney shot Billy a disparaging look and said, "That was KIND of funny the first time." Billy shrunk down in his seat and left soon afterwards.)

So there you have it, my first "famous persons" story. Heartwarming, isn't it? (And you were gonna buy a novel.)

Anyway, there I was at Fern's, night after night, singing sensitive 'sixties and 'seventies songs for people who were minutes away from either throwing up or going into cardiac arrest from snorting just a little bit too much cocaine. One night, fed up with the inattention I was getting, I used one of my breaks to come up with a parody of the then current Bee Gees hit, "Staying Alive." In keeping with the falsetto voices they used in the song, I called my creation "Singing Too High":

> *"Well you can tell by the way I wear my pants*
> *That I am a guy, I don't take no chance*
> *But when I sing I sound so dumb*

Like I've just been snorting helium...

> *Nobody today can tell what I am saying*
> *'Cause I'm singing too high, singing too high*
> *My career is zoomin', but I can't get a woman*
> *'Cause I'm singin' too high, singin' too high..."* etc. etc.

I didn't know what kind of reaction I would get, and I really didn't care. I just did it to break up the relentless monotony and frustration of being ignored by a roomful of people. As it turned out, the reaction was amazing. People stopped talking. They started listening. Some of them paused mid-puke so they could hear the lyrics. I was actually getting laughs. Something I had done just as a goof to alleviate the boredom was actually getting a positive and enthusiastic response. I started writing more parodies. John Denver's "You Fill Up My Senses" became "My Songs Make Me Nauseous." Donna Summer's "Love To Love You Baby" became "Pass the Kaopectate." Lou Rawls' "You'll Never Find (Another Love Like Mine)" became "You'll Never Find (a Penis Long as Mine)." Sophisticated comedy for the discerning listener.

I began dedicating one set per night to this. I would do some song parodies, then tell a few jokes I'd come up with, then open the floor to requests. This would consist of people basically yelling out songs or singers for me to do, and me trying to come up with a witty, funny parody right on the spot. Sometimes it would work. Sometimes they would just look at me. Sometimes the more intoxicated patrons would hear the songs and go, "Hey, those aren't the words." Often these were the club owners.

Largely as a result of my success, Fern's Harness Shop began to dedicate one night a week to comedy. I was to be the main attraction, they would call it "Comedy Night," and charge admission to come and see the show. The price they decided on was fifty cents, a sum that made it literally impossible for me to feel good about myself. Nevertheless, "Comedy Night" became a hit, and during this time some stars of the future could be seen doing sets there. Paul Reiser, Carol Leifer, Bob Nelson and Rob Bartlett all headlined at Fern's...for fifty cents. Rumor has it they make a lot more now.

Meanwhile, after a few months of song parodies and jokes and general fooling around, I found that I had somehow made the transition from singer to comedian. And it was at this time that I decided to make the move and audition at one of the clubs in Manhattan. As it turned out, the club I picked was "Dangerfield's."

Chapter 2.
Dangerfield's

By this time, Peggy and I had decided that two people as odd as we were belonged together, so in October of 1979 we moved into an apartment on 65th Street and First Avenue in Manhattan. The rent was $274.00 a month, very cheap for such a stylish neighborhood. Actually, 274 bucks a month was cheap for any neighborhood in Manhattan. I remember taking a cab ride after we'd moved in. The cab driver was a Bulgarian guy named "Czhznyxzkian Sldwbvidxxzyyinzsky," which in Bulgarian means "John Smith." He had a thick accent and a knack for not watching the road except when we were stopped, which wasn't often. In the course of conversation, right after I had screamed for him not to hit the lady with the twin baby stroller, he asked me what my rent was. When I told him, he said, "Two seventy four? Wow! You hit the bingo with that one! You put crazy glue on your shoes and stick to that place!"

The reason our rent was so cheap was that our apartment was in a rent-stabilized building, and the previous owner had lived there for about ninety years. The building had also been constructed, by all appearances, during the Revolutionary War. The apartment itself was a six-floor walkup atop a winding stairway that was made out of cheap tungsten and broken dreams. It had one bedroom that measured approximately six-by seven feet, unless you put furniture in, in which case it was one-by-two. (At one time they had considered turning the building into a penitentiary, but decided that it would be too cramped for the prisoners.) Interestingly, the bathtub was in the kitchen, not in the bathroom, which I suppose made the room technically the "bitchen." The place was run-down, stuffy and dismal. Cockroaches refused to live in it, preferring instead the crack den across the hallway. But it was ours, it was in a great neighborhood, and it was a mere four blocks from "Dangerfield's," Rodney's legendary nightclub.

Touring with Legends

Sunday night at Dangerfield's was audition night. This was the night when young and not so young show-business hopefuls would gather in the bar area, awaiting a chance to go onstage, bring down the house, be discovered and go on to a career of fame and fortune. The fact that no performer had as yet ever been discovered at Dangerfield's deterred no one. After all, there was always a first time.

And what a group of hopefuls it was; comedians, jugglers, magicians, ventriloquists, comedy-magicians, juggler-ventriloquists, singer-impressionist-plate-spinners...you get my point. It was a diverse and motley group, one that would make the clients of the Woody Allen movie "Broadway Danny Rose" appear normal by comparison.

One Sunday night I made my way down to the club at eight o'clock and mingled with the other performers, hoping to get on. The MC was a curly-haired Englishman named David Copperfield. As you might suspect, that wasn't his real name. I think he'd changed it for show-business purposes. I never could figure out why he chose the name "David Copperfield." If he had wanted to name himself after a fictional character, why not choose a name that wasn't already being used by a world-famous magician? Why not call himself Oliver Twist? Or Thurston Howell? Why take the chance that people in the audience might be expecting you to make the Statue of Liberty appear at any minute?

Anyway, I kept waiting for "David" to put me on. As ventriloquist after comedian after fire-eater went onstage, he kept assuring me I'd be next. Apparently, the word "next" at Dangerfield's was loosely translated as "sometime near dawn." At one A.M. I was still waiting. I began to realize that maybe I was being jerked around, that I would never make it onstage that evening, and that the only thing left was to take drastic action. I would need the services of....a gorgeous woman with enormous breasts.

A friend of mine named Tony Pinkey had come to the club to see me that night, and had brought with him a lovely English woman with the aforementioned breasts whose name I don't remember but to whom I credit my entry into show business. She walked up to David, grabbed him gently by the tie, and whispered into his ear that she and her boyfriend had come here specifically to see me. Then she gently inquired if he could see what he could do about putting me on soon, as she nonchalantly rubbed her leg against his thigh.

I was onstage in four minutes.

I did my routine, and fortunately the crowd (or what was left of it) responded so well that I was hired on the spot to be the official opening act at Dangerfield's the following week.

And so began a long association with some of the biggest and best acts in show business. All because of a leg rubbing against the thigh of a fictional character.

Chapter 3.
Jackie Mason

As it turned out, the scheduled headliner the next week was Jackie Mason, one of the funniest people ever to grace a stage anywhere. For those of you who don't know him, Jackie had been a brilliant up-and-coming star in the days when the legendary Ed Sullivan Show was on the air. Ironically, it was that very show that would prove to be his temporary undoing.

During his appearance one night on the show, Jackie became annoyed that an off-camera stagehand was counting down on his fingers the seconds Jackie had left for his performance. Jackie raised his own finger in a gesture that Sullivan interpreted to be obscene, but that Jackie to this day contends was totally innocent. When you watch the tape of the show in question, it actually doesn't seem to be the middle finger at all. Sullivan, however, thought otherwise, and banned Jackie from ever appearing on the show again. In those days, that was the equivalent of death, the end of a performer's career. Jackie labored in relative obscurity for years, until his infamous one-man Broadway shows in the '90's and beyond catapulted him once again into the much-deserved limelight.

But those days were in the future, and Jackie was still not a household name as he worked at Dangerfield's to somewhat sparse audiences. It wasn't unusual for there to be less than fifty people on a weeknight, which seemed to annoy Jackie to no end. He would sometimes come down off the stage in the middle of the show and walk around the room, counting the people to make sure he wasn't being screwed out of his money by the management.

Many performers, no matter how well they're doing, steadfastly believe they can be doing better. Jackie is no exception. We were hanging out in Las Vegas once when he saw the huge crowds exiting the Siegfried and Roy Show which was then playing at the

Mirage hotel. He couldn't believe the size of the crowds. "What's so fantastic about this show?," he wondered.

I explained that it was a huge spectacle, complete with costumes, effects and, of course, white tigers.

Jackie was befuddled. "This is a big attraction to people, these tigers?," he said. "You mean if I came up to you in Las Vegas and said, 'Listen, you wanna watch a Jew fight tigers for an hour', people would come?"

Jackie (and his friend and accountant, Jessie) always liked to hang out wherever and whenever they could. If you ever wanted to find Jackie after a show, you'd invariably head to the coffee shop. He'd be there, talking to a pretty waitress. Or if he was appearing at a hotel, you'd head to the lobby. He'd be there, talking to a pretty desk clerk. Or the gift shop, talking to the pretty lady behind the counter. Jackie always liked to hang out, and he also liked pretty women. And if there were no pretty women, he'd hang out anyway, although not as long.

Jackie has always appreciated lovely ladies. There's a story about Jackie Mason that goes this way:

After his show one night, a beautiful, sensual young woman came up to Jackie with tears in her eyes, begging to talk to him for just a few moments. Jackie listened silently as she spoke to him....

> BEAUTIFUL YOUNG WOMAN: "Jackie, I just need to tell you...My mother and father are survivors of the Nazi Death Camps. For the longest time they couldn't get over the horror of their experiences there. They were depressed for years, I would never once see them laugh or smile. Finally, after years of seeing them despondent and in agony, I convinced them to go to a Jackie Mason show. And I have to tell you, watching you, I saw my poor, sad parents laugh for the first time, laughing so hard that tears came out of their eyes. And from that moment on, things got better for them, and they were able to take some measure of joy out of life.

The woman by now was completely overcome by emotion.

> BEAUTIFUL YOUNG WOMAN: "You saved my parents' lives, Jackie Mason! You saved them with your humor and your humanity and your wonderful show that night! You saved their souls! And for that, Jackie, I will always be eternally grateful! I just wanted you to know that."
>
> Jackie looked at the woman for a long time as she wept silently. Then he softly said,
>
> "So what are you doing Saturday night?"

I will always remember my first encounter with Jackie that fateful evening at Dangerfield's, on my first night as the house opening act. I did my show which went very well, and when I came off stage I headed to the bar, where Jackie was sitting with one of his many hangers-on. I heard his voice immediately, calling me over to say hello. I went over to him tentatively. This had been my first experience performing, not only at a respected New York nightclub, but also opening for a big celebrity, a true star, a comic icon, and one that I had always admired. I hoped he had liked my show. I hoped he had SEEN my show.

Here is what he said, a quotable quote that I use on my website to this day:

> JACKIE: "Hello! Are you the guy who was just on?"
> ME: "Yes."
> JACKIE: "You're very funny...for a gentile."

To this day, whenever I'm in New York, I call Jackie and try to arrange to spend time with him. It's a challenge too, even at his advanced age, just trying to keep up with his incisive mind, trying not to feel dumb or overpowered by his intellect. You must also be careful not to engage him in small talk, or even worse, talk that he disagrees with or opinions he finds stupid. Because if you do, you'll hear about it.

I was in the coffee shop with Jackie at the Mirage hotel in Las Vegas one night. Jackie was there with his friend Mel and a woman from a local strip club whom he had met. Jackie had just signed to host a talk show in New York, and we were discussing that and other things when the conversation naturally turned to politics. I offered an opinion about the nature of the Presidency and how people don't respect the duties and the integrity of the office as much as they used to, and Jackie responded with his own thoughts on what I said. To the best of my memory, his comments (best read in his thick Yiddish dialect) went as follows:

"That's the stupidest thing I ever heard. Only a stupid person would think such a thing. You have to be a complete moron to have such an opinion. I can't believe I hang out with such a totally demented person that would come up with something so idiotic. It makes me nauseous to think that such a stupid thing could come out of your mouth..."

I'm not paraphrasing.

After his tirade ended, the table was deathly quiet for a few moments. Finally, I turned to the woman from the strip club and muttered, "So...how are you?"

That seemed to break the tension. Everyone laughed, including Jackie, who turned to Mel, pointed at me and said, "He would be great on the T.V. show."

Yeah, right. Every TV show needs a resident moron.

Being attacked verbally and abusively by Jackie was almost an honor, kind of like the way I imagine it would have felt to be insulted by Groucho Marx. Somehow, it was impossible to take it personally, because Jackie attacked everyone that way, especially his closest friends. If Jackie never called you an idiot or a stupid person, it meant you weren't contributing to the conversation. It was like being called a hockey puck by Don Rickles. I figured I'd made a friend for life.

Jackie didn't reserve his acid tongue for just his friends. Anyone was a potential victim. I remember one night walking into the Carnegie Deli in New York. It was 1986, and I had just done my second Tonight Show. Jackie was sitting at a table with Jessie and a comedian who often played Dangerfield's. The comedian had seen my appearance, as well as my first Tonight Show appearance about six months earlier, and used this occasion to let me know that he felt my first shot had gone better than my second. Jackie put down his pickle, turned to the comedian and said:

"I can't believe you said that. Only a sad, bitter comedian would say a thing like that. What kind of an idiot are you, to put a person down like that? You Nazi bastard. You're jealous and nauseous that another person can have success, so you have to put a person down to make yourself feel good about yourself. What a sleazy, obnoxious, lowlife vicious person you are. Tell the waiter I need more mustard. "

Not all of Jackie's verbal gyrations were acerbic. He could just as often kill you with his own brand of kindness. I remember standing around on a Manhattan street corner, jabbering away with Jackie and yet another of his cliques of hangers-on (Jackie always attracts a diverse array of fans and buddies that run the gamut in appearance and philosophy. At any given time he can be surrounded simultaneously by a distinguished lawyer, a disheveled bag lady and an old-time Borsht Belt comedian complete with mismatched clothes and a bad wig. There is no single, unified Jackie Mason demographic. His humor appeals to everybody regardless of race, creed, age or hair style.)

The desire to be clever and funny around Jackie is sometimes overwhelming, and on this occasion I came out with a remark that I thought to be a gem, a shining example of comic gold. I forget exactly what the remark was, but I was sure it would get guffaws from the entire group. I finished my sentence and waited for the showers of praise and appreciation. Instead, I was met with silence, the awkward kind of silence where people look down and stare at their feet as opposed to looking into your eyes and saying, 'What the fuck did THAT mean?"

Jackie looked at me for a few tense moments, nodding slowly, taking in my remark. He opened his mouth, but instead of sticking in the knife, he said this:

"There was something funny about what you just said. I'm not sure what it is yet, but there's something there. If this was a scavenger hunt, we could find the humor in that statement."...which broke the tension, produced chuckles all around and allowed us to continue on our way into the Carnegie Deli. The man has a way with words.

Hanging out with Jackie was always one of the greatest things you could do, just to hear him talk and to be in his presence, because it would always be memorable and you would always have a story to tell.

One incident I will always remember was when Jackie and I decided to take a walk around Manhattan one night. He was talking away, going on about everything, and was clearly not in the mood to watch out for oncoming traffic whenever we crossed a street. Jackie would be going on and on about something that interested him, oblivious to everything else, and step out onto Seventh Avenue or 55th Street or some other busy intersection with no regard for the red light. I think I counted twelve separate times when I had to pull him physically back onto the curb so as to avoid the front page of the New York Post the next day saying "Jewish Comic Killed By FedEx Truck While Discussing Best Place for Pastrami."

On that night he was telling me the story of his first one-man show on Broadway, "The World According to Me," which virtually changed his career and made him a huge success. The powers-that-be had been trying to make Jackie understand why he needed a director. He had been doing stand-up shows for his whole life and didn't see the need for a director to tell him what to do, but the producers were adamant. "They told me this was Broadway," Jackie said. "No one wanted to see a Jew standing there like a schmuck and talking for two hours...they had to have me leaping and jumping and twirling around to make it interesting." And so he had agreed to go with a director, although he wasn't happy about it. He continued, once again, in that unique heavy Yiddish dialect...

"They gave me a pointer and built scenery and they told me to move left and then right and then go backwards and do a summersault... it was ridiculous. Then the director comes over and says, 'Okay Jackie, here's how it's gonna go. You'll do three jokes next to a sofa, then you'll walk two steps and do five jokes next to a lamp post, and then you'll cross over backwards and do seven jokes in front of a third of a staircase...'"

"Third of a staircase"...that killed me. I can see it in my mind's eye, Jackie being told to walk over to a spiral staircase prop that only went halfway up. I laughed so hard I almost forgot to save him from the speeding motorcycle that just missed him as he stepped off the curb.

Jackie Mason has always been one of my favorite show business people. He's truly brilliant, someone I've always looked up to. He also disproves the adage that you have to be a cutthroat bastard to make it big. He is a far cry from being one of those all too common show business types who are only interested in themselves. As of this writing he's in his 90's and doesn't perform much anymore, but in his heyday he was always willing and ready to help out anyone who needed it, because he's always been secure enough in who he is and what he does that he would never consider other performers a threat to his own livelihood or position. He is still also one of the most naturally funny people in America.

Now, if we can only keep him out of traffic...

Chapter 4.
Seinfeld Et Al

As I've mentioned, the early eighties witnessed a rise of comedy clubs across the country like no one had ever seen. There were basically two varieties of clubs, not altogether different from the present day:

"Headliner" clubs ran shows which consisted of an MC who would open for ten minutes, then introduce the middle act who did fifteen, and then the headliner who did about an hour or, if it was Robin Williams, a decade.

The second type of club was the "Showcase" club. These included places like Catch a Rising Star ("Catch") in New York or the Improv in LA, where a number of comics would come in and each do about twenty minutes or, if it was Robin Williams...

In Fort Lauderdale there was a club called "The Comic Strip," affiliated with the club of the same name in New York. The New York club would take five or six of their favorite comedians and send them down to Ft. Lauderdale for a two-week gig consisting of two shows a night. In 1980 I was new on the circuit but garnering a bit of a following at Dangerfield's, so the Comic Strip tapped me to be one of the six comedians to perform at the Florida club. On the bill with me were Carol Leifer, Bob Nelson, Peter Bales, Rich Hall, Paul Reiser and Jerry Seinfeld.

I've always been very grateful to Peter Bales. If it weren't for Peter, I'd be the least famous person of those six. Although by the time you're reading this Peter, who was a very funny comic, may have gotten his own talk show or reality show or cable network, and I'll be dead last.

Even in those days, you could tell Jerry Seinfeld was on a track for success. Besides having material that was smart and funny, he had an air of confidence about him. He was good, he knew it, and so did everybody else. You just had a feeling that things were going to happen for him.

Rich Hall had an air of confidence too, but it was hard to spot because he was never around. While the rest of us would hang out together during the day, going to malls or the beach or just watching "Gilligan's Island" reruns, Rich was nowhere to be found. No one was ever quite sure where he went. We could only assume that he was either out shopping for the weird props he used in his act, or, as Jerry Seinfeld theorized, he was being raised by a family of wolves.

Rich always had an arsenal of strange props that he used in his show, one of them being a head of lettuce that he would remove from a suitcase and plop down onto a stool in front of him. It was always enjoyable for me to imagine Rich at the supermarket, comparing heads of lettuce and asking the clerk which one he thought was funnier.

Paul Reiser was an all-around nice guy. We were fairly good friends back then, and even began collaborating on a song, which to this day we have never finished. Peg and I used to hang out with Paul fairly often. We went to see him perform at the Friar's club in New York, and open for the Pointer Sisters when he was starting to get some notoriety.

The story is told that one day Paul and a fellow comedian friend of ours went shopping for underwear, as all comedians do when they're bored and need to fill up some time. After they were done, the comedian invited Paul to accompany him on an audition for a movie he was up for. The comedian didn't get the part, but the casting people spotted Paul, thought he looked right for the role, and called him in. He got the part. The movie was "Diner," one of the most successful movies of the eighties.

I always wondered if the comedian who went for the audition with Paul that day ever felt a little like Pete Best, the Beatles' drummer just before Ringo.

Paul Reiser went on to fame and fortune with his sitcom "Mad About You" and appears on TV and in movies today.

Dennis Wolfberg, who some may remember as the infamous "bug-eyed" comedian, appeared at the club about a month after I did. About this time I received a letter in the mail from a rental car company, asking me to pay for the damages inflicted on my rental car from the recent accident I'd had. Since I hadn't had an accident with this car, I contacted the rental company to find out what drugs they were taking. As it turned out, Wolfberg was the one who had been involved in the accident. The reason they were coming after me was that I had handed my rental car off to Paul Reiser, who had handed it off to Wolfberg, who had apparently wrapped it around a tree. It took weeks to straighten it all out, and from then on I've practiced the fine art of keeping my rental cars to myself.

Seinfeld was the first of any of us "comedians of the eighties" to do the Tonight Show. He'd obviously been gearing up for that night for years because not only was he prepared, he was also supremely relaxed and smooth. It was the beginning of a long, successful career. Jerry was revered by just about everyone, always. I cannot remember a time when almost every standup I knew either wanted to be Jerry Seinfeld or wanted to throttle him for being so consistently focused and unflappable. I could always imagine him as an infant, standing up in the cradle, calling his mom and dad over and saying, "Okay, here's the plan. By twenty-two I'm headlining, twenty-five I do my first Tonight show, thirty I'm doing concerts and thirty-six I'm doing a sitcom, although I haven't figured out the name of it yet."

I wish that in the interests of this book I could tell you that Jerry and I used to pal around a lot, but we really didn't. Even then, Jerry was part of a kind of exclusive club that included only those who were deemed the best stand-ups, and as a "guitar comic, I was not under serious consideration for membership.

Back then in the eighties, there was sometimes a tendency among certain monologists to look down their noses at comedians who they don't consider "pure comics." By that I mean comics who use props in their acts, or guitars, or pianos, or puppets, or anything that distracts from the "purity" of just standing on a stage and talking. I was certainly a victim of this at times in my career, and I always found it both hurtful and arrogant. Comedians like Carrot Top have suffered from this prejudice in the past... as if using a prop in your show gave you some kind of an unfair advantage. Maybe it's true in a way, but to me, I always felt that you should use whatever you have at your disposal when you're up on that stage. Monology is a big part of my show, but I always reach for my guitar at the end and it creates a level of energy that people truly enjoy and always remember. And sometimes, especially when an audience is just dead and needs a jolt, it really comes in handy. So why not use it?

Fortunately I encounter that sort of prejudice very rarely these days, and have taken great comfort in the fact that funny is funny, no matter what you do or how you present it. And great comedians such as Jackie Mason and Rodney Dangerfield and Joan Rivers and George Carlin have been fans of my work, which validates it in my mind completely.

I never knew for sure what Jerry Seinfeld thought of me as a comedian. Sometimes I would get a whiff of disdain from him, and sometimes I would get no feeling at all. But he was always friendly enough to Peg and me, and certainly deserves all the success he's had.

I'll tell the story of my first Tonight Show appearance in a later chapter. I managed not to throw up, but it was touch and go for a while.

Two Related Stories...

The majority of comedians...at least the ones I know...are basically normal people, who just happen to be filled with angst and anxiety and at least ten or twelve separate and distinct neuroses that vie constantly with each other for supremacy, and who in addition to being uncomfortable with people are totally absorbed with themselves and their careers to the exclusion of all else, and are never happy even when they reach the pinnacle of success...

Alright, let me start over.

The majority of comedians...at least the ones I know...are complete oddballs.

To succeed in the field of comedy, even more so than in music or film or any other area of show business, you need an ego the size of Jabba the Hut's trench coat. I say more so because, while the musician or the actor has many other people on whom he can depend for support, the comedian is alone. He's not only alone on stage, but also in his quest to make a roomful of strangers laugh, which is the hardest response to evoke from an audience. It's a hard job, a hard road, and a hard life. So to tackle such an undertaking, it helps to be insane.

And many of us have egos to match. Not me, of course. I'm talking about other people. People who are nowhere near as good as I am. Peasants all of them.

There is a story about a comedian who has become famous in recent years. He was known, at least in those days, to have an air of condescension toward many comics and oftentimes toward audiences. Shortly after he had appeared on Johnny Carson's Tonight Show, but still years before he became famous, he was working at some comedy club in the Deep South. He was, in the terminology of the comedy world, bombing. Badly.

Finally, in the middle of his show, having gotten absolutely no laughs, he turned to the audience and snarled, "You know, ladies and gentlemen, Johnny Carson loves this material."

Whereupon a member of the audience snapped back in a deep southern drawl, " Well, Johnny Carson ain't here."

There is another comic who has had some success doing commercials and sitcoms who is by no means a household name but feels he should be. He came into a comedy club at Harrah's hotel in Las Vegas one night and demanded that he be allowed to do a guest spot. "Guest spots," where an unscheduled comic comes in and does ten or twenty minutes, are generally frowned upon in Las Vegas because the shows are rigidly timed so that the gambling audiences can return to gambling. The name of the game is "keep the show tight and get them back to the slot machines." So guest spots are not really an option at these clubs.

When this comic came in for his guest spot, the club manager immediately rebuffed him. His ego damaged, the comic said to the manager, "Hey, if Jerry Seinfeld came in and wanted to do a guest spot, what would you do?"

The manager looked at the comic and pointedly said, "If Jerry Seinfeld came in, I'd bump the fuckin' headliner."

The comic left with his tail planted firmly between his legs.

Chapter 5.
Rodney:
The Early Years

Let's go back to those heady days at the beginning of my comedy career in the eighties, shall we? When we last saw our hero, he had just embarked on his adventure as the house opening act at a little club called Dangerfield's.

I had been appearing at Dangerfield's for several months now and was becoming pretty comfortable with my role. Jackie Mason's audiences were terrific, especially on weekends.

The weekdays weren't always quite as terrific. In the days before Rodney's rise to fame due to the movie "Caddyshack," the club tended to be a bit underpopulated on weekdays. And on nights like those, the people who did show up sometimes seemed unaware that they were in a comedy club. I remember one couple sitting ringside during my portion of the show who did nothing but make out and hump each other the entire time. They didn't laugh, they didn't clap, and apparently had no idea that there was a show going on. I assumed they thought I was an aquarium.

So I always looked forward to Saturday nights at Dangerfield's, when the electricity and the energy were infectious. There's nothing like a hot audience to erase the taste of one or two bad shows.

It was on one of these great Saturday nights when Rodney himself stopped by his club for a visit. I'll never forget the first impression he made on me. I was sitting at the bar waiting to go on when Rodney walked in, sweaty, tired, a mess. One of the people working there asked the kind of standard rhetorical question everyone asks anyone, "Hey Rodney, how ya doin'?" Rodney took him literally and answered, "Not so good. I been goin' to the bathroom loose." The man could paint a picture.

He was dressed in his standard issue light blue safari shirt with epaulets on the shoulders, dark blue shorts and sandals with socks. Rodney always dressed like that, every time anyone ever saw him. It had become known as "The Rodney Collection"... safari shirt, shorts, socks & sandals. The only deviation from this outfit (except for his signature stage clothes) was when he would replace the blue safari shirt with a white safari shirt.

(Interesting aside #2: Once a T.V. crew followed Rodney around for a week, filming his activities for a special they were doing about him and his skyrocketing career. The producer told me during editing that he was concerned people would think Rodney wore the same clothes every day. I told him it wasn't the same shirt and pants. It was different shirts and pants, they just all looked the same. The producer said, "I guess we'll have to put that in the credits." I suggested writing the days of the week on his clothes as he wore them.

I once asked Rodney how he came upon his black suit and red tie. I was truly wondering if it had been mapped out, if there had been some meticulously crafted plan that had led to the iconic Rodney outfit. There was nothing of the sort, and his answer was pure Rodney. He said "I was never good with clothes, I never knew what went together, so I figured how can you go wrong with a black suit and a red tie?")

Anyway, I went on and did my show that evening, and it went well. The audience was cheering as I came offstage. Rodney, whom I had never met before, stepped up to me and in his signature New York baritone said, "They obviously like what you do." I stood there and said thanks and nodded nervously a few times. Then he said, "So...What do you do?"

I told him what I did - song parodies, jokes, pretty much anything that would get a response. He responded by grunting and turning away. A week later I was opening for him as he returned to headline his club.

Dangerfield's was in many ways the perfect headquarters for Rodney. Unpretentious to say the least, the club itself and the characters, both employees and patrons, would easily seem at home in a John Waters movie. Upon entering the club, the first thing you'd notice is that taste... in the "Home Beautiful" or "Architectural Digest" sense...was not a priority. The overriding motif of the club was "dark"; dark, worn-out red carpeting embellished with dark draperies and dark, fake-wood paneling. The club's main wall was a pictorial gallery of Rodney's showbiz history; Rodney with Dean Martin on his variety show, Rodney with Jack Benny, George Carlin, Richard Pryor, and a great photo of Rodney on the panel of the Tonight show in the 1970's with Johnny Carson laughing as Rodney sat there with his famous put-upon expression. (This photo was unfortunately stolen by an overzealous fan. I think I saw him recently on "Judge Judy.")

As you kept walking and thought the club couldn't possibly get any darker, wham! Welcome to the showroom. To enter this area safely, you needed a guide with a miner's hat and a lantern attached. The shaded candles that adorned each table shed just enough light to enable the customer to see his seating area, or more accurately, nook. Each table was about the size of a ceiling tile. If a party of four each ordered a cup of coffee, you wouldn't see the tabletop again until they cleared it.

Bobby Campbell, the maitre d', had a habit of giving prime seating to the patrons that tipped him well. Many of the patrons that came to Dangerfield's, however, were either unfamiliar with the custom of tipping or familiar with it but not big fans of it. The result of this was that on many weeknights, Bobby would seat everybody who came in for the show to the extreme right of the stage, even if the audience numbered no more than ten people (which it often did). Consequently, one of my standard weeknight onstage comments was, "I guess I won't be joking to my left this evening."

Bobby was one of the many eccentric characters that populated the club in those days. His unique seating method was only one of his many endearing qualities. The microphone he used to bring on the acts was located on a ledge by the telephone. After introducing the act, Bobby was supposed to then turn off this microphone so that sound from the bar wouldn't bleed into the showroom and disrupt the show. The odds of him actually remembering to do this were slim. Bobby almost always left the microphone on.

Bobby used the telephone to confirm credit card orders. Since the microphone was on, everyone in the showroom would be treated to this exchange. The comedian would be onstage setting up a joke. He'd build to the punchline, and just as he was about to deliver it the audience would hear over the loudspeaker, "American Express, 4115-233-00971, expiration date 9/82."

To this day, people who saw me perform at Dangerfield's come up to me and say, "Hey, aren't you the guy who did that American Express joke? I never got it, dude."

There were many headliners who worked at Dangerfield's. One of the most interesting was David Frye, an impressionist who owed much of his popularity in the seventies to his uncanny impressions of politicians like Lyndon Johnson, Hubert Humphrey and especially Richard Nixon. In the middle of his act, David used to run a five-minute film of Richard Nixon walking along the beach, shaking hands with citizens, and finally resigning from the presidency in disgrace. Throughout the film David's recorded voice sang "My Way" as Nixon. As it played, David would leave the stage and go off somewhere, returning just as the film was ending. I never knew where he went, until finally someone told me that David, who was fond of drinking before the show, would always use the five minute interlude to run to the men's room and pee. I can only assume this is true, since I never went down there to check.

Then there was Murray Langston, "The Unknown Comic." Anyone who remembers "The Gong Show" will remember him, the rapid-fire joke teller with the paper bag over his head. At Dangerfield's, Murray would come onstage and do half the show with the bag on, then take it off halfway through and finish the show as himself, "unbagged." Apparently he did this because he was tired of going up to women, telling them he was the Unknown Comic, and having them constantly say, "Yeah, right. And I'm Meryl fuckin' Streep."

Paul Newman in the House!

One of the most memorable nights of my life was when I opened for the legendary Sarah Vaughn at the club. Just before I went on, one of the waiters casually whispered to me "Don't be nervous, but Paul Newman is in the audience."

Yeah, I calmed right down.

I did the show. It was a good show. I had no idea what Paul Newman thought of it, but I thought it went well. As I left the stage, my waiter friend came up to me and said, "Slow down, Paul Newman is running after you." *Running after me*? Shit. Had I offended him in some way? I didn't remember doing any off-color Joanne Woodward jokes. Maybe he was a huge Bee Gees fan, and I was about to be knocked on my ass.

He caught up to me. I cowered. He put out his hand and said, "Hi. I'm Paul Newman." Like he really had to introduce himself.

Now of course, being a typical star-struck fan and a nerd by nature, my inclination was to grab his hand and pump it furiously while screaming "OH MY GOD, MR. NEWMAN, I AM SUCH A BIG FAN OF YOURS, I'VE SEEN EVERY ONE OF YOUR MOVIES, YOU'RE HUD, FOR CHRISSAKES!" But a little voice inside my head nudged me gently and said, in so many words, "try not to be an asshole, would you?" And so instead of making a fool of myself, I somehow garnered the presence of mind to calmly shake his hand and say, "Uh...hi."

Thinking that would be the end of it, I headed downstairs to my dressing room. To my complete amazement, Paul (as I'd now come to know him) followed me, and pumped me with questions; "How do you do what you do up there? Do you change the show every night or is it basically the same? Is it hard to come up with material?...," etc., etc. I continued to follow the advice of the little voice in my head and answered all his questions calmly and rationally; "It's just something I'm able to do, I change the show around to suit the audience, the song parodies come easier than the actual jokes," etc. etc. At that point I realized I was having an out-of-body experience, because a part of me was monitoring this exchange and thinking, "Damn, I can't believe you're talking to

Paul Newman without wetting yourself." I was somehow staying cool, and not giving in to my natural impulse to say, "CAN MY DAD MEET YOU? WHAT WAS IT LIKE WORKING WITH GEORGE C. SCOTT? YOU WERE IN "THE STING," FOR CHRISSAKES!!" And I was truly impressed with the fact that he wasn't treating me like a nobody. He was honestly interested in finding out how a comic's mind works and in what I had to say, almost as if he were researching for a part. It was pretty darn cool!

When we got downstairs (Paul and me, me and Paul, my good buddy and I), he looked me in the eye and said, "You did a terrific job." I think that's what he said. It was either that or "I wish my table was larger." I don't know. All I know is that at that precise moment, I could tell how incredibly blue his eyes were, and I've never paid attention to that in a man before.

Then off he went, into the sunset. Or the men's room. It was one of those two things.

The next thing I remember is one of the waiters, who was gay, was licking my hand, the one that had shaken Paul's hand. Who could blame him? I was licking my OWN hand.

HE WAS BUTCH CASSIDY, FOR CHRISSAKES!!

Shufflin' Man and Other N.Y Stories

Dangerfield's was, of course, in New York City, and consequently a good selection of typical New York City crazies used to come and go. One of my all-time favorite memories was my brief encounter with the shufflin' man.

I was talking to Bobby the maitre'd outside the club about what my plans were for the coming week. As we talked, out of the corner of my eye I noticed a thin, shady figure shuffling toward us, hobbled and bent against the chilly night air. As the figure came closer, I could see it was an old black man with an overcoat and fedora, heading down the street in our direction.

The old man had reached us now and was about to pass us when Bobby asked me, "Where are you and Rodney going this week?" I began to reply, "We start out in Phoenix, then Tucson, Billings Montana, Reno..."

The man turned in our direction without slowing his gait and in a thin, raspy voice yelled out, "Why don'tcha go to California and make yerself some real money?" ...then turned and continued on his way.

I think that man is now managing Jimmy Fallon.

Manhattan was, and is, always full of characters like that, and it made living in the city a unique experience. Whenever I saw some typically off-kilter person talking to himself, I would always try my best to overhear what he was saying. I spotted one guy having an energetic solo conversation, and made my way in front of him so I could hear. All he kept saying to himself was, "Barbados is nice. Yeah, Barbados. Nice. Barbados is nice"

I have to include my favorite NY story here, told to me by my friend Jack Regan. There was a man - dirty, disheveled, his hair in dreadlocks - who used to pound his drumsticks on the pavement in the middle of 48th street while humming loudly and incoherently. One afternoon Jack decided he was going to make this man's day.

Jack went into a nearby music store and purchased two brand new drumsticks, then walked outside and tapped the man on the shoulder. The man stopped playing and wheeled around toward Jack, annoyed at the interruption. Jack handed him the drumsticks.

The man took them, examined them closely, then shook his head and handed them back. In a loud voice he croaked,

"Can't use 'em. They got fiberglass tips!"

And continued playing his trusty old wooden sticks.

* * * * *

One of the reasons people identify with certain comedians is that they sense the honesty behind the material. Whenever Rodney Dangerfield said "I don't get no respect," people believed it. Even when he was in his prime, doing sold-out concerts and movies and T.V. specials and making literally millions of dollars, people would still come up to him on the street and say, "Rodney, how ya doin', ya doin' alright?" And usually Rodney would answer, "Goin' along."

"Goin' along" was Rodney on a good day. Of all the comedians and performers I've worked with, Rodney was by far the least able to find happiness. Even when the movie "Caddyshack" had catapulted him to superstardom and he was selling out two and three-thousand seat theatres all across the country, Rodney just couldn't enjoy the experience. It seemed that he'd always been, to put it in his own words, a "down cat with a down head. Fame and fortune don't change what's in your head, man." At least part of the reason for this was that Rodney always lamented the fact that he'd made it so late in life. Caddyshack and his subsequent rise to the heights of show business didn't happen until he was fifty-seven years old, "late" by show-business standards.

And so the sadness persisted, which ironically seemed to serve him well, because the "no respect" image fit him perfectly. People sensed that this was not just an act or a gimmick. "No respect" was the truth of Rodney's life. And that perception of the truth and honesty behind his jokes and his act helped fuel his tremendous rise in the eighties.

I'll always remember one day in particular that illustrated this facet of his character.

We were booked to do a show somewhere in New Jersey. It was sold out, and the limousine picked me up at my apartment, then picked Rodney up at his place. Rodney was in a foul mood that morning. As he got into the limo, he dispensed with the small talk and began to complain about how he hadn't slept and how tired he was and how all this show-business stuff was bullshit. He'd met all sorts of famous people, he'd done tons of T.V. shows and a hit movie and had an album that was #1 on the comedy charts, and it was all meaningless, "we're all gonna die anyway, so what does it all matter?" This was before I'd had my morning coffee.

Rodney couldn't even give himself any respect. But his fans did, and everyone who knew anything about comedy did, and pretty much everyone in America did. At least he had that.

I'll never forget the first time I opened for Rodney in a big theatre. It was in Philadelphia, 1980. Before this I had never done comedy in a place bigger than a nightclub. Now I was about to face three thousand people. People who loved Rodney. People who were fanatical about Rodney. People who had consumed enough beer to fill the Grand Canyon and still have several six-packs left over. People who had no idea there was an opening act about to come out.

Let's review.

Everyone in the theatre has paid the equivalent of two day's salary to see a comedian or a singer or a band that they idolize and that they've been dying to see for weeks, sometimes months. So here they are, minutes away from this big event in their lives, when the lights go down. The moment is at hand. The crowd roars in eager anticipation. The words "Please welcome..." ring out over the P.A., and pandemonium reigns. This is it! Fantastic! Unbelievable! The moment we've been waiting for! Then they announce a name no one's ever heard before..

In my case, this geek with a guitar strolls out onstage. It's the opening act., and he's gonna do thirty minutes. Isn't that wonderful? Thirty whole minutes from a guy we've never heard of.

Let's kill this son of a bitch.

On this balmy night in Philadelphia, the lights went down. The crowd roared. And the announcer said, "Please welcome Rodney Dangerfield's opening act..." Except all the audience heard was "Please welcome Rodney Dangerfield..." They had drowned out the "opening act" part with their delirious cheering. So when I walked onstage, the crowd was....well, "surprised" would be a kind way of putting it. "Royally pissed" would be more accurate.

"Hey. That ain't Rodney!," someone observantly yelled.

As I strode to the microphone and the crowd hissed and booed, I began to imagine what it would feel like to have an arm ripped from a socket and used as a club to beat my skull. My opening line at the time was "This looks like a disco crowd," whereupon I would launch into my Bee Gee's "Singin' Too High" parody. This was during the infamous "Disco Sucks" era. It was a "Disco Sucks and so do Guitar Comics" crowd in the hall that night. They screamed. They yelled. The phrase "get off" was uttered, along with "where's Rodney," "go home, asshole," and various things about my mother. It was magical.

Luckily for me, I was able to rescue myself before the first platoon stormed the stage. the Phillies had just won the World Series, and I quickly used that fact to my advantage. "So," I said as

I heard the audience members loading magazines into Uzis. "This is the home of the World Champions, huh?" Huge cheers. Thunderous applause. Some of them actually dropped their grenades so they could high-five each other. Then I put on my stereotypical effeminate voice and said, "I love the Phillies. They always come from behind!"

Okay, it was crude and insensitive and a cheap, easy laugh, but I was young and stupid and politically incorrect and fighting for my life up there. And it also made them not want to kill me right away. From that point on, I did fine. Rodney's audiences in those days were tough, and they could eat you alive, but if you broke through the preliminary hostilities and made them laugh, they were also the greatest audiences in the world.

(Yet another "opening act" horror story:)

My friend Max Alexander, a fine standup comedian and actor as well, told me his own personal tale of woe about the time he opened for Steve Lawrence and Edie Gourmet at Westbury Music Fair in New York.

It was going to be a special evening. Max's father was in the audience that night, and Max was backstage, pacing nervously up and down and hoping everything would go smoothly.

As the lights went down and the orchestra began to play you could feel the eagerness and anticipation in the air. The announcements began...

"Ladies and gentlemen, welcome to the Westbury Music Fair..."

Max stood there, adjusting his tie.

"Tonight, an evening of music with Steve Lawrence and Edie Gourmet..."

Max peeked out to see his proud father sitting in the audience, beaming.

"Please welcome Steve and Edie's special guest, Max Alexander!"

And at that moment, a lady in the audience loudly exclaimed, for everyone to hear; "OH SHIT!"

Max told me it was all uphill from there. Where else could it go?)

Chapter 6.
James Brown

One of the good things about being associated with Rodney when he was red-hot in the eighties was that a lot of cool, impressive celebrity types would come to see him and, by default, also wind up seeing me.

One night, James Brown was in the audience at Caesar's Palace, sitting ringside. I don't remember if I was nervous knowing he was there. I was sick as a dog that night and was more concerned with not heaving on the first row than worrying if James Brown would like me or not.

I guess he did, because several months later I was tapped to host a fledgling award show in New York called the "New Music Awards," and my co-host for the evening was...James Brown.

I was not even out of my twenties and here I was hosting a show with James Brown. Because he loved my show with Rodney Dangerfield. So...when was my mom gonna wake me up from this dream and tell me I'm late for school, and why was I singing "I Feel Good" in my sleep?

I showed up for rehearsal before James did. As we started going through the schedule, I noticed that the young and apparently ill-informed producers had allotted time in the schedule for James and I to "kibitz for ten minutes." Y'know, "kibitz." A word which meant, loosely, ad-lib and joke around. Me and James.

As gently and diplomatically as I could, I informed them that James Brown, the Godfather of Soul, was not particularly known for his *kibitzing* abilities. And furthermore, even people who were known to kibitz now and then couldn't really be expected to kibitz for ten minutes! They reluctantly dropped the "kibitz" clause from the schedule.

James arrived with his wife and entourage, and told me how much he'd enjoyed the show at Caesar's Palace that night. This relieved me to no end, because it would have been really terrible for the Godfather of Soul to have thought I sucked.

Or as he would have put it, "*Hey*!!! You sucked!!! *Hey*!!!!"

As time wore on, it became painfully obvious that no one associated with putting this show together really knew what he or she was doing. Cues were being missed, names of bands were being mispronounced, things were being dropped and rearranged all over the place. At one point, James turned to his wife and said, in his raspy James Brown voice; "Honey, I'm goin' back to the ho-tel. When these people got their shit together, call me." He left the hall, and we didn't hear from him again until one minute before show time.

By the way, the show didn't run anywhere near smoothly. At one point, James and I were onstage presenting the award for something like "The Band with the most Visible Open Sores," and I announced the winner. No one came up. No one moved. We just looked like idiots waiting for a non-existent band to show up and accept their award. The acceptance music just kept playing. I turned to look at James, who was standing next to me, smiling with those beautiful teeth of his. Without letting his smile waver one bit, he leaned toward me and whispered, "Do somethin' Dennis. We lookin' like assholes up here."

So I turned to the crowd and said, "Well everybody, 'Bent Scrotum' couldn't be here tonight, but if they were here, they'd probably say...(in a deep Cockney accent)..'Yeah, right, award, yeah, well, right, thanks, yeah'."

I don't remember the rest of the evening. Most of it's a blur. I remember a lot of loud music, a lot of broken glass, and a lot of hostile stares from people with safety pins in their noses, and that's about it.

But sharing the stage with James Brown, I have to admit, was cool.

Chapter 7. Paul Anka

Another person who saw me perform with Rodney in Las Vegas was Paul Anka. At the time, I used to do a parody to his song, "You're Having My Baby." It went:

"You're having my baby
What a wonderful way to say I need better protection..."

I did the parody that night, and Paul was in the audience, unbeknownst to me. I came offstage, and I was handed a note in my dressing room: "Paul Anka wants to talk to you. Room 3876." Oh, shit. Did he hate the parody? Was I about to encounter my first lawsuit? I went back to my room and apprehensively dialed his number. He picked up.

"Hello?"

"Hi, Paul?"

"Yeah?"

"Uh, hi, it's Dennis Blair. I opened for Rod..."

"Dennis? Hey, great show, listen, you wanna open for me?"

"Huh?"

I was stunned. I was expecting a tongue lashing at the very least. Instead I got this hyper-enthusiastic guy who wanted me to open for him, even though I had just trashed his most recent hit.

"Uh, open for you? Sure, if I ..."

"I'm doing thirty dates this summer, I want you to do all of them. I love you, man, I think you're terrific, you gotta do it!"

"Well, thanks, but I'm touring with Rodney now, so I've gotta check my schedule..."

"Yeah, yeah, check your schedule, I can give you a ton of work. Let me know as soon as you can, I want you to work with me!"

"Okay, I'll let you know, thanks!"

He hung up. It didn't look like I was getting sued.

Paul invited me to his show the next night and I met him backstage before he went on. He shook my hand and talked to me like we were old buddies. He told me he hoped we could work a lot in the future, and he could hardly wait. As it turned out, the only one of Paul's dates I could commit to without conflicting with Rodney's schedule was an upcoming weekend at the Universal Amphitheater in LA. That was fine with Paul, and I signed on.

The Universal Amphitheater was a beautiful, classic venue. It sat approximately 6,000 people, with state-of-the art sound and lights. The backstage area was comfortable, and it was great to be there.

(Note: Many of the backstage areas in theatres around the country are, to put it kindly, hellholes. If you get a table and chair with a mirror that isn't covered with dried makeup from some vaudeville production of "Forty-Second Street," you're lucky. Rodney used to ruminate about what the audiences out in the theatre, which was usually ornate and beautiful, were imagining the backstage area to be like. He'd say, "They probably figure we got a ten-piece band playing back here, with red carpets and candelabras and a big pig roasting on a spit." Not so. Most New York City subway platforms are more elegant than the backstage areas at these old theatres.)

The first thing I noticed after I was introduced and walked out on stage was that I was, for lack of a better term, tilting forward. Paul traveled with his own portable stage, which someone had forgotten to tell me sloped gently downward. This made the performer feel at all times like he could slide into the laps of the people at table one at any given moment. And to make things worse the stage was apparently made out of some sort of malleable, sponge-like substance. I guess this was okay for Paul, who always held his microphone in his hand. But I always kept the microphone in a stand, and every time I moved my feet on this sponge-stage, it would cause the mic stand to wobble and shake. So not only was I in constant danger of losing my footing, but I had to make sure that the microphone didn't bash out several of my teeth during my Mick Jagger takeoff.

Other than that, the show went well. We did three nights, and each performance was fun to do. On the last night, I went backstage to find Paul, whom I had never gotten a chance to talk to. I was buzzed with adrenaline, and was eager to thank him for the first of what I figured might be tons of gigs in the future. I mean, he loved me, right? I knocked on the door of his dressing room, but it didn't open. Pressing my ear to the door, I could hear lots of loud voices inside, talking and laughing. I pushed harder, then slowly opened the door and walked inside.

It seemed like half of L.A. was there. There must have been hundreds of people in the room. It looked like the cover of the "Sergeant Pepper" album. Former Mouseketeer Annette Funicello was among the throng, congratulating Paul on his show. I half expected to see Frankie Avalon and Troy Donahue eating cocktail franks in a corner somewhere, chatting with David Niven and Nikita Kruschev. I made my way toward Paul, hoping he'd put his arm around me and tell me how many shows we were planning to do next year. Maybe he'd even introduce me to Rex Harrison and Pope Pius XXIII.

I finally reached him. I put out my hand and said, "Hey Paul, thanks for the gig," He looked at me, still smiling from a recent congratulatory remark. He peered into my eyes, and said;

"Who are you?"

I'm not making this up. He literally had no idea who I was. I guess his memory chip had expired. I just stared back at him, unbelieving.

"I'm...I...Uh...never mind."

I walked out of the dressing room and out of the theatre. I never heard from Paul Anka again. Good thing I didn't give up the gig with Rodney.

There's no people like show people.

(For some reason, it always seems as though the more these headliner types told me they liked me and wanted to work with me, the more of a chance there was that I would never hear from these people again. I don't know if there's a name for this phenomenon or if it applies only to me, but I would know instinctively that each time a celebrity told me "we're gonna work a lot together!," that's the last time I would ever see this person.

I worked with Dionne Warwick for two nights at a theatre in the Midwest. On the first night, I did my show and came offstage. Dionne was standing there, smoking a cigarette, waiting to go on. She didn't say a word to me. Nothing. Just a quick glance my way, then she snubbed out her cigarette and went on. "Boy, I sure did impress her!," I thought as I went backstage. Dionne's manager and staff were there, and they also didn't say a word to me. "Boy, they really like my work, too!," I thought, as I slunk off to my hotel room.

Second night, same thing; I did the show, came off. Dionne was there, puffing away. But this time, she looked me up and down, and as she was being introduced, she said,

"You are a sick motherfucker."

So this time, I went backstage and the atmosphere was decidedly different. Her manager came up to me and told me how much Dionne loved my act and that we were gonna work a lot in the future.

I never heard from them again.

The same thing happened with Marvin Hamlisch. Marvin had seen me MC a benefit in New York and decided to use me to open up a few of his shows in Rhode Island that fall. I did the shows, and Marvin came up to me and said, "I want you for all my shows from now on. You're on the 'A' list!"

Apparently, the 'A' stood for 'Absentee' or 'Avoid' or 'Anti-Dennis-Ever-Working-With-Me-Again'. I never heard a peep from Marvin. For years afterward, I would get an occasional call from my friend (and former Joan Rivers road manager) Kevin Jones, asking me if I'd heard from Marvin Hamlisch yet. When I'd say no, he'd cackle viciously and say;

"Hey, don't worry, you're on the 'A' list!"

These days, I like to work with people who think I suck. At least that way I know I've got job security.)

Jump ahead about 28 years, to 2010. Peggy and I were invited to see a performance at UCLA by none other than Marvin

Hamlisch. We got to talking with the woman who got us the tickets and happened to mention the circumstances of how I had worked with Marvin all those years ago. She immediately handed me a pen and paper and told me to write him a note, which she would promptly deliver backstage to Marvin's people. I tried to cut this off at the outset, but she was insistent. "It will be like a reunion!," she gushed.

We watched the show, which was excellent, and then waited at the backstage door for Marvin to come out, and I think you pretty much can guess what happened. In a way, it's a good thing he didn't show up. There was a good chance that had I seen him, I would have tackled him to the ground, screaming at the top of my lungs, 'Hey Marvin! Remember me? .'"A' LIST, BABY!!"

Chapter 8.
The Beach Boys

The Beach Boys never saw me open for Rodney, but it was through my association with him and my success as an opener that my agent (yes, I'd signed with one) booked me at Caesar's Palace in Lake Tahoe to open for them. It was 1980, which meant their drummer Dennis Wilson was still alive and Brian Wilson had returned from his forced hiatus from touring and show business.

I met the Boys briefly before the show. They seemed nice and unassuming, especially Carl and his brother Dennis, who struck me as being tremendously sweet and very shy. I found it odd that a member of the Beach Boys would be shy, especially around me. I mean, besides being the least intimidating person in the room, I also had the distinction of not having done "Pet Sounds," one of the greatest albums in rock history. If anyone had a right to be shy, it was me.

Brian Wilson was pleasant enough but seemed a little out-of-sorts. He shook my hand quickly and looked at me, but I got the distinct impression he never actually saw me. As far as he was concerned, I was a hologram.

Brian was definitely interesting. As I found out later from my Peggy, while I was onstage doing the first show Brian had wandered over to her while she was watching me from the wings and said, "Who are you?" She replied, "I'm the comedian's girlfriend." He paused to let this sink in, but it obviously didn't quite register fully. So he then said to her, "I'm gonna need five cups of coffee on my piano." She stared back at him, stunned. Then she said, "So what, are you looking for a person with a really big hand?"

According to Peggy, he stared back at her for a long time and then just wandered away.

One thing that happened every night was that while I was performing, nearing the end of my show, Dennis and Brian for some reason would start tuning up behind the curtain WHILE I WAS

STILL ON. As a result, I would plainly and clearly hear notes from the piano and "thunks" from the tom- tom intermittently throughout my show, Consequently, my act would go something like this; "You ever see those late night commercials..." - WHACK! WHACK! TINKLE! - "Everything's always $19.95..." - BAM! NOODLE NOODLE! THUDWACK BAM!

Great. I was getting unrequested rim shots from the Beach Boys.

I watched them perform from the spotlight booth after I was done. Their fans were ecstatic, everyone loved them. Dennis was obviously having trouble with the thin Tahoe atmosphere (5,000 feet above sea level). He would finish drumming on one song, then reach down and take huge gulps from the facemask of a nearby oxygen tank. Brian was onstage for the whole performance, except for the times he would occasionally just get up in the middle of a song and walk off, only to return a few minutes later. I noticed that on the top of his piano someone had placed five styrofoam coffee cups. Someone with a large hand, I guess.

The engagement went fine, and they wound up using me several more times over the years. One of these times was at the Sands in Atlantic City.

The lead singer on most of their songs, Mike Love, had a reputation for being a bit more mystical and otherworldly than the others. Whenever I worked with them, I noticed there was always one dressing room with a sign that read "Meditation Room" set aside for Mike and his friends. Mike was a mellow guy.

Maybe a little over-mellow sometimes.

Each night when I ended my show at the Sands, I would walk off, the curtain would part and the Beach Boys would immediately start playing.

Usually.

One night I came offstage to complete pandemonium. The pre-recorded intro music was already playing out in the house, and the curtain was just about ready to part. But instead of the band being on stage and in place, everyone backstage was scrambling around in a panic looking for Mike Love; "Where is he?," have you seen him?," "God dammit, you look downstairs, I'll check the bathrooms!," etc. After about a minute, in the midst of all this unhinged chaos, Mike came wandering calmly onstage from God Only Knows where, seemingly oblivious to the near-riot he was causing. He looked at me, then at the stage, then back at me, and in a very mellow voice said,

"Are you off?"

I nodded my head. Mike and his band mates got together. And the show began, finally.

Mellow out, dudes.

Chapter 9: Rodney's New Protégé

I've mentioned how Rodney Dangerfield could sometimes seem like the unhappiest person in the world, but that's only part of the story. Yes, he had personal demons, but he also happened to possess a good deal of warmth and generosity. If he liked you, and could help you out in any way, he would. That's exactly what he did for Roseanne, Sam Kinison, Andrew Dice Clay, and numerous other comedians who have all acknowledged that Rodney helped get them their first big break. I will always be grateful to Rodney for giving me my start, and although my break turned out to be not as big as some of the others, I credit him with starting me out on a satisfying career that might never have panned out at all without his help.

There are plenty of people in show business who are in a position to help out lesser known artists but would never do it. Rodney was not one of those people. In the early eighties when I toured with him, I was pretty much known in the industry as Rodney's protégé, and that was a pretty accurate assessment. He took me under his wing, he guided me and my career almost like a manager, and he really cared about what happened to me even though he didn't need to.

For instance, when I was starting out and almost completely unknown, Rodney would sometimes have to fight to get me on the bill with him. Caesar's Palace in Las Vegas in particular resisted having me open for him, contending that I was a "Rock & Roll comedian" (whatever that meant) and that my parodies and references would be too "hip" for a Las Vegas audience. (Look at any photo of me from that time. Do I look like I'd be too hip for anybody?) They just kept refusing to let Rodney bring me along on the bill, and finally demanded that he come up with a list of alternate opening acts that would be satisfactory to him. He thought for a moment, then said, "You want a list? And I have final approval? Okay, here's the list; Get me either Bob Dylan, Billy Joel or Mick Jagger."

They let me open.

Rodney also did things like having Jack Rollins come to see me. Jack Rollins at the time was one of the most powerful managers in show business, representing people like Woody Allen and David Letterman. Rodney didn't have to put his reputation on the line like that, but he did.

Rodney also became fiercely protective when he felt I was being mistreated. His partner at Dangerfield's had signed me to a long term management contract which I had signed hastily during my overeager beginnings in comedy, and he had never done anything to advance my career since I had signed that piece of paper. I had finally realized my mistake and asked to be let out of the contract, but he stood firm and refused to let me go. Rodney was so appalled by this that when it came time to do his best-selling "No Respect" album, he chose to perform it at "Catch a Rising Star" down the street rather than his own club as a statement of his loyalty to me. I found that to be amazing.

There was also an incident where I had recorded some musical novelty songs at a friend's studio to use as outgoing messages on my phone machine. They were takeoffs on fifties songs, classical pieces, etc. Cute stuff. I guess they were cuter than I thought, because I turned on the TV one night and heard my messages being sold on one of those cheesy late-night commercials for $19.95. My "friend," the owner of the studio, had stolen my ideas and recordings, even though I had introduced him to Rodney and paved the way for him to produce Rodney's next comedy album at the studio.

One night Rodney and I were coming out of the Improv in Manhattan when we ran into this studio owner/ex-friend. Unbelievably, the guy went to give Rodney one of those typical bullshit "I Love You Man" showbiz hugs we all know and puke over. Rodney recoiled and showered my former pal with expletives; "You fucked my friend Dennis, you fuck! Fuck you, you're an asshole, get the fuck away from me!" The hilarious thing to me was that this guy looked genuinely hurt that Rodney felt this way. "So ," the guy said as the final "You sleazy motherfucker" escaped from Rodney's lips. "Uh...does this mean the album is off?"

It bothers me that Rodney and I parted on a sour note that was never fully reconciled. I'll go into detail about this later, but for now I'll just say he got angry and had a falling out with me for reasons that are, to my way of thinking, both absurd and untrue. (Let me just say that Rodney fired me as his opening act because...well, it involves a dog, a pool and Howard Stern. All will be explained in subsequent pages).

One of my most pleasant memories of those Dangerfield years, long before things turned sour, was of hanging out with Rodney in his dressing room, just talking about all kinds of stuff. We would hang out for hours, mainly because we enjoyed each other's company. Rodney was one of those people who was funny without even trying to be funny. He was a lot like Jackie Mason in that respect. Jackie could tell you a story about what he bought in the produce department that day and have you on the floor dying of laughter. Rodney had the same gift, and some of the stuff he said has stuck with me to this day. Some examples...

We were on an elevator in a hotel one time. Both of us had rooms on the top floor, so naturally we had to stop each time someone needed to get off. As soon as the last person had left the elevator, Rodney turned to me and said, "That's what I hate about being on the top floor. You always have to take someone else's ride."

When I started touring with Rodney, there were several agents from the William Morris Agency who wanted me to sign with them. I was excited. I was honored. I asked Rodney if he thought I should do it. He looked at me like I was nuts. "You wanna know what that agency will do for you?," he said. "You know the money you're making with me now? They'll take ten percent. That's what they'll do for you."

He also had some keen observations about fame. On a ride back from a gig, I was talking in my young and naive way about how nice it must be to be famous. Rodney set me straight, telling me it was mostly bullshit, about how most of the famous people he knows were miserable and bitter. "If you ever get famous, you know what the difference will be?," he told me. "You know all the stuff you're doing now in your act? When you're famous, everyone will say it's brilliant and they knew it all along. That's the difference."

Rodney could never quite get over how famous he'd become in the eighties. He marveled at how celebrities were treated, and at how much they could get away with. "When you're famous, they think everything you do is great. I could take a crap in the hotel lobby, and they'd laugh and say, 'Look at Rodney, he's taking a crap in the lobby!'"

Another thing I remember from hanging in the dressing room is Rodney trying out new jokes. It was always amazing how he could take a new, unpolished joke and cut it down, throw out the "fat" as he called it, the extra words and phrases that slow the joke down and make it not as funny as it could be.

One of my more enduring memories was when Rodney showed me his cache of "Tonight Show" jokes.

It seems that the most successful comedians are the ones that are the most methodical, obsessed with stockpiling and honing and organizing their work. George Carlin was an obvious example. George had files of jokes and thoughts, and subcategories of jokes and thoughts and ideas that are never-ending, all set down meticulously for present and future reference. This was one of the reasons why George was able to come up with fourteen HBO Specials, not to mention books, albums and countless TV appearances. By comparison, I'm happy if I can match my socks.

I forget exactly how it came up, but one day at his apartment Rodney wound up pulling out a large stack of well-worn papers from a file cabinet somewhere in his bedroom. It turned out to be all of his Tonight Show appearances, mapped out on paper. It was a list of all his standup jokes, followed by a list of the jokes he did on "panel," sitting in the chair next to Johnny Carson's desk. It was a case study of a master comedian's work ethic. I asked him if his first Tonight Show was in that pile somewhere. He shuffled through the papers and produced it; a piece of scratch paper so old and tattered it looked like a frayed map of Africa, with the same basic format he had used on all his other appearance notes - his standup jokes for the show, followed by his panel jokes.

It occurred to me to ask him if I could have that very first Tonight Show page, but I couldn't bring myself to do it. It almost seemed too much to ask, irreverent almost, for someone other than him to own such a souvenir. But I'll never forget it; a tangible artifact from the workings of one of the best comedians of our time.

(By the way, this anecdote does have a happy ending of sorts, although it involves another comedian entirely. Soon after I started opening for George Carlin, I asked George if I could maybe have something from his vast stockpile. I didn't care what it was, just something, a keepsake, maybe an old discarded note or an unused bit of material that he would've just thrown out anyway. George said sure, he'd find something and give it to me. The next day he handed me an envelope. I opened it when I got home and found out that it contained, neatly typed out, his original "Hippie-Dippie Weatherman" routine. I have it in my files at home in a fireproof box, one of my more treasured possessions. I threw out my original Picasso sketches to make room for it.)

I usually don't write jokes for other people, but early on in my career I did try my hand at writing a few for Rodney. One of them went like this; "She was fat, I tell ya. Every time she went swimming, she left a ring around the lake." Rodney told me he liked that one and that he was going to try it out onstage at the club that night. I was excited as hell, and eagerly watched from the back of the room as Rodney performed to a packed house. At a prearranged point in the show, amid a cluster of "My wife is fat" jokes, he dropped mine in; "I mean, when she went swimming, she left a ring around the lake."

It bombed. Utter silence. Not one laugh. Rodney wiped his brow, peered into the lights and said, "Thanks, Dennis. Thanks a lot for that shitty joke." People in the audience looked around the room, trying to find the perpetrator of this obviously hideous one-liner that had brought the show to a screeching halt. Ducking under chairs and behind tables, I slithered back into the bar as quietly as I could and ordered several large Heinekens. I never attempted to write jokes for Rodney again.

(I did get involved with writing TV Specials and a movie for him, and those were fruitful and interesting experiences. Maybe if I'd kept on trying, I would've given him a one-liner that he could have used, but that one bad experience kind of soured me on it forever. And yet, when his first special aired on ABC, I was watching one of the sketches, and guess what joke was in there? The infamous "Ring Around the Lake" joke! Good things come to those who wait...)

People would always send Rodney jokes, and he read them all. If he found one that he liked, he would sit there and say it, then rephrase it, reworking it over and over until he got it exactly right. I remember sitting and watching him work on a joke for about ten minutes. He'd sit there practicing it, bouncing it off the wall in the dressing room, stopping and starting over again until it sounded perfect to him. Then the next show he'd go onstage and drop it into the show, and nine times out of ten he'd get a big laugh with it. His instinct for what would work was amazingly accurate (except for that one time with mine. Did I tell you he wound up putting it in his special?...).

No one can be right 100% of the time, and one afternoon Rodney called me to tell me about a joke he had tried out onstage the night before that he was sure would get a big laugh.

ME: "What was the joke?"

RODNEY: It was: "My wife is dumb I tell ya. I took her to the movies, and she wanted to go backstage and meet the stars."

I thought the joke was funny, and so did Rodney, but he said the audience just stared at him like squirrels at a folk concert. Rodney eventually figured out that it was because going backstage to congratulate actors after a play is something only people in show business do and that normal citizens wouldn't make that connection. He may have been right, but we'll never know. He never tried the joke again.

One of the funniest incidents I remember happened backstage at a theater we were playing. I was sitting in my dressing room when I heard the unmistakable sound of Rodney in his slippers shuffling down the hall. He appeared at the doorway, wearing one of his many bathrobes and his reading glasses, a bemused look on his face. He was holding a sheet of jokes someone had sent him. He said;

"Someone just sent me a hundred of the stupidest jokes I've ever heard.," he said. "They're not even jokes! All this guy did," he continued," was write down something bad that happens, and then put 'No Respect' at the end of it. Listen to this..."

He adjusted his glasses and began to read down the list:

"I went to the refrigerator, there was no food in it. No respect.

"I was driving the car, and I ran outta gas. No respect.

"My doctor called, he hadda cancel my appointment. No respect.

He read a few more, then just couldn't go on. He took off his glasses and looked at me, incredulous.

"I could write a thousand of these myself. What do I need him for?"

One observation Rodney made is that when people sent him jokes, for some reason the best ones were usually handwritten, hardly legible, on greasy, crinkled-up loose-leaf paper with food spots on it. The ones that were neatly typed, double-spaced, on clean white typing paper were, more often than not, shit. Cleanliness may be next to Godliness, but it's not all that funny.

Yet another backstage factoid: Rodney often wore bathrobes, everywhere; in his room, backstage, in the steam room, in the hallway, sometimes in a restaurant or casino. What made this even more interesting was that, usually, Rodney wore absolutely nothing else underneath the bathrobe. And since he was in the habit of never tying the robe closed, you and anyone else in the vicinity would be treated to the sight of Rodney's "jewels" hanging out for the entire world to enjoy. When other comics who'd had encounters with Rodney find out I used to work with him, they will always have a story about the bathrobe, as if I didn't know this information firsthand...

>COMIC: "I knocked on Rodney's door once, and he came to the door wearing a bathrobe and..."
>ME:..."his junk was hanging out?"
>COMIC: "Yeah. How'd you know?"
>COMIC #2: "I was in the lobby of a hotel, and Rodney came walking by with a bathrobe opened up, and you'll never guess..."
>ME: "Testicles?"
>COMIC #3: "I was in a restaurant two months ago, and..."
>ME: "...Rodney was there wearing a bathrobe and you could see his nut sack?"
>COMIC #3: "Uh...no. I had the best hamburger I ever ate. Who's Rodney?"

If Rodney were ever knighted, I'm pretty sure he would have shown up for the ceremony in a bathrobe. The guy liked to be comfortable. And the Queen would say, "I hereby dub thee...Sir Ballsalot!"

Chapter 10.
The Magic Bus

By 1982 Rodney had gotten so big that he started to consider alternate travel options. He wasn't particularly fond of flying or going to the airport, so he decided that if a show we were doing was within a 4-hour drive from New York, he would hire a tour bus. He figured it this way: "By the time you get to the airport, check your bags, wait to board the plane, board the plane, get off the plane, get your bags, and ride to the venue, you've wasted 4 hours anyway. Why not do it all in one shot??

You've probably seen one of these buses on a highway somewhere, big and sleek with a huge painted insignia of an eagle or a mountain or a girl with big boobs on the side. The interior of these things was pretty cool... a sofa, a table and some plush chairs, a microwave oven, bunk beds for the occasional nap. You could ride for hours in luxury and comfort, and a famous comedian could put his feet up, put on a bathrobe and "let it all hang out." So that's how we would travel to the gigs in New Jersey or Pennsylvania or Connecticut...in a big ol' rock star bus..

There were a few things about this new development that struck me as hilarious. First of all, Rodney would always tell the bus driver to pick Peg and me up first, so this gigantic tour bus would be parked in front of our run-down tenement on 65th Street and wait for us to come down.

I remember a specific incident where we were on our way down the stairs from our apartment and we ran into a neighbor who was following us. He saw me carrying my guitar case and said, "Are you on your way to a gig?" As we reached the street-level landing I said, "Yep. The bus is waiting for us outside." The neighbor gave us a confused look and said, "Uuumm...don't you mean you're waiting for the bus?" At this point we all exited the building, where the huge tour bus opened its door for us. We watched our neighbor's mouth drop open as Peg and I hopped on. The last thing I heard our flummoxed neighbor say was...

"Uuuuuh...so....where are you going?"

"Baltimore.," I replied, as the bus door closed and we slowly pulled out.

Our neighbor just watched in awe as his fellow tenement dwellers pulled away in a vehicle that could have easily fit the cast of 'A Chorus Line" inside.

The second thing that was funny to me was the fact that this enormous bus was only carrying three people at any time; Rodney, Peggy and me. Every once in a while Rodney would want to stop at a gas station or a convenience store along the highway to buy cigarettes or gum or a bag of cheese doodles. I completely relished the thought of this bus pulling in to the parking lot and people standing around gawking, wondering which famous rock band was inside..."Is it the Eagles? The Who? Crosby Stills and Nash? Will they give autographs when we see them?"...and the door would hiss open, and out would shuffle this old Jewish comic with a blue safari shirt looking for the snack section and muttering, 'I might as well take a piss while I'm here."

Cheese doodles and cigarettes? $5.95. The disappointed looks on peoples' faces? Priceless.

Chapter 11.
Sam Kinison and other stories

It's common knowledge that Rodney was always a fan of young comedians, especially good ones. He had told me once about a guy he'd seen in Houston who was real funny and had a unique style, kind of like a manic comic preacher.

One night a guy named Sam Kinison came to the show at Dangerfield's. We started talking after the show, and he told me that he was a comedian from Houston and that Rodney had come to a club he had worked one night. I did the math and realized this was the guy Rodney had mentioned. I told Sam that Rodney loved his work and brought him down to meet him. They hit it off immediately, and Rodney eventually put Sam on his first Young Comedians special. The rest is history.

Sam always gave me credit for introducing him to Rodney, a key factor in igniting his career. When Sam was still unknown he was a regular MC at the Comedy Store in L.A., and he told me he would get me spots there whenever I wanted them. I took him up on the offer frequently, and he always came through. Whenever I ran into Sam over the years, he always greeted me with a big ol' bear hug. He was a nice guy.

I was working in Las Vegas with George Carlin when I heard about the car accident that killed Sam. George dedicated his HBO special that year to him. It was certainly a well-deserved and noble gesture. I also remember that George was planning to drive home the next night along the very same route where Sam had died. Peggy told George that maybe he should re-think his plans. George replied, "You know, the chances of two famous comedians dying in a car crash on the same highway two nights apart is re-e-e-ally fucking small."

I remember being in Rodney's dressing room soon after "Caddyshack" had come out. Caddyshack was far and away the catalyst in Rodney's rocket ship of a career. Even though everyone was funny in it, Rodney pretty much stole the movie in a part that was tailor-made for his one-liners and unique delivery. His performance especially resonated with young people who could identify not only with the humor but also with the image of the homely-looking guy who went up against the stuck-up country club elitists and won. From that point on, Rodney would play big halls and venues all across the country, often selling out two three-thousand seat shows in one night.

Rodney was still performing at Dangerfield's, but not for long. The once-underpopulated nightclub was now full to capacity every night he was there, with lines stretching around the block on weekends. It was becoming impossible and unfeasible for Rodney to work there anymore with his newfound popularity. (Often during this period, when people would ask him if he ever worked his club anymore, he would say "No, I had a fight with myself.")

Naturally, Rodney at this time was being courted to star in a movie of his own. All he needed was a premise, and he discussed that with me as he got dressed for what would be one of his final shows at his own club. "See if you can come up with an idea for a movie that I would star in," he said to me. "You think you can do that?"

I had the idea in ten minutes.

The movie was "Easy Money," which I'll discuss in its own chapter.

Most of us, of course, would kill to be in a movie. We couldn't begin to imagine that anyone would complain about having a successful film career. Rodney, of course, felt differently. After Caddyshack came out and was a huge success, Rodney summed up his feelings about doing movies this way;

"If you wanna punish a kid, you make him write something on the blackboard a hundred times. That's what making a movie is like." He didn't enjoy the endless takes, the waiting around, the whole process. Yet here he was, about to go through the whole thing again. But what else could he do? He was a superstar now, and he wasn't about to let this opportunity, not to mention this financial windfall, pass him by.

There was a hilarious example of how big a celebrity he'd become, and how ridiculous the whole experience can be. He had made it big already, doing the huge one-nighters, the TV shows, becoming a household name. He had plenty of money by this point, and probably could have retired at any moment if he wanted to. He certainly could afford to turn things down. But along came this offer from out of left field. The rich CEO of some company whose name escapes me had a son named Jason who was about to celebrate his thirtieth birthday, and he wanted to throw a party that his son would never forget. He had figured he'd hire Billy Joel to come play the piano and sing for an hour for a fee of $100,000.00. Billy turned down the offer (I mean, who can live on $100,000?), so the CEO dad turned to America's hottest comedian, Rodney Dangerfield. For $50,000.00, could Rodney come to his house and perform twenty minutes of standup? You know, just stand there in the living room and tell jokes to Uncle Jim and Aunt Edna and, of course, the birthday boy. Rodney thought it was the most insulting and absurd and ludicrous thing he'd ever heard of.

He took the offer.

He was still a little shocked and embarrassed that he did it, but he summed up his feelings succinctly on the limo ride to the guy's house: "It's $50,000.00. *For twenty minutes!* I don't care how big you are, how the hell do you turn down $50,000.00 for twenty minutes?"

Good point!

The fact that Rodney Dangerfield was about to perform in a split-level ranch style house with shag carpeting for a surprised audience of thirty or so uncles and aunts was funny enough. What made it even funnier to me was that he had insisted that I come along to open for him. For ten minutes. For $250.00. I don't care how big you get. How the hell do you turn down $250.00 for ten minutes on shag carpeting?

You don't. Especially when Rodney insists. Which he did.

When we got to the house, Rodney was met by the ecstatic CEO dad, who ushered us into our respective guest bedrooms to get dressed. Rodney got himself decked out in his full show garb. I put on a vest and made sure my fly was zipped up.

"Showtime" arrived. Someone flicked the dimmer switch on and off. The CEO dad came out and announced that in honor of Jason's thirtieth birthday, he had arranged for a special surprise performer to be there tonight. But first, there was an opening act.

I stepped out of the bedroom onto the living room landing. Someone handed me the microphone. The only problem was that, since I played the guitar in my act, I required the microphone to be placed in a stand. But there wasn't a stand. There was just the microphone. I asked one of the caterers if he would hold the microphone to my mouth while I performed. And he did. Reluctantly. Actually, he was pretty pissed off about it, and glared at me throughout my entire ten-minute show.

I have to admit I don't really remember much about the performance or how it went, since my primary emotion during it was supreme embarrassment tempered by bouts of nausea and anxiety. All I know is that eventually it ended, as proven by the fact that I am now writing about it. I do remember that for my entire show, no one bothered to stop eating their cake.

After my triumphant performance, the CEO proudly announced, "Ladies and gentlemen... and Jason...Rodney Dangerfield!"

Rodney came out of the bedroom and hit the living room to squeals of shock and delight. He then proceeded to do twenty minutes. The photographer took pictures. Hors d'ouerves were served. Party favors were given out. It was the most ridiculous thing I'd ever seen, except for what I'm about to tell you next.

Rodney and I had worked out an arrangement for when he and I performed at the big theatres. I would do my show, then I would put on a baseball cap and sneak out into the audience when he came onstage. About five minutes into his show, Rodney would be talking about the small town he grew up in ("it was a small town, I tell ya!"), at which point I, disguised as an audience member, would yell out, "How small was it!!?" Then Rodney would launch into a series of small town jokes. The reason this worked, of course, was because in the theatres I blended into those big audiences, and in the darkness no one could tell that the guy yelling "How small was it" was the same guy they'd just seen onstage a few minutes ago. Rodney had come to rely on this routine, and wanted me to do it at the CEO's house as well. The problem was that I wouldn't exactly be able to blend into the crowd here in the living room at Jason's thirtieth birthday party. But Rodney, as I said, had come to rely on it. So he asked me to do it. I finished my show, and then in full view of everybody came down into the living room to watch Rodney. For some reason I'd put on a baseball cap, as if that would disguise me in a ten by twelve-foot room. Rodney went along until he got to the part where he started talking about the small town he grew up in.

And I yelled out, "How small was it!!?"

Everyone turned around and looked at me, and I could see in their faces that they were thinking, "Isn't that the guy who was just on? Why is he heckling Rodney?"

I slunk off, vowing never to do anything like this again, no matter what. Luckily, that was the only time an offer like this ever came along. But who knows? If a 7/11 opens up and they need a comedian...

One thing I will always remember was that I've never seen two comedians get into a limo as fast as Rodney and I did after that show was over. As we sped away, Rodney sunk back in his seat for a while, then started to mutter softly..."I mean...How the hell do you turn down $50,000.00?"

Speaking of limos; (another amusing limo story)

We were on our way to a show in Dallas once, and the limo was late picking us up. To make matters worse, we immediately got stuck in heavy traffic, and it looked as if we'd be late for the show. Rodney told the driver to go up on the shoulder of the highway and bypass the other cars. The driver was reluctant to break the law in this way, but after some gentle coaxing by Rodney ("I'll pay for the damn ticket, just go!"), the driver took the shoulder route. Motorists were yelling and screaming at us as we passed.

After about ten minutes we hit a nail or something and got a flat tire. So here we were in this huge stretch limo stuck on the side of the highway, with all the motorists we'd passed now passing us, snickering and yelling obscenities and flipping us the finger. Rodney hid his face in his hands, embarrassed by the whole thing.

But the fact remained that we were still running late and had to get to the theatre somehow, so Rodney decided to bite the bullet. We grabbed our bags and got out of the limo as Rodney tried to flag down anyone who would stop. I couldn't help noticing some of the expressions on the faces of the passing motorists. They seemed to say things like, "Jeez, that guy looks like Rodney Dangerfield. Nahh, couldn't be, he'd be in a limo.," as they kept right on going.

Finally, he flagged down a guy driving the most godforsaken, dilapidated pickup truck I'd ever seen. It was covered with grime from at least 1962 and spat out gray, noxious smoke from the tailpipe. There were actually rust spots on the windshield. But it was a ride, and we were desperate. The driver, who from the looks of him had probably appeared as a regular on "Cops," spat out some tobacco juice as he let us in, while exclaiming, "Hey, you ain't that Roger Dangerford, are ya?" Then he pulled out, his truck backfiring all the way down the Interstate. He just couldn't believe he had a celebrity in his vehicle. "Hell, my wife's gonna die! Roger Dangerford, in my truck! My wife's just gonna shit! Hey Roger, you wanna beer?"

"No thanks, man," Rodney said as he began to cough uncontrollably. "Just get us there before these fumes kill us, okay?"

He did. We made it. And I guess that night, our driver's wife just shat.

A limo / hangover story ...

Rodney used to tell this joke in his act:

"Ya wanna really confuse a guy? Join him while he's taking a leak in the street."

One night Rodney, Peggy and I were riding home in yet another limo from yet another gig. After about forty-five minutes, we couldn't help noticing that instead of heading towards New York, we kept seeing signs that said "Cleveland, 80 Miles," which we quickly figured out meant we had been going the wrong way for forty-five minutes. Rodney tore the driver a new one about this error for about ten more minutes, then had him stop the car so he could reorient himself and get back on track. I figured I'd use this opportunity to relieve myself on the side of the highway. I guess Rodney thought this was a good idea, because a few seconds later he was standing next to me doing the same thing.

At which point I looked at him and said, "What are you trying to do, confuse me?"

Inside the limo, I heard Peg and the driver laughing at this. Rodney just chuckled, then zipped up and we all took off down the road.

The next day we flew to Los Angeles because Rodney was scheduled to appear on the

Tonight Show with Johnny Carson and we went with him for moral support and to provide any sort of assistance he might need. One of the places we ended up was the Improv in Hollywood, where Rodney went up and did his Tonight Show set to laughs and applause. He was feeling pretty good about things that night. Maybe a little too good.

After his set, Rodney and Peg and I hung out in the bar area where Rodney proceeded to have a martini, and then another martini, and another, and another, until he started to get so drunk we thought he would pass out and miss not only his Tonight Show spot but also his next seven personal appearances and several weeks' worth of memory. Peg and I took the young girl he had been talking to aside and convinced her to take Rodney home with her for the night, to tuck him in and make sure he didn't have another drink. The young girl did exactly that, and the next day we headed over to the NBC studios with a woozy, bedraggled Rodney who at least was able to stand upright.

Rodney's hangover was so bad that during his performance on TV that night he had to stop a few times and find his place. It was not his best performance to say the least, but at least he got through it and did well enough so that the audience didn't really notice his condition. Most of them assumed him losing his place was part of the act.

* * * * *

Rodney had become a huge star. He was recognized everywhere. One day in Milwaukee we decided to leave the hotel and go to a local supermarket for some fruit. Peg and I watched in amusement as Rodney squeezed melons while customers did double and triple takes upon realizing who he was. Not many people approached him, but he caused a stir just the same.

The store clerks noticed him pretty quickly. As Rodney wandered over to check out the bananas, he was spotted by a group of teenaged workers. Eager to alert their friends that a celebrity was in the store, they took out their little walkie-talkies and whispered discreetly...

"Hey, Joe. Rodney Dangerfield! He's in the store, right now. Yeah! He's in produce!"

Our Biggest Gig

Rodney was so hot now that he was getting offers to play 20,000 seat arenas and even the occasional 60,000 seat football stadium. Venues of this size are fine for rock & roll events, with their pyro and light shows and elaborate stage setups, but they don't exactly provide the kind of intimate setting that comedy needs. Something is definitely lost when there's one guy on stage telling jokes and, to the people in the cheap seats, he's the size of a sesame seed. Still, I suppose some of these offers were too big a financial windfall for him to turn down. Rodney accepted an offer to perform at the Minneapolis State Fair, smack dab in the middle of a racetrack surrounded by bleachers. I don't know exactly how many people this site can hold, but I do know the official estimate is "a whole shitload."

We were to perform on a stage built in the center of the track oval. This was during the pre-jumbotron era too. There would be us, then the racetrack, and then the bleachers, so basically the people in the first row were at least a hundred feet away from us. Nice and intimate.

Another terrific aspect of this show was that I was scheduled to go on before the sun went down. Now as I've mentioned before, it's hard enough being an opening act under the most ideal conditions. But when you have a darkened room and a spotlight shining on you, it at least focuses the audience's attention so you have a shot at building some momentum. Not only was I going to have to perform outdoors, without the benefit of a ceiling and walls to have the laughter bounce off of (sucks); and not only would I have to project enough to reach something like fifty-thousand people (blows); but I'd have to try to accomplish this in the glaring, blinding, ambient light of our friend Mr. Sun (kill me). In the kindest terms available, it was an interesting show. And I still have spots on my retinas.

Rodney's portion of the show was also interesting. The show promoters had requested that he keep his performance squeaky clean, since this was a very conservative part of the country and they didn't want the audience members to be offended. Rodney didn't cherish being restricted in this way, but he agreed to it and kept his jokes free of any objectionable content.

One set piece of his show in these days was to bring up the house lights and ask for questions from the audience. Since the closest audience member was basically in another time zone, they had set up microphones in the aisles so that people could speak into them and ask Rodney questions that way. When that segment of the show came, Rodney did his usual "does anyone want to ask me some questions?" routine. As people began stepping up to the microphones and asking their questions, it became clear that these folks weren't quite as conservative as the show promoters had thought they'd be. Sometimes there's nothing worse than an audience member with access to a loudspeaker, and the stuff that came out of these people's mouths proved the point conclusively. If I remember correctly, questions about Rodney's genitalia were the most frequent, followed by suggestions of what he should do with his genitalia, dirty jokes, inarticulate ramblings, filthy insults, underarm fart noises, and limericks about incest, fecal matter and animals. Rodney just stood there listening to all this stuff, and finally just said, "I'm glad they told me to clean up my fuckin' show."

I remember reading a review of the show in the morning paper. The headline of the review read "Dangerfield Show For Immature Audiences Only." It was the only review I've ever read where the performer was spared and the audience got slammed.

Chapter 12.
Easy Money

"Caddyshack," the film comedy starring Chevy Chase, Ted Knight, and Bill Murray, was a turning point in the life and career of Rodney Dangerfield. When I began working at Dangerfield's, Rodney was enjoying moderate success as a comedian. His club was usually full on weekends, but was often less than half that on weeknights, even when he was appearing. Then came "Caddyshack."

The movie became a big hit, and Rodney was singled out for his performance as a loud, crude, socially inept character who didn't fit in at all with the snobs at the golf club. His "no respect" image had sustained him for years, but the exposure this movie provided for him and his image struck a chord that resounded all across America.

Now Dangerfield's had become too small to hold the crowds that wanted to get in to see him perform. He'd outgrown his own club and started being booked to perform in the big theatres nationwide. In 1980, Rodney Dangerfield was the hottest comedian in America.

So naturally, the movie offers started pouring in. One night at the club, he told me that Orion Pictures wanted him to come up with an idea for a movie he could star in. He told me (in his dressing room, as he was putting on his pants - Rodney always felt comfortable with me I guess) that if I could come up with an idea, he would give me a "story by" credit on the movie.

This was one of the things that really was great about Rodney. I was a relative unknown. My entire experience with the movies was buying tickets and popcorn and finding a seat. And yet here he was, offering me the opportunity to create what was sure to be a major film starring one of the hottest guys in show business. This kind of thing doesn't happen a hell of a lot, and I was eager and ready to capitalize on it.

As I mentioned before, the idea came quickly to me because I knew Rodney pretty well by now. I was familiar not only with his image and his style, but also with the real personal struggles he had, the constant battles to try and control his weight, his smoking, and his drinking.

So I thought; What if he were to play a guy who smokes, drinks, gambles and partakes of the seven deadly sins (and maybe two or three more that weren't even covered in the Bible)? Then what if, suddenly, his hated mother-in-law dies, and stipulates in her will that her no-account son-in-law stands to inherit her entire ten million dollar fortune, but only if he stops smoking, drinking, and gambling for one full year?

I was extremely excited about this, and hurried over to the club that night to present the idea to Rodney, hoping he'd like it, hoping he'd be knocked out by the concept. To the best of my memory, I told him, he listened, and replied, "Yeah. Good. Okay."

High praise indeed.

I was thrilled. I'd been a standup for less than a year, and already I had a movie in the works. I figured they'd make the movie, Peggy and I would go to the premiere, and that would be that.

Well, not quite.

Estelle Endler, Rodney's manager at the time, had hired two writers to do the script; her husband, Michael Endler, and a then-writer for the National Lampoon named P.J. O'Rourke, who has since gone on to national renown as a social commentator with several books and essays and numerous cable television appearances to his credit. The two writers finished the script and gave the draft to Rodney, who called me up in what could kindly be described as a pissy mood:

"They just gave me the script for the movie."

"Oh yeah? Is it good?"

"I want you to read it and tell me what you think of this piece of shit."

"Uh.......okay."

Through simple intuition, deductive reasoning and retention of the phrase, "this piece of shit," I concluded that Rodney felt the script might need a rewrite.

I read the script, and told Rodney I honestly felt that it was okay. I thought it could use some punching up and funnier jokes here and there, but it was after all a first draft and all first drafts needed reworking. Apparently (as I found out much later) Rodney called Estelle immediately and told her I had confirmed what he thought. According to Rodney, I felt, as he did, that the script was a complete piece of shit and that the writers, her husband included, had the comedy instincts of a crouton. Oh, and by the way, he also told Estelle "I want Dennis to be a writer on the movie. Maybe he can help make it funny, not a piece of shit like these other two made it."

Imagine how pleased Estelle, Michael and P.J. were to see me on that first day of rewrites at Rodney's apartment. If looks were laser beams, my brains would have melted in the Dutch oven that had once been my head.

By the way, at this point I had no idea what Rodney had told them my reaction to their script had been. I had no inkling of the fact that this threesome thought I had savaged their work. All I knew was, gosh oh gee, now I'm a writer on Rodney Dangerfield's guaranteed-to-be-a-hit next movie, and wasn't life a big kick in the head and weren't we all lucky and happy to be here together working on this project kumbaya my Lord, kumbaya! I sat there like Barney the dinosaur, blindly unaware that across the table three people were probably imagining what I'd look like with a chalk outline around my bullet-riddled body.

I may not be the most perceptive guy in the world, but by the end of that first rewrite session, even I could tell that Michael, Estelle and P.J. would have rather accepted ideas from a porcelain frog than from me. Every contribution I made was greeted with cynical derision tempered with a healthy dollop of scorn. Thinking back on it now, they must have been in a weird position. Here was this guy who supposedly had trashed their skills, talent and effort, and they were forced not only to be in a room with him, but actually WORK WITH THE SON OF A BITCH!! I hate me just thinking about it, and I generally like me as a rule.

I eventually got an opportunity to talk with them all and straighten out this huge misunderstanding, and after that everything went much more smoothly. But that first six months? Donkey dung.

By the way, yes I did say "first six months." That may seem like a long time to work on a rewrite, but let me assure you, I WISH IT HAD BEEN THAT SHORT. Rodney had clear ideas on what he wanted, unyielding reactions on what he hated, and strong opinions on how the lines of dialogue should be said, even the lines that weren't his. Many times in fact, at the end of a day, the five or six pages of dialogue we had finished all sounded like Rodney...his delivery, his timing, his inflections. Through sheer force of his personality and will, all the characters in the script started to sound like him. We were faced with someday releasing a movie starring Rodney Dangerfield, Joe Pesci Dangerfield, Jennifer Jason Leigh Dangerfield, and Taylor Negron Dangerfield.

Since Rodney's world had always consisted of jokes, jokes and more jokes, it was tough to get him to realize that all the scenes in the movie didn't have to be a series of one-liners and zingers. That's the natural way that he thought, that's what had gotten him this far in his career, and that's all he felt the movie needed in order to be funny; jokes, jokes, jokes, like a 90-minute vaudeville routine on film. Of course there needed to be jokes, but it was a tough sell to convince him that sometimes characterization or nuance or just the situation was enough to get laughs.

When Joe Pesci signed on to play Rodney's friend, we of course were all thrilled. Joe had just been in "Raging Bull," and everyone was understandably excited to have him in our movie. Joe, of course, came from a different place than Rodney. The actor naturally would build a character, and Joe was always trying to get Rodney to hang out with him "in character" so they could truly get into their roles. "Rodney," Joe said once.... "Let's you and me go to a fight and hang out as Monte and Nicky" (their characters in the movie). Rodney turned to Joe and looked at him like he'd just asked him to put on a spandex halter top.

"I don't do that, man. I don't do that method shit.," he said. Joe looked at him dumfounded as he continued. "Here's the way I do it. You throw a line at me, I throw a line at you. Back and forth, that's it. Okay, man?"

Rodney's reliance on "the joke" was all encompassing. Michael Endler told me that he and Rodney went to a screening of "Tootsie" once, and that all around them in the theatre, people were howling with laughter at one of the scenes. The scene was all visual and situational, with no jokes at all, and Rodney could not understand what everyone was laughing about. "Where are the jokes, man?" is all he kept saying. "This isn't funny. Where are the jokes?" Even though an entire audience was laughing hysterically, Rodney was convinced that the movie wasn't funny. Such is the devotion to the art of the joke, the joke, nothing but the joke.

I heard later on that Joe Pesci was extremely frustrated by Rodney's notion of acting and how he felt it affected the movie. Almost every day Joe would go to Estelle and say, "Is it over?" When Estelle asked what he meant, he'd say, "My career. Is my career over yet?"

* * * * *

So with all the struggling and arguing for scenes and against scenes, for jokes and against jokes, and just the usual haggling that I suppose goes on with many projects like this, the rewrites for the movie that would become "Easy Money" took about two years. And that's not counting the constant rewrites on the set.

As for the actual filming, even with all the craziness, I have to admit it was one of the most exciting and rewarding experiences I've had in my life, even though I've come to learn that it might not have been that way for the other actors in the film. As far as I'm concerned, few things can compare to going from being a singer in a sangria-soaked wine and cheese eatery to being on the set as one of the writers of a major motion picture. I was actually hanging out with and helping to put words into the mouths of actors like Joe Pesci and Jennifer Jason Lee. Although it wasn't required, I would try to be on the set every day, just in case they needed a rewrite or a turn of phrase or someone to eat for free. They have free food at these things, you know. Tons of it. Completely free of charge.

I also got to appear in two scenes; as a fashion critic during the "Regular Guy Look" fashion show; and as a gasping, bed-ridden hospital patient in a scene with Joe Pesci and Jennifer Jason Leigh. (I got to sneeze on her head. It's in my résumé.)

Probably the most memorable thing that happened on that set, at least from the standpoint of the diligent, hard-working, and considerably horny crew members, is the day when the Playboy Playmate of the Year showed up to do her scene. Naturally, she was beautiful, and naturally, she had big breasts. No, make that huge breasts. To borrow a phrase from Firesign Theatre, she had a balcony you could do Shakespeare off of.

In her scene, she was lounging in her backyard almost completely naked. Rodney/Monte came onto the landing to throw out his garbage, took one look at her, bugged out his already bugged-out eyes, and almost decided to blow the inheritance right then and there. On the day they filmed that scene, not only did every guy involved with the movie show up, but the line producer actually sold tickets to the room in the house that overlooked the backyard.

I think he's still living off the money he made.

Speaking of "Easy Money"...

A few weeks after Easy Money had wrapped. Rodney and I performed a show in Chicago. Roger Ebert, the famed movie critic, was at the show and invited Rodney and me out to dinner afterwards at the world-famous Pump Room restaurant.

One of Rodney's quirks was that he could be congenial and engaging and entertaining as an offstage host, but once he started eating something came over him. It was hard to describe, but suffice it to say that his eyes would glaze over and he would be in another world, in a trance, uninterested in anyone and anything except the meal at hand. So on that night at the Pump Room, as soon as dinner arrived, Rodney, Roger and I were seated at the table, but only two of us were present. Roger and I were engaged in conversation. Rodney was busy eating and drinking on his faraway planet, oblivious to everything except his turkey leg and mashed potatoes.

Roger was in the midst of expounding on the craft of film acting, explaining all the major theories, Stanislavski, Stella Adler, the Method, etc. etc. After about three minutes of this, Rodney had finally had enough. He put down his fork and carving knife, wiped his mouth and said;

"What's all this bullshit about acting? It's bullshit. If you're supposed to be mad, you pretend you're mad. If you're supposed to be happy, you pretend you're happy. That's all you gotta do, it's not rocket science. "Schools of acting"...it's all bullshit. Pass the fuckin' potatoes."

Then Rodney returned to "Planet Appetite" and continued eating. Roger just stared at him with his mouth hanging open. The Rodney Dangerfield Theory of Acting...'It's All Bullshit!" Priceless.

Chapter 13: T.V. Land and Other Rodney Adventures

"Easy Money" had a good showing at the box office, and Rodney's concert career was through the roof. Offers were pouring in from everywhere, to do more movies, more albums, and of course television specials. Rodney and I co-wrote most of the material for his TV specials in the early eighties. I went out to L.A. with him for the first taping, and incidentally accompanied him and sat in the audience for an appearance he was making on the Tonight Show.

He had appeared on Johnny Carson's Tonight Show throughout the years, but since he had become a superstar the excitement in the audience was incredible when he appeared. It must have been similar to the electricity that was in the air the night the Beatles appeared on Ed Sullivan. And Rodney had better hair.

Rodney had asked me to yell out my usual "how small was it!?" from my perch in the audience so he could launch into his string of small town jokes. Of course, he knew how much I wanted to be on the Tonight Show myself someday, so he jokingly told me "And do me a favor, Dennis...Don't yell out, 'How small was it, Johnny put me on the show!'"

One enduring memory from that night (aside from seeing Johnny and Rodney in action live in the studio) was of watching the show during the commercial breaks, which of course you never get to see at home. At each break Johnny would take out a cigarette and smoke like a fiend. He literally would smoke it all the way down to the filter by the time the break ended. Then he would take one final drag and tap it out a millisecond before he came back on the air.

By the way, I did yell out "How small was it" and nothing more. But I am insisting that since my voice was heard on the broadcast,

I can say that technically I was on the Tonight Show with Johnny Carson that evening and I'm putting it on my résumé, dammit, along with sneezing on Jennifer Jason Leigh's head.

Rodney did two specials for ABC. They included guest stars such as Bill Murray, Robert Urich, Andy Kaufman, Angie Dickinson and Valerie Perrine. We wrote a song parody for the first special called "The Lord High Executioner" which featured Bill Murray. In the piece, Rodney played a king who has a list of everyone who had done him wrong and who he summarily would bring forth, sentence, and have put to death. Bill played Rodney's brain-damaged servant. It was his favorite sketch in the entire special, and when Bill found out I'd co-written it, he approached me one night at an after-hours bar I had begun to frequent called J.P.'s and raved about it. I was always a fan of his, and it was fairly cool to have someone you'd admired for such a long time come up to you and praise your work. Another reason the moment was so memorable was that while Bill was speaking to me, some drunk decided to chime in (actually, a friend of mine at the time. Ok, actually, the guy who'd stolen my Phone Answering Machine ideas). He was hanging on Bill's arm and going on and on about how he loved him and could he have an autograph and "hey Bill, didja hear the one about the Jew and the quadriplegic?" Bill's concentration never wavered the entire time. He never even glanced at my "friend" or acknowledged his existence in any way. (I'm sure to this day my old friend must still be telling the story about how he and Bill Murray used to hang out at the bar and talk for hours.)

The second ABC special was memorable for two reasons.

First of all, Rodney was scheduled to do some standup to start the show off, and they brought a live audience in for it. They had requested that I assume my warmup role and keep the audience entertained until he came out. What they'd neglected to tell me was that they hadn't constructed the set for the standup segment yet, and had in fact planned to build it all around me while I was performing.

It's hard enough to perform for a roomful of strangers, but it's even worse when there's hammering and sawing and workmen yelling things like, "Hey Vinnie, where's the fuckin' tape measure?"

Walls, banisters and a makeshift stage were literally put up as I was delivering punchlines. I finally realized that if I were to survive at all, I'd need to throw away the standard act and just go off on what was happening all around me, which I did and which worked just fine. To the best of my recollection, the last thing the audience heard before Rodney hit the stage was "Thank you ladies and gentlemen, enjoy Rodney," "Is that curtain crooked? Aww, fuckit."

The second memorable event was when Rodney was talked into doing his own stunt, to disastrous effect. We had written an opening scene where Rodney was on the ledge of a building threatening to jump unless he got his own special. At the last minute, the president of ABC (played by me) showed up and told him he got his special, then gave him a congratulatory slap on the back, which sent him falling off the ledge.

The director had talked Rodney into doing the fall himself. He was about three feet off the ground, and he would fall onto a thick, soft mattress below camera range. Nothing could possibly go wrong, and besides, there was no other way to do the scene effectively. We did the scene. I appeared at the window, slapped him on the back, and Rodney fell. And he didn't get up.

I can still remember the hush that fell over the set. It was so quiet I could hear the blood rushing past my ears. He lay there for almost a minute, and we thought rational thoughts like, "is he dead?" Then finally, he slowly began to move and clutched his neck, saying, "I think I need to go to the hospital."

From what I can remember, I think he hit his head, blacked out momentarily, and came to with a severe neck ache. He was fine after a few days rest and continued working the following week.

Could you imagine the media frenzy though if it had been more serious? "Opening acts who kill their headliners, today on Oprah."

Atlantic City Gypsies

Rodney and I performed many times in Atlantic City, and it remains the home of my favorite family of characters, a family I will refer to here as simply the Atlantic City Gypsies.

I was hanging out with Rodney at the hotel when I got a phone call. It was my wife Peggy on the line (yes, I'd married that girl), and the call wouldn't have been noteworthy except for the fact that she was in hysterics and could not stop laughing. It seems she had wandered into a rug and knick-knack store on the boardwalk and had now been kidnapped by the owners.

Okay, let me back up a bit.

First of all, for those of you who have never been to Atlantic City, let me first say that its famed boardwalk is bordered by the strangest assortment of stores you could ever imagine. Each store seems to be selling the same thing, which is, basically, anything they can find. It's not uncommon to have one store that specializes in "I'm With Stupid" T-shirts, but also happens to sell radios, cookware, photo albums, paintings and pool equipment. And if you don't like the merchandise in this particular store, you can go one door down to a store that specializes in radios, which also happens to sell all of the previous items at the exact same price.

I never understood this "exact same price" thing as a marketing gimmick. I'm no businessman, but to me it would seem that if you're going to open up three hundred similar stores with similar items, someone should be able to come up with the notion of, say, beating the competition's prices. Well, apparently not on the boardwalk. The overriding merchant motto seems to be "Same Price or your Money Back!!!" I really don't follow the logic;

"Hey, y'know there's a store down the block that's selling fake vomit for $2.99."

"Oh, yeah!? Well, we'll sell fake vomit, and we'll also charge $2.99. Ha! We'll show them!"

Anyway, The store Peg had wandered into was called "Bellrose Galleries," so-named I suppose because the name "T-shirts and Vomit" had been taken by everyone else. I'm not sure how they decided on the "Galleries" part, since there were no paintings there. Although there was a nice collection of big porcelain Buddha figurines on sale, right next to a table full of squirt guns and "Retired Old Fart" baseball caps. I would be tempted to say that one reason Peg chose this store was the "Lost Our Lease/ Everything Must Go!" sign in the window, except for the fact that almost every other boardwalk store has the same sign. There's one store that's been going out of business since the first moon landing. I have a feeling that "Lost Our Lease/Everything Must Go" is just a disguised way of saying "How Can We Get People To Think This Crap is Cheap?."

   Peg had spotted a rug in the Bellrose Galleries window that had caught her eye. Another thing that had caught her eye in the window was the ample butt of one of the store managers, Schultz, who was fixing a display. She had asked the price of the rug, and Schultz had discussed it with his butt pretty much in her face the entire time. When another store manager spotted her and asked her whom she was talking to, she replied, "some asshole in your window."

Since there was a dearth of customers that day, the denizens of Bellrose swooped down on her and brought her inside, plying her with coffee and showing her rug after rug after rug. When they began pressing her for a decision, she came out with every store manager's nightmare customer response: "Let me think about it. I'll be back." Having heard this exact sentence uttered no doubt twelve million times before, they held her captive in the back and forced her to call her husband. When I got on the phone, they told me that they had my wife in custody and that they would not release her until I came down there personally and persuaded her to buy a rug.

I hung up and told Rodney that my wife was a hostage in a rug shop and I'd be right back. He was intrigued by this and decided to accompany me on my ransom mission.

When Rodney and I walked in, there was Peg, in the rear rug area surrounded by velvet ropes. Rodney took one look at the store and the weird characters running it and said, "What are you? Gypsies?" They of course recognized him immediately and asked for autographs, and Rodney got into the absurd spirit of the situation. He said he would give no autographs until they released my wife, and that they should not try to force her to buy a rug. One of the gypsies, Joe, turned to Rodney and said,

"You finger your ass too much?"

Rodney said, "What?"

Joe said, "You figure we ask too much? For the rugs, I mean."

Rodney looked at him for a moment and replied, "That's not what you said the first time."

Now everyone was laughing, including Rodney, who for whatever reason really got into this "finger your ass too much" joke. I mean, he *really* got into it. All that day and night.

After the gypsies released Peg and got Rodney's autograph, Peg, Rodney and I began walking down the boardwalk to our hotel. We would've gotten back a lot sooner if Rodney didn't constantly stop people along the way to riddle them;

"Hey, Rodney, how ya doin!"

"Good, man. Hey, let me ask you something. Did you just eat at that restaurant over there?"

"Huh? Uh...yeah, why?"

"Do you finger your ass too much?"

"Excuse me?"

"I said, do you figure they ask too much? You know, for a meal."

(Relieved) Oh, no. It was very reasonable."

On and on it went, people coming up to him or him stopping people, asking them variations on his new favorite theme;

"Hey Rodney, we're coming to your show tonight."

"Oh yeah? You finger your ass too much?"

"What?"

"Do you figure they ask too much? For the tickets?"

(Relieved) "Nahh, they were a gift from my uncle."

The hardest part of this whole thing by far was for Peg and I to keep a straight face while he was doing this. If we had succumbed to our natural inclination to roll on the boardwalk laughing, the joke would have been ruined.

The funniest was when we got back to his room. A sweet-faced female security guard came by to check on his broken door lock.

Guard: "Okay, Mr. Dangerfield, it's all been fixed. Have a nice day."

Rodney: "Hey, let me ask you something. You worked here a long time?"
Guard: "Uh....yeah, about six years, Mr. Dangerfield."
Rodney: "You finger your ass too much?"
I'll never forget the look that came over that poor woman's face at what she thought she'd just heard. Her jaw dropped twelve feet. Her eyes became glassy, and her entire body went stiff. Apparently this particular kind of situation had not been covered in the manual. Peg and I had to duck out of sight and stuff pretzels in our mouths to stifle the laughter.
Guard: "Uh.....Um.....Uh.....Eh.....Excuse Me?"
Rodney: "For the rooms. You figure they ask too much for a room here?"
Her whole being relaxed and her jaw swiveled back up from the floor.
Guard: "Well....I do!"

Of all the times I've spent with Rodney, this was by far the funniest day we ever had.

By the way, whenever Peg and I are in Atlantic City, we still stop by to visit our favorite gypsies. And occasionally buy an "I'm With Buddha" T-shirt.

The Birthday Party

In 1982 Rodney had a party at Dangerfield's for his 60th birthday. It was a great night, and I mention it briefly here only for the fact that the guest list of people who showed up to honor Rodney on his 60th birthday was amazing. Among the guests that night were Chevy Chase, Steve Martin, Robert Klein, Danny Aiello and John Belushi. That's how big a star, and how highly regarded, Rodney had become.

One of my best memories of that night was performing a parody of "I Write The Songs" onstage and Peggy telling me that Steve Martin had watched and was laughing the whole time.

I also remember going down to the dressing room during the party to get some film for Peg's camera, and sitting there in the midst of a discussion were Rodney's room mate Joe Ancis and John Belushi. John scowled at me a little bit, making me think I was interrupting, so I left as quickly and quietly as possible.

One month later, Belushi would be dead from a drug overdose.

Robert Klein

I also remember that being the night when comedian Robert Klein came over to me, put his arm around me and said loudly, "Hey Dennis, I used to be Rodney's protégé. I guess you're the new guy now!" He was half-joking I'm sure, but I remember feeling badly that he may have felt a little hurt that I was the one getting so much of Rodney's attention lately. Rodney was an early admirer of Robert's keen comedy mind and had taken him under his wing years earlier, and you couldn't blame him. Robert was and is a brilliant and influential comedian, often and accurately credited for being the originator of the brand of "observational" humor that was later adopted by such stalwarts as Jerry Seinfeld and the like. He had so many great and memorable bits, groundbreaking albums (the iconic "Child Of The Fifties" among others), and numerous appearances on TV, in movies and on Broadway. I really never wanted to feel that he resented me for any reason, and since he was always nice and supportive and friendly to me whenever we would run into each other, I came to realize I'd been silly and there was no reason to believe he harbored any ill feelings. I was thrilled that when he briefly hosted a radio show in the early eighties in New York he graciously had me on to do a guest spot.

Robert and I had a pleasant reunion at a show he did in Las Vegas in 2019 at the Southpoint hotel. He was as funny as ever and I was glad we got to hang out for a while.

Chapter 14.
The Rescue Comic (rescues the Pointer Sisters, Eddie Rabbit and Ben Vereen)

I got booked fairly often on my own in Atlantic City as an opener for performers besides Rodney. One of these bookings was as the opening act for the Pointer Sisters at Caesar's on the boardwalk. The Pointers were really nice people, with good, responsive audiences. They were also the tallest women I've ever met. It was a good gig, and we got along very well.

One night before the show I got word that June, one of the sisters, had gotten food poisoning and might not be able to go on. Jokingly, the other sisters, Anita and Ruth, came to my dressing room and started sizing me up, wondering how I'd look in a dress and asking me if I knew their songs. (I could see the headline: "Blair Abandons Comedy, Becomes Black Female Singer"). June was indeed too sick to go on, and the Pointers had to cancel their show. Herb Wolfe, the entertainment director, came to me and requested, since the audience was already there, that I salvage the evening by doing a one-hour show of my own. I agreed.

Caesar's made an offer to the audience over the loudspeakers; they could get their money back and leave, or they could stay and watch me do a show. Amazingly, most of the audience stayed, and I did a good, solid one-hour performance. David Spatz, the reviewer for the Atlantic City Press, was there and reviewed my show favorably, headlining his article "Dennis Blair to the Rescue," and detailing how I'd stepped in for the ailing Pointers at the last minute. From then on, for at least the rest of that year, I became known as "The Rescue Comic." The reason for this was not just because of the Pointers' show, but a series of weird events that took place over the ensuing months where I would be called upon to fill in for a succession of ailing headliners.

A few weeks after the Pointer Sisters incident I was in Atlantic City again, opening for Rodney at the Resorts Hotel. Ben Vereen was scheduled to appear and to host a telethon at Caesar's that night, but had broken his leg and couldn't go on. Herb Wolf called and asked if I could somehow get over there for the two scheduled shows and fill in for a while. Of course I could, I replied. Don't you read the papers? I'm the RESCUE COMIC.

It was like some unreleased Marx Brothers movie. After my first show at Resorts, Caesar's would send a car to shuttle me and magician Jeff McBride over and do the show there. After that show, they'd haul me back to Resorts, where I'd do the second show, then head back over to Caesar's to do their second show. It was fairly tiring, but the weirdest part about doing four shows in one night was the repetition factor. By the fourth show I was so confused and disoriented that I was never completely sure whether the joke I was about to do was one I had just done a few minutes earlier.

By the way, Ben Vereen had hired a full orchestra to be onstage at Caesar's, and they just sat there while I performed. At one point during the telethon segment I decided to do my "New York, New York" parody and asked them to join me, which they gleefully did. About twenty minutes after I came off, Andy Williams showed up to sing a few songs. The last song he did was "New York, New York." Unfortunately, my parody was still fresh in the audience's minds, and they kept giggling all through Andy's rendition of the song. I could see by the look on Andy Williams' face that he had no idea why the audience was laughing at him. I could almost hear him thinking, "Is my fly open?"

A few weeks later in Milwaukee I was scheduled to open for Eddie Rabbit, the country singer. The show was cancelled the first night, because Eddie got strep throat. I kept waiting for them to call me in as a replacement, but the call never came. DIDN'T THEY KNOW WHO I WAS!!?

Celebrities were dropping like flies all around me during this period. I started thinking of myself as a jinx. It was during this time that I was in L.A. to do the ill-fated TV Special where I slapped

Rodney on the back and he wound up in the hospital. Also, this was when I was to open for Paul Anka at the Universal Amphitheater. In light of all that had happened with these celebrities I was involved with recently, Peg turned to me before the Universal gig and said, "Hmm. I wonder how Paul Anka's feeling these days."

Fortunately, my spell wore off. Celebrities miraculously stopped getting sick and injured, and my reign as the Rescue Comic came to an end. But just in case I'm ever needed again, I'm still holding on to the costume and cape.

Chapter 15: Best-Selling Author Robert Ludlum

No, I never opened for Robert Ludlum. True, he was a famous novelist, but novelists are not generally noted for their live performance skills. The reason I bring him up is because he and his wife Mary lived in the house across the street from Rodney in Westport Connecticut. Rodney had become friends with the Ludlums, and subsequently Peg and I became their friends as well. They were extremely nice people (I was very saddened when I heard Robert had died). It was apparent that Mr. Ludlum had done quite well from his writings, because his house was large and beautiful, and had a large pool, which overlooked a stream, which overlooked Long Island Sound. (I used to tell him that he was the only guy I know who had Poolfront/Riverfront/Lakefront property.)

As you could tell by reading his books, he had a fascinating mind, inquisitive and probing, with an affinity for details and intrigue. This was made clear one time when he came to see Rodney and me perform in Atlantic City. We all went to the lounge to have some drinks after the show, and the man who was in charge of slot machine operations came over to say hello. Robert started grilling him immediately about how the slot machines work, and asked him about how one could go about rigging a machine so as to get an illegal payout. Like the guy would actually tell him. But what the hell, it was worth a shot.

One afternoon after Easy Money had come out, the Ludlums threw a little impromptu party at their house with Rodney and Peggy and me and a few other friends of theirs. We were all hanging out by the pool, relaxing and having a very nice time. Robert knew I'd co-written Easy Money, and, having had a few drinks that afternoon, was feeling expansive and loose. He also kept buttering his tie.

He began talking about movies and scriptwriting and what I thought about the idea of adapting certain things for the screen, such as, for instance, novels by really famous authors.

At one point he disappeared into the house and came back a few minutes later, clutching one of his novels in his hand. He gave it to me and said, "Read this and tell me what you think."

I knew he was pretty drunk by now, but the words had come out surprisingly clearly. Although I didn't fully understand what he meant.

"Tell you what I think about what?"

"You know. If this book would make a good movie or not."

"You mean this best-selling novel with your name on it as the author?"

"Yeah."

"Why are you asking me?"

"'Cause if you think it would make a good movie, you can write it."

Okay, so Robert Ludlum had just basically offered me the task of possibly making one of his million-selling books into a screenplay for a movie. Now remember, just a few years earlier I was singing James Taylor songs in broken-down hippie-taverns for thirty bucks a night, and now I was looking at maybe, oh I don't know, THE CHANCE OF A LIFETIME?

"No problem, Robert.," I said, as calmly as I could. "I'd be glad to give it a look."

I figured, sure he's a little tipsy, but maybe.....Okay, he's shitfaced , but y'know, some people handle being shitfaced very well. And who knows, tomorrow when he's sober he might even remember this conversation we're having now...About doing a Robert Ludlum movie...Millions of dollars...summer blockbuster...total respect in the industry...Leading to other scriptwriting offers... Working closely with Spielberg on our third project...

"Dennis!? Are you there? You seem far away."

"Huh? Oh no, I was just thinking, Robert. Would tomorrow morning be soon enough?"

"Overnight? You can read a whole book in one night?"

"Yeah, well, I'm a little pumped."

"Sure. Let me know tomorrow morning. Then maybe we'll discuss, you know, terms."

"Sure, uh huh. Terms would be good."

I was completely out of my body by this point. If Paul Newman had shown up, I would've imploded. That night, I stayed up till about five A.M., getting through most of the book. I awoke bleary-eyed but full of ideas for a great movie.

Peg and I had breakfast with Rodney, then I walked across the street and knocked on Mr. Ludlum's door. He answered tentatively, haltingly, as if he might have a slight headache.

"Hi Dennis. What is it, morning?"

"Afternoon, actually."

"Ah. Must've been sleeping, then. What's up?"

"Just wanted to let you know that I read the book."

"Okay. Good for you. What book?"

"The one.....the book that....yesterday, when you..."

I didn't need a guy with a megaphone to tell me that Robert had indeed forgotten our conversation, and that the offer had obviously been made under the influence of forces he could not control.

"Umm....never mind. Hey, good party yesterday. Thanks for having us over."

"Okay."

He closed the door and I walked back to Rodney's house. I imagined Robert inside, shuffling up to his wife and saying, "Mary, did we have a party yesterday?"

Years later, when I was appearing in Las Vegas with George Carlin, Robert came to town and saw my name on the marquee. He called me and asked me to come visit him and Mary in their hotel suite. I did, and we had a great visit, laughing and talking over old times. The infamous novel-to-screenplay conversation never came up. I'm sure if he remembered it at all, he would think it was a dream he must have had. And anyway, why force the issue?

Somewhere in a box in my garage I'm pretty sure I still have the copy of the novel he gave me, with the words he scribbled in his own hand on the title page: "Dennis - tell me."

Chapter 16:
The Big Kiss-off
(or "How I Lost My Gig")

On New Year's Eve 1983, Rodney decided to fire me.

A few things led up to this forced separation. For one thing, Estelle Endler had turned against me, mainly due to lies that her assistant Kathy had told about me and things that I had allegedly said (but never did). You all have heard about how slimy this business can be, and how certain people will do things for their own advancement even if it's to the detriment of others. I won't go into detail about what happened to me, since Estelle is long dead and as far as I know Kathy is out of the business. Suffice it to say that I was a victim of typical show-biz backstabbing, and let it go at that. Another reason that Rodney fired me is Joan Rivers, whose opening act I was to become for the next two years.

Rodney hated Joan because he felt that she had basically stolen his act; not so much the exact jokes, although he felt she had done that as well, but also his style and his delivery. Although they both dealt in rapid-fire one-liners and shared some of the same subject matter ("ugly" jokes, spouse jokes, "I'm not sexy" jokes, etc.), to me their styles and delivery were very different. Rodney was the put-upon guy, moaning about how he could never get a break, while Joan was the gossipy vixen who took the audience into her confidence by dishing celebrities, herself and her husband Edgar. Rodney didn't see it this way, and there really was no room for discussion. In his view Joan Rivers, along with David Brenner and certain others, had stolen his jokes, and when someone steals your jokes, according to Rodney, it's like "slapping your kids."

(Interesting aside # whatever: In the world of standup comedy, there is no real way of protecting jokes. If you do a joke onstage and an unscrupulous comedian is in the audience, he can steal that joke and use it in his act, even do it on television or YouTube or on social media or whatever. The only recourse the original comedian would have is to confront the "thief" and tell him not to do the joke anymore or, as happened once to a very famous comedian who had a reputation for stealing material, corner the thief and beat the shit out of him. Standups are on an honor system not do other comics' material, and the majority abide by this unwritten rule. The relatively few comedians who do steal are generally well-known and ostracized by the comic community, and are usually wished an early and violent death.)

One thing about many celebrities I've come in contact with is that it's extremely hard to win an argument with them. So often the ego accompanying the drive that leads to fame is also fueled by an overriding belief that the celebrity is right and everyone else is wrong. This was no less true with Rodney. According to him, Joan Rivers was stealing his stuff, and that was that. It was fruitless for anyone to argue, especially since in my case it would have meant "sayonara" to my gig. And anyway, I never felt the need or desire to argue about Joan one way or another.

Until her manager called me with an offer to open for her.

Bill Sammeth, who at that time managed Joan Rivers and Cher, had apparently heard about me through the maitre' d at Caesar's Palace in Las Vegas. He called me at home to ask if I'd be interested in opening for Joan for ten nights on the road. The offer was attractive for several reasons. First, Joan was at that time the regular guest host of the Tonight Show, every comedian's dream gig, and a chance to appear on that show as her guest was a definite point to consider. Second, what Joan was offering to pay on her gigs was twice what Rodney was paying me. Third, for some reason which remains a mystery to this day, for her shows Joan always used two opening acts instead of just one, and I would be on the bill with her and Garry Shandling. I admired Garry a great deal and would be pleased as punch to work with him.

Now, here was the drawback to this whole thing: RODNEY HATED JOAN RIVERS. So naturally, if I were to accept dates with Joan Rivers, I could be fairly certain that I could kiss my gig with Rodney goodbye. Nevertheless, it was worth a try. Tentatively, I

Touring with Legends

approached Rodney when he was in a relatively good mood and broached the question. I remember the conversation went something like this:

    Me: "Hey Rodney, how you doing?"
    Rodney: "Goin' along. What's that in your hand?"
    Me: "Oh, this? It's a magnum of Dom Perignon and a season's tickets for the Yankees. They're for you."
    Rodney: "Really? Thanks. What's the occasion?"
    Me: "Nothing. Hey by the way, Joan Rivers wants me to open for her."
    Rodney: "Oh yeah?"
    Me: "Yeah. Anyway I gotta go, see ya tomorrow...."
    Rodney: "You should do it, man."
    Me: "Huh?"

That last part was for real. He really said I should take the gig. "It would be good for you, she'd probably put you on the Tonight Show."

I couldn't believe it. He hated her guts, but he was gonna let me tour with her? I needed some confirmation, just to make sure I was hearing what I thought I was hearing.

    Me: "That's what I thought too, but I figured with the way you feel about her...."
    Rodney: "No man, do it. It's a good career move."

I was floored, but incredibly happy and deeply grateful. Peg and I called Bill Sammeth the next day and accepted the gig. A contract was drawn up and we signed it.

Not long afterward, Rodney changed his mind.

We were in the limo, halfway to a gig somewhere, when he turned to me and said, "I've been thinking about it, man. I'd prefer that you not open for her. I don't like her."

What? "Uh....but Rodney, we signed a contract. The deal's been made. You said..."

"I don't care what I said. I don't like her, and I'd prefer if you didn't open for her."

Well, what a fine mess I'd gotten me into. I don't remember anything about the gig that evening, probably because I was in a neurotic stupor the entire time. I do remember that on the ride back I raided the limousine's private liquor stash and got completely wasted. I have a dim but solid memory of arriving back at Rodney's new Westport house and lying across the living room sofa in a beer haze as he turned out the lights and said something like "If you need to puke, here's a wastebasket."

I did wind up doing the ten nights with Joan, and a lot more nights as it later turned out. I was contractually obligated to do the gig of course, and my choice boiled down to risking Rodney's wrath or a breach of contract suit. Even though the lawsuit would have probably been less stressful in retrospect, I chose Rodney's wrath.

You may be thinking that working with Joan Rivers was the final nail in the coffin of my association with Rodney. That was a contributing factor to be sure, but the actual, final thing that did me in was - how can I put this delicately? - the final thing that did me in was, I firmly believe, ONE OF THE LAMEST MISUNDERSTANDINGS IN THE HISTORY OF SHOW BUSINESS.

For more, please read on.

On a bright, sunny day in the summer of 1997, as I was blissfully pushing my daughter on the swing at her preschool, my friend and fellow parent Curtis asked me if I was aware that I had been discussed on the Howard Stern Show that morning. "Why no," said I, "I wasn't." And since I wasn't exactly the kind of non-celebrity person that would normally be utilized as grist for the Stern mill, I wondered aloud what the topic of this conversation could possibly have been.

It turned out that Rodney Dangerfield had been the in-studio guest that morning, and with one thing leading to another (and his on-air foil and head-writer Jackie the Joke Man having been an old friend of mine), the subject of our falling out had come up. I got a tape of the broadcast, and heard Howard tell his version of why he thought Rodney had fired me. It was so completely wrong that I thought I might take a shot at setting my version down in this book, since I was actually there when it happened.

First, a bit of background. After Rodney's phenomenal success with his movies, albums and live appearances, he figured he would get himself a nice home in the country. So he bought the house in

Westport Connecticut, and hired a contractor to build an indoor Olympic-sized swimming pool and jacuzzi. Since I had developed a close relationship with him, Peg and I found ourselves at his Connecticut home quite often, either to work or to just hang out. In those days, before Peg and I had even thought about having children, we had a dog named Daisy. I never believed we would actually ever be parents ourselves (I liked kids, but only in certain situations, such as when they didn't belong to me), so Daisy had become our surrogate daughter. Okay, you're probably thinking we were just like all those other annoying dog owners who kissed their dogs on the mouth and let them sleep on the bed and used those high squeaky baby voices to talk to them, but the truth of the matter is, alright, that's exactly what we were like.

Since we were on the road so much, and hardly got to see Daisy to begin with, when Rodney would summon us to his house we requested that we could please bring the dog along, and he consented. We would leave her in the garage or tied up in the front yard, and everything was fine. At least we got to have her around.

One evening, when we were swimming in the pool, Rodney decided to go to his room for a quick nap. Before he left, we asked him if we could bring Daisy into the pool area so she could hang out with us. He said okay, but she could just hang out, not go swimming or anything. We told him don't worry, we weren't the kind of people to bring a dog swimming in his pool. So he went inside and Daisy got to roam around poolside. She was ecstatic to be in this warm area and to have us nearby. Whenever we'd surface from an underwater dip, she'd be there licking our faces. You know how those semi-neglected dogs are.

When we left the pool to hit the jacuzzi, there was Daisy, right on our heels. Peg got in on the farthest side of the jacuzzi from Daisy, which caused the dog to begin whining and howling for one more kiss. Peg called her over, and Daisy walked the narrow ledge of the jacuzzi for a quick face lick. As she turned back around to go, she lost her footing and fell in.

As I was lifting Daisy quickly out, I saw the following in quick succession; Peg looking up toward Rodney's bedroom window, which faced the pool room; Peg's look of abject terror as she saw

Rodney awaken and peer through his window, apparently right at our wet dog; Peg's next expression combining abject terror with what must have been both of our lives flashing before her eyes; Peg's mouth forming the words "Get the dog out of here!" as she pushed me out of the jacuzzi toward the garage clutching Daisy, who now looked like a drenched bedroom slipper.

I quickly found myself outside in the cold night air, tip-toeing toward the garage so as to stash the dog and make a clean getaway. No such luck. The garage door was locked, so I had to go back inside. Rodney was already there, yelling at Peggy about what he'd seen. And it didn't make matters any better when I came in holding the dripping dog.

"You took the dog swimming in the jacuzzi!"

"No we didn't. She fell in."

"That's bullshit, man!"

"It's not bullshit, Rodney, why would we bring a dog swimming in a Jacuzzi, especially after you'd told us not to?" Back and forth it went, us trying to convince him of the truth, him practically reading us our Miranda rights.

As I said before, you can't win an argument with a star who's used to people sucking up to him day in and day out. According to his accusatory mind, we had taken our dog for a swim, and that was that. By the way, to Rodney's way of thinking this was, for some reason, a big deal. It was as if we'd stolen his credit cards and used them to buy crack. I'd never seen him this angry before.

We eventually stopped arguing, because it was pointless to continue. But believe it or not, instead of throwing us out of his house he insisted we stay over that night. It was too late for us to leave, and besides, he wanted me to work with him on his TV special the next morning.

Yeah, Peg and I slept really soundly.

By the time we awoke in the morning, Rodney had actually called several of his friends to tell them what we'd done and what horrible people we were. And as soon as he saw us, he laced into us again; "I just want to tell you that what you did was disgusting. It really shows what kind of people you are. I've told everyone what you did, and they all agree with me that was a horrible thing to do, and I'm very, very angry at you. You're terrible, dishonest, despicable fucking human beings. Now, let's write some comedy."

I'm not making this up. He really expected me to be able to write jokes after the tongue-lashing he'd just given us. Peggy was in tears and had gone upstairs to pack our stuff and get us out of this madhouse, which we did. We said our good-byes as diplomatically as we could, but there was no way we were going to stay around after that. Plus it's a little hard getting in the mood to write mother-in-law jokes when you've just been compared to Jeffrey Dahmer.

And that, believe it or not, was the beginning of the end of my relationship with Rodney. All because of a wet dog.

* * * * *

A few footnotes to this story:

First of all, many of the friends who Rodney called to tell what hideous serial-killer types we were, and who had incidentally become our friends as well, did not think we were horrible people because of this. Most of them, we found out later, humored Rodney and laughed to themselves, thinking it would all blow over in a few days when he calmed down. They hadn't counted on Rodney's deep, religious attachment to his jacuzzi.

Secondly, allow me to elaborate on the 1997 Howard Stern broadcast. Jackie "The Joke Man" had confronted Rodney on that show with the fact that Rodney had had falling-outs with a lot of comics, including me. Jackie claimed that I'd borrowed five thousand dollars from Rodney and never paid him back, and that was why we weren't friends any more. I don't know where this information came from, but the only thing I ever borrowed from Rodney was a pen and a waffle iron.

Howard weighed in at this point that he'd heard my dog had peed in Rodney's pool and that he'd had to drain the whole thing to get rid of the tons of dog hairs that had clogged up the pipes.

Shit, man. We are horrible people!

Chapter 17: Howard Stern

I never opened for Howard Stern (see "Robert Ludlum" above), but I do have a quick story about why he got pissed off at me. (Rodney and Howard are the only celebrities that ever got ticked off at me - it's not something that happens to me all the time. Really.)

After Howard got fired from WNBC radio in New York in the early eighties, the station was in a frenzy trying to find a suitable replacement. Of course, no one was ever going to "replace" Howard Stern, but they had to find someone to fill his slot. So the call went out to virtually every standup comedian in New York. A friend of mine who worked at NBC put in a word for me with the powers that be, and I was invited to audition for the slot.

Now I may be a bit naïve at times, even a little spacey, but I'm not stupid. Even I realized that whoever took over Howard Stern's old time slot would be subjected to ridicule and scorn from Howard's loyal fans, even if he or she was good at it. Disgruntled New York listeners would probably be calling in every seven seconds to offer words of encouragement such as "You suck!" and "Get off the air, dickhead!" and "I'm gonna blow you're fucking head off!"

And if he or she was truly *bad* at it......No, I can't even think about what would happen without going into a cold sweat.

But I was a young, ambitious, hungry comic, and I figured it couldn't exactly hurt my career to go in and meet some high-powered NBC honchos. So I went into WNBC to meet with the station manager, Dale Parsons. While I was waiting in the reception area, Gary Del'Abbate (Baba Booey, Howard's producer) came in to clean out some stuff from his old office. He recognized me from Dangerfield's, said hello, and asked me what I was doing here. I innocently (and dumbly, I suppose), told him, "Duuh, I'm auditioning for Howard's old time slot."

Gary apparently went back and told Howard he'd run into me, because word got back to me that Howard was livid that I would do such a thing, stab a fellow humorist in the back like that.

Huh?

First of all, he'd already been fired weeks ago, so my being there had no bearing on him whatsoever. Secondly, I had no intention of being a radio personality. That would have been unrealistic and naïve on my part. No, I was going to be a huge television and film star.

Nevertheless, to this day I wonder if Howard still holds a grudge about me trying to get the job he'd already left. I like to think he's mellowed so much over the years that he had gotten past it long ago. Or if he'd even remember who I was.

I have to admit, in both these cases, with Rodney and with Howard, I never did understand the thought processes that could lead them to these strange and twisted conclusions. Maybe there's some Book of Skewed Celebrity Logic that I'm not aware of. Maybe becoming famous just derails your brain waves, no matter who you are. Whatever. But I do know one thing; I'm not getting any more dogs until I'm out of show business.

* * * * *

As I mentioned earlier, Rodney fired me on New Year's Eve, 1983. After the "Drenched Dog/Joan Rivers/Estelle Hates Me" shitshow had happened, things had become a bit tense. But I continued working with him for a little while, so I assumed he'd reconsidered his feelings about all of it. I was wrong. In Fort Lauderdale at the Sunrise Theatre, a few minutes before I was to go on, Rodney came up to me and said, "Y'know, I think it would be best if you and I were to part ways for a while."

Immediately, my head started spinning and nausea began to set in. This was not a good time for this to happen, because five minutes later I was introduced and had to go out and do comedy in front of two thousand people. For the first time in his life, Rodney had lousy timing.

That was the only night in my whole career I can ever remember being unable to complete a show. I was dizzy and sick to my stomach, and instead of doing my usual thirty minute set, my head started spinning and my vision started blurring and I wound up doing twenty before saying "Thank you, goodnight." I rushed off the stage, ran to my dressing room and immediately threw up.

And that was it. Peg and I went back to New York and started calling agents. Aside from ten upcoming nights with Joan Rivers, I was an unemployed standup comedian.

Chapter 18: Treading Water

Luckily I had some agents that were able to get me work during this down period, although little of the caliber of what I'd been used to for the last three and a half years. Still, it was the eighties, and the aforementioned "comedy boom" was still going strong. So after the initial shock of Rodney cutting me loose wore off, I was able to get booked into some of the approximately seventeen billion comedy clubs around the country, which were actually paying decent money in those days. And there were other gigs for me in those days, too.

How Do You Get To Carnegie Hall?

I was fortunate enough to get booked into the world - renowned Carnegie Hall. Well, I *thought* I was fortunate.

Playing Carnegie Hall would be, of course, the realization of just about any performer's dream. It was certainly no less true with me. As a young college punk I had seen two of my early idols here, James Taylor and Paul Simon. I had dreamed of what it must be like backstage, all velvet and oak with butlers and antique furniture and Pre-Raphaelite paintings. And how incredible it must be to walk out onto that stage and face that audience. Someday, I thought, I too will walk those hallowed halls.

So here I was, seven or eight years later. My then-agent Randy had booked me to open for two nights for the singer Shirley Bassey (she was best-known for singing "Goldfinger," the theme for that James Bond movie). Shirley Bassey at the time had a large, devoted gay following. Now I was many things, but a comedian that gay people could love apparently was not one of them (as I was soon to find out). First of all, my bubble was burst fairly early that night. I entered the aforementioned hallowed backstage halls and was greeted not by velvet and butlers and oak and magic, but by a squadron of beefy, beer-bellied union guys. These guys couldn't care less if it was Carnegie Hall or Folsom Prison as long as they got paid, and they had the attitudes to match. Every question I asked and every request I made was met with a loud, beefy grunt.

"Excuse me, where's my dressing room?"

"Uganuh."

"Uh....is there a stage manager?"

"Humph."

"Thanks for your help."

"yeahblowme."

Well, I was sure at least that when I went out on that magical stage, it would all be worthwhile.

Nope.

Shirley's audiences...how can I put this? They didn't really.....they weren't the most....they hated my bony, guitar-playin' ass. I don't know why or what I did wrong, but the biggest laugh I can remember getting that whole night was when a guy up front yelled sarcastically, "Oh, *that* was funny." Classic, unbridled opening act hell. Unbelievably, Randy actually thought I'd done well. "Maybe I shouldn't have done the Bee Gees parody, with those high voices and everything.," I wondered. "Maybe they thought I was poking fun at stereotypical images of gay people or something."

"No, that was great!," he insisted. "They loved it! Do it again tomorrow night! You do very well with the gays!"

"The gays?" He'd actually said that. "The gays." Something my uncle Morty would have said at a Shriner's convention.

The following night went no better than the first night. Randy was as good at gauging an audience as Michael Richards was at word selection. Except in that case, I think the audience was less hostile. I never thought I'd be so glad to get out of Carnegie Hall. Sometimes no matter what you do or how hard you try, you just have to offer it up to the comedy gods as another horror story you'll file away for the book you'll write someday. Not a bad idea, actually.

(Interesting aside: I never once got to meet Shirley Bassey. I think she was one of these diva types who can't be seen before the show or something. Or maybe she didn't want whatever I had that night to rub off on her. Anyway, I hear I'm on her "A" list.)

As I mentioned, there were lots of gigs for comedians in those days, so this post-Rodney period for me wasn't all bad. I worked - clubs mostly. And other gigs. Weird gigs. I had one agent who booked me in the Catskill Mountains. For those of you who don't know, the Catskill Mountains are located in the Adirondacks in upstate New York, and at that time were home to a number of vacation resorts which featured, among other things, live entertainment. (Fans of the series "The Marvelous Mrs. Maisel" will have a good idea of what I'm talking about). Over the years, due to economic and other conditions, just about all of these places have closed down permanently and there are only a handful left, but in the eighties they were still flourishing. The clientele at these places were predominantly Jewish and quite often elderly, and the entertainers that went over best were usually older, more traditional singers and comedians who catered to that demographic. For instance, old school (VERY old school) performers like Henny Youngman, Myron Floren, Steve and Edie, Shecky Greene, Vic Damone, etc. would rule in those rooms. Newer and hipper acts like, for instance, Peter Lemongello might not do quite as well.

Also, the audiences at these places had a reputation for being, to put it mildly, brutal. I don't know for sure why this was. Most performers from those days that I've talked to say it was because the show wasn't usually part of the hotel package. For one price you'd get a room, meals and the show, so people weren't really paying for a ticket to see a specific performer like fans do. If you were playing the Catskills, usually the show was just bundled with the meal. Conversations in the dining room were fascinating;

PATRON: "Excuse me, the southern fried chicken dinner - what does that come with?"

WAITER: "Englebert Humperdink."

My then - agent at William Morris, Lee Salomon, was a true fan of mine and thought I was good enough to make any audience laugh, even a Catskills one. I told him I'd had bad experiences in the Catskills before (see the Melissa Manchester story earlier) and begged him not to book me there. He replied that he was headlining me on a "singles" weekend in front of what he said would be a much younger crowd, and promised that I would have a great show. Since I was basically unemployed, I reluctantly agreed to give it a try.

The big night arrived. My opening act was a singer, and while she was on I peeked out from behind the curtain to survey the crowd. There was definitely something wrong here. Most of the men had white hair, and the women pale blue. If this was a singles weekend, these were the oldest singles I'd ever seen. I found out later that Lee had gotten his dates screwed up. Singles weekend was *next* weekend. He had apparently booked me for a Maalox convention. So I was introduced, and I went out and told my first joke. Then my second joke, third, fourth. No laughs. Not one. And I hadn't even gotten to my rock & roll stuff yet. The only laughs I got were, just like before, from the band behind the curtain. They were doubled over. They'd never seen an act bomb so badly before. After ten minutes of this, shell shock set in and I began to laugh as well.

I also could hear, beyond the footlights and in the audience, the unmistakable sound of shuffling footsteps. First a few, then several, then hundreds. Shuffling away from the stage. Rodney had once told me that in the old days, an act was rated as being anywhere from a one-door to a four-door act, depending on how many doors people were walking out of. That night, they were carving out a fifth door for me. People couldn't get out fast enough.

After forty-five minutes of this torture, I said goodnight to the one remaining deaf couple in the audience and got offstage. As the band members were congratulating me on the fine job I'd done, the backstage phone rang. It was someone from the bar who had seen me, told me I was hysterical and invited me for a drink. It turns out that a group of people who still had pulses had watched my show from the bar upstairs and thoroughly enjoyed it. The only problem was the bar was enclosed in glass, so I couldn't hear them laughing. If I'd known this, I would've gladly paid to have the glass removed myself.

Later, as Peg and I were having a drink and licking my wounds, I noticed among the list of coming attractions that the comedian Sandra Bernhardt was scheduled to appear one weekend the following month. I couldn't believe it. For those who don't remember, Sandra Bernhardt was a regular on Late Night with David Letterman, provocative and controversial and edgy and not beyond using profanity. I told Peg that if I hadn't been already booked at a comedy club for the coming week, I would give my right arm and part of my spleen to see how Sandra would do with a typical Concord audience that weekend.

I remember that for some reason I was back at the Concord one year later (the audience probably demanded a return engagement), and I asked the entertainment director how the Sandra Bernhardt show had turned out. "Oh, her?," he replied matter-of-factly. "She had to be escorted off the grounds surrounded by bodyguards."

Funny Catskills horror stories abound in comedy circles. A comedian friend of mine named Abby Stein told the story of the time she was booked to do one of the hotels up there whose audiences were used to exclusively Yiddish acts and nothing else. Abby was not aware of this fact as she was introduced to a small smattering of applause. As soon as she came out and said "Good evening, ladies and gentlemen," a lady in the audience loudly and disappointedly exclaimed, "Oy! It's in English!"

Abby forged boldly ahead with her "in English" act, generating not a single laugh. After what seemed an eternity, in the middle of her show the audience suddenly responded with cheers and wild applause. Abby thought, "Wow, I must've finally registered with these people!" No such luck. The reason the audience was going wild was because the dessert table had just arrived.

One of my first bookings during my exile period out of Dangerfield's was at the Raleigh hotel. Having never been to the Catskills before, I had no idea what to expect in terms of response, and this show was where I got my first taste of what to expect. They seemed like nice enough people, smiling and applauding warmly when I came out. And they didn't seem to mind that my act was in English. What they did seem to mind was that they didn't get my jokes. My references at the time were very current and mostly references to '80's pop music, Bee Gees, Donna Summer, Barry White, etc. I had not built up enough of a stockpile of traditional jokes that I could fall back on as yet, and since the audiences at Dangerfield's liked what I did, I hadn't realized the need for it. I sure wished I had those kinds of jokes now as I sweated through ten, twenty, thirty minutes of stony silence from the befuddled folks before me. As the show finally drew to a close, I thought "at least now I can do John Denver," a parody which I always relied upon to close my show and which always got a great response. "They must know who John Denver is," I thought.

They did. As I put on my little round glasses and introduced, "John Denver," I heard the audience members sigh adoringly, uttering things like, "Oh, John Denver," "I love John Denver," "Oh good, he's gonna sing a lovely John Denver song!" Everywhere I looked I saw eager anticipation from them for the first time, waiting raptly for me to do what they assumed would be my tribute to John Denver, not the "My Songs Make Me Nauseous" takeoff on his big hit "Annie's Song" that I always did. So what did I do?

I did an impromptu, "heartfelt" tribute to John Denver.

I sang "Annie's Song." Straight. No joke. Not the parody words, the actual words to the actual song. I didn't have the heart to disappoint those gleaming, rapturous faces. Not to mention that the way the night had been going, if I did the parody they would have looked at each other as if to say, "Are those the words?" I got a standing ovation. Just from doing that song.

The weird gigs I was getting were by no means confined to the Catskills. I was booked to perform at a private party in Atlantic City. I wasn't given any information about the people at the party or what the party was for, but I figured I didn't need this information anyway. I was a comedy veteran now, dammit! I was seasoned, I was tempered, I'd played the Catskills and lived! I figured, hey, if I can make audiences in the Catskills almost laugh, then I can make audiences anywhere almost laugh! So I showed up eager and ready to entertain this small room of fifty or so people. I walked in, bounded onto the stage, and began my show.

Touring with Legends

The first thing I noticed was that these people didn't seem... happy. In fact, they seemed...pissed. Not pissed at me, not pissed at anything in particular, just...pissed. And most of them had pinkie rings. Big, shiny, gaudy pinkie rings. Even some of the women had pinkie rings. And, from the looks of them, penises.

I started with my world-famous, knock-'em-dead, Bee Gees' "Singin' Too High" parody, the one that always got audiences going, the one that always worked.

Nothing. Crickets chirped. Glares intensified. I quickly moved on.

I launched into my Donna Summer and Barry White parodies, followed by my time-honored Country Music hunk.

Nothing. Not a laugh, not a chuckle, not even a cleared throat. But did I panic? Did I back down? Did I give up? Immediately.

I took a good look at these rough-looking people with their turtlenecks and cigars, quickly sized up the situation, concluded that this was a bad booking for a comic like me, and told a series of dirty golf jokes.

The place went nuts. They hooted, they laughed, the suddenly loved me. I racked my brains for every filthy joke I could remember and told them all to these beefy tough guys and their ladies for the next ten minutes. I had them in the palm of my hand! So I decided that, now that I had loosened them up, I could go back into my standard routine. I hit 'em with Lou Rawls, Kenny Rogers and Michael MacDonald.

You guessed it. Zilch.

So back I went to the dirty jokes and limericks. Right back to the hoots and hollers and raucous laughter. And just when I'd used up every filthy joke I'd ever heard and remembered, the gig was mercifully over. A big, fireplug of a guy came over to me, told me to sit down, and hooked his arm around my neck. He started to squeeze me as he said, in a deep, raspy baritone, "Hey, you're a fuckin' funny kid, you know that? Fuckin' funny. Them jokes you was doin'? Funny. I don't know what that singin' shit you was doin' was all about, where you got the words wrong, but them jokes? Funny." He reached into his pocket, handed me my check and a business card. Then he slapped me on the back, dislodging my spine and part of my pancreas as he left the table. "You call me anytime you need somethin', you hear me good?"

I looked at the card. It read, "Tony Mazzarino, "Director of Solid Waste."

I don't care how successful you are in life. I don't care how big or famous you become in show business. It's always good to know someone in the solid waste business.

Chapter 19: Gilbert Gottfried

In the early eighties, standup comedy was so popular that not only were there stand-alone comedy clubs everywhere, but also a large number of restaurants and bars that put up makeshift stages and held "comedy nights." It wasn't at all uncommon to walk into a local eatery in New Jersey, for example, and see a sign that read, "Tonight: All you can eat shrimp bar $3.99, and Emo Phillips." You'd be surprised at how many comics, who have since become very successful, would appear at these places. Some of these gigs, sleazy as they may have seemed, actually paid fairly decent money. And besides, a gig was a gig, and you could never underestimate the benefit of practicing your craft in front of a live audience, even if they were hopped up on Coors Lite and buffalo wings.

One night I got booked to do a bar in New Jersey with Gilbert Gottfried. I had been a fan of Gilbert's even before I got into standup myself, so I was looking forward to doing this show. And since I had been chosen to do the driving for this hour-long trip, I was also looking forward to talking with and getting to know Gilbert on a personal level. At the appointed hour I picked him up outside of Catch a Rising Star on 78th St.

The first thing he said when he got in the car was, "I hate doing these fucking shows. I hope they don't want me to do a lot of time."

That was a real ice-breaker. As we drove in my turd-brown Datsun B-210, Gilbert sat in stony silence for about ten minutes, obviously distracted and depressed. I would try to pierce the silence every once in a while with attempts at conversation, but got only grunts or minimalist answers in return.

"Have you ever worked at this place before?"

"No."

Silence.

"How long do you want me to do?"
"Dunno."
Silence.
"Do you want to listen to the radio?"
"Mnnfh."

I found myself wondering if he had ever been a stagehand at Carnegie Hall.

I wound up turning on the radio and listening to music for the whole trip. Occasionally I'd try to interject with some small talk, just to get a conversation going, but Gilbert had either decided he hated me or he was too depressed to reciprocate. Whatever the reason, I just continued to drive and scan the channels.

We finally arrived at the place, a typical TGIF Wannabe in the Jersey suburbs; sawdust on the floor, red-and-white checked tablecloths on the tables, the day's specials and our names written on a blackboard. The Big Time. Who the hell needed Rodney?

I went on and did thirty minutes, then Gilbert hit the stage. Judging by his attitude in the car, I figured he'd do maybe twenty or thirty minutes and just throw the show away. As it turned out, and as often happens, something came over him once he got up there and he wound up doing over an hour of some of the most energized and brilliant material I'd ever seen. The audience went crazy, and he got a standing ovation when he finally got off the stage. It had turned out to be a damn fine show all around, and we each got a free bottle of Coors Lite and buffalo wings to boot.

Actually, hanging out before and after the show in the dressing room (kitchen), Gilbert had lightened up considerably. We talked and did bits and made each other laugh, and the car ride back to Manhattan was a lot better than the ride to Jersey. I didn't really understand what happened on that ride out to the gig, but with time and experience of doing hundreds and hundreds of gigs, I finally get it. Gilbert has said that when he books a gig, when the night finally arrives, his fondest wish is that the club owner would walk into the green room and say, "Sorry, the show's been canceled. Here's your check." I often feel the same way. I'll book a gig, and it looks good on the calendar, and feels great that I'll be making money, and when the day of the first show comes, I wonder what ever possessed me to book the show in the first place. The anxiety builds up until show time, especially if the middle act is killing the crowd, and the insecurity is palpable... "I suck. I'm not funny. They're gonna hate me. I've got nothing." And then you go on, and 95% of the time it goes really well. And you're alright again. Just chalk it up to the innate weirdness of comedians in general, I guess. Even ones as great as Gilbert Gottfried.

What, and give up Show Business?

For those of you who don't know the joke the above line derives from, here it is: There was a guy named Joe whose job it was to follow the circus elephants around and shovel up the droppings. It was the worst job you could imagine, and one day one of the performers went over to this guy and said, "Hey Joe, you can do so much better than this. Why don't you quit and get a better job somewhere?" To which Joe replied, "What, and give up show business?"

It summarizes the way I often felt as I scrambled for work during my post-Rodney stress-syndrome period. I was clearly reminded of this joke as I pulled into Benton Harbor Michigan to do a one-night stand at a comedy club there. Well... The phrase "Comedy Club" would be a bit of a stretch in describing this place.

Peg and I flew into Detroit, rented a car and pulled into a truckstop along the highway in Benton Harbor. The truckstop was filthy, disgusting, a hellhole, but at least we could get some coffee and then be on our way. Except we found out it wasn't a truckstop. It was the comedy club.

Actually, it was a hotel with a coffee shop that "became" a comedy club at night. There was no marquee or billboard announcing the show, but right outside the coffee shop was one of those black felt signs they use to show the day's lunch specials. Stuck onto this sign was the following:

"Comedy Show Tonight: The Star of Easy Money : Denis Blare."

The *star* of Easy Money? Wow. I must be rich.

Peg and I went in to have some lunch. I introduced myself to the woman at the counter as that night's comedian, and she gushed, "Oooh! The star of Easy Money!" A cleaning lady nearby overheard this, turned to me, shook her finger in my face and said, "You'd better be clean tonight! I'm takin' my mama to the show, and I don't want her hearin' no cuss words. So you better do a clean show!" Yes, ma'am, I thought. I sure wouldn't want to piss her off and come back to my room and find she'd short-sheeted the bed. And I sure wouldn't want to piss off a lovely regular-paying customer like her and run the risk of never being booked back into this prestigious, luxurious hellhole.

As we ate our scrumptious meal of some kind of meat covered with some sort of gravy on a bed of some type of vegetable, two elderly farmers were at an adjoining table finishing up their coffee. They spoke in a laid-back southern drawl, and we could overhear their conversation:

"So, you gonna go to the show tonight? They got the star of Easy Money."

"Nah, I got me a case of beer with my name on it in the refrigerator. I'm gonna pop open a few and watch "Return of the Jedi.""

Now maybe if I'd been the star of "Return of the Jedi.."

Peg and I realized how bad things had gotten when we went to our room to try to take a nap. The room was filthy, with stains on everything including, if I remember correctly, the soap. It also had the distinct odor of stale cigarette smoke, which was interesting because this was a non-smoking room. I kept thinking about that cleaning lady we'd met, and wondering......WHAT THE HELL DOES SHE DO HERE?

After a futile attempt at spreading our clothes out on the sheets so we wouldn't have to actually come in contact with them, we tried to get some sleep. This never came about for two reasons. First of all, we kept hearing this loud and constant noise, like thousands of people talking and laughing and clinking what sounded like silverware. We didn't know where the noise was coming from, but it seemed like it was right outside our window. Of course that couldn't be. How could people be eating outside our window? Suddenly the curtains in our room, for no apparent reason, fell down. It seemed we'd been given a room not with a view of the lake, or the pool, or even the parking lot. No, our room overlooked the dining room, where at this very moment a huge buffet for some convention was being held... RIGHT OUTSIDE OUR WINDOW. Even worse was the realization that, since our lovely, crud-stained curtains had just fallen to the floor, all these conventioneers could now look directly into our room and see us. In our taking-a-nap mode. Half naked.

We tried calling housekeeping to fix our curtain, but the cleaning lady couldn't come. She was in a room down the hall, stuck to the mattress.

Oh Rodney, why the hell did you let me go?

By the way, the show that night was memorable for one particular reason, other than the fact that it was technically being held in a coffee shop and I had to time my punchlines so they didn't coincide with the hissing of the cappuccino machine. During the show, some guy who had been heckling me on and off all night finally couldn't nurse his beer anymore and got up to go to the bathroom. When he came back, he thought he would just be heelarious and return to his seat wearing a roll of toilet paper around his head. I guess he thought he would show me, by crackee!

No sir. I couldn't believe it. It was as if God himself had handed me a straight line. I took one look at beer-boy and his little toilet tissue hat and said, "Hmm. Nice hat. I guess that would make you a shithead."

The place went nuts.

Hey, they didn't make me the star of Easy Money for nothing.

Chapter 20: Enter Joan Rivers (and Garry Shandling)

Being fired by Rodney really wore me down. Ours had been a three-and-a-half year relationship, which had permeated virtually every aspect of my life. Not only did I suffer from the loss of what had literally become a lifestyle, but also from the realization that it happened for no reason, or at least for no logical or sensible one. But it was over, and it was time to move on.

Fortunately I had a gig lined up; ten nights opening for Joan Rivers. And as it turned out, the engagement was scheduled a very short time after the split-up with Rodney, so happily I wouldn't have too much time to wallow in self-pity before packing my bags and hitting the road.

Peg and I traveled together to Boston to hook up with Joan for the first night. I had never met Joan. I wasn't even sure if she'd actually seen my act or was just relying on the recommendation of her manager, so I had no idea what she would be like. Would she be happy to meet me, marginally curious or completely indifferent? After the experience of Paul Anka gushing about me opening for him and then not remembering who I was, nothing in show business would surprise me at this point.

A car awaited us at the airport to bring us to the hotel and venue in the city of Framingham, a Massachusetts suburb. The venue was the "Chateau de Ville," a reconverted furniture warehouse that had been bought out and turned into a theatre. It was slightly ironic that this would be my first post-Rodney show, since he and I had performed at the Chateau de Ville several times during our run. But it was comforting too in a way, because at least it was a familiar place with familiar faces working there, including Mario, the owner.

Mario was an interesting man. I had met him in the past of course when I worked with Rodney, and he had always been pleasant and friendly. He seemed to be very accessible, a generous and open sort of guy. So Peg and I found it fairly amusing when Mario had us picked up at the airport in a car that was being driven by what could only be described as a henchman. I forget this guy's name, but my first impression was that he seemed something other than just Mario's driver. He seemed more like a personal bodyguard or a member of the secret service or a bank robber on the lam. He greeted us, but his eyes never quite met ours. They were too busy darting this way and that, looking over his shoulder, as if Peg and I were in danger of being assassinated at any moment by someone who'd seen me at the Concord. I also noticed a slight, telltale bulge near his jacket pocket, and became instantly convinced that had Peg or I made any sudden, anti-Mario-like moves, we would've been riddled with bullets right there in baggage claim.

This behavior continued when we got in the back of the black town car. Our illustrious driver sped off and darted in and out of traffic, checking his rearview and sideview mirrors approximately three hundred times per second. Any attempts by us at normal conversation were met with terse, monosyllabic answers. It felt like we were riding with a robot, but without the warmth. One of the ice-breaker type questions we asked was, "So….you're just Mario's driver, or do you do other stuff for him, too?" He looked left, then right, then left again, cleared his throat and replied, in a hushed, intimidating voice,

"I watch Mario's back. Capeesh?"

We pretty much didn't ask him any more probing questions after that. He dropped us at our hotel, helped us with our bags and shook our hands, after first checking them for weapons. We never saw him again, but when I heard Osama Bin Laden was assassinated, I was convinced he did it.

Opening for a new celebrity was a little nerve-wracking. With Rodney it had been a gradual and natural progression, from working his club to meeting him to opening for him there to working the theatres (and living rooms. and racetracks). This was a different experience entirely. I had no idea what to expect from a Joan

Rivers audience, or what they would find funny from my act, if anything. Rodney's mostly young, mostly raucous, often beer-drinking crowds had laughed at my stuff, but what if Joan Rivers attracted Mormons? Would they respond to my fart and V.D. jokes in quite the same boisterous way? And of course, what would Joan be like? As I'd found out by now, many performers are not at all like their sweet, onstage selves. Would she be a pleasure to work with or a bitch in Bob Mackie?? And more importantly, how did she feel about opening acts owning dogs?

One thing I did know. Joan was a different sort of headliner, at least in one major way; as I mentioned before, she used not one, but *two* opening acts. And the acts she used were not obscure names but often pretty well known ones in those days; The Smothers Brothers, Jim Stafford, Nell Carter, people who were fairly well established in show business. I had never asked her why she did this. I also never figured out why she felt the need to have fully fifty minutes of comedy and music before she even hit the stage. All I knew was that for these ten nights I would be opening the show followed by Garry Shandling, who had been touring with Joan for some time and whose work I greatly admired. Hopefully this would be a pleasurable experience. I could sure use one.

About thirty minutes before showtime, I was hanging around the backstage/greenroom area when Joan, her husband Edgar and Garry showed up. Joan put me at ease immediately, joking around, telling me how funny she thought I was (I guess she *had* seen me), basically making me and Peg feel like part of her inner circle and part of the show. She was the kind of person who took immediate charge of a situation and made you feel like you'd not only known her for years, but were very possibly even a long lost family member. Our impression of her was as some sort of celebrity den mother (I think one of the first things she did when she met Peg and me was ask if we'd eaten and offer us a bagel chip.)

Edgar made me feel at ease as well. He came right up to me, extended his hand and, in a clipped, raspy voice that made him sound like some sort of British Delta blues man, said, "Don't fuck up, Blair."

(People have asked me what Joan's legendary husband Edgar was like. I never got to know him all that well, but I could say with certainty that although he wasn't exactly the warmest person in the world, he had charm. He also had a dry sense of humor and a deadpan face that made you constantly wonder, when he would say things like "Don't fuck up, Blair," if he was kidding or if he really meant it. I think the definitive answer to that question would be, "I had no idea.")

Garry said hi and was polite enough, but was a little less ready to roll out the red carpet immediately. He had heard of me I guess, but obviously had never seen me perform and was reserving judgement until he did, which was completely understandable. I was certainly aware of the way comedians could sometimes behave around each other, with equal parts admiration and suspicion, especially when they were thrown together into a working situation without being familiar with each other's work. These were the days long before YouTube where you could just go online, type in a performer's name and check out clips of their performances or TV shots. In the eighties, you had word-of-mouth, reputation, or nothing at all to go on.

Garry didn't know me, and he certainly had no reason to be relaxed around me yet. He also knew I was going on first and that he would have to follow me whether my show sucked or not. No matter how good a comedian is, there's nothing that fills him with more dread than wondering if he's gonna have to follow someone whose act is riddled with expletives and diarrhea jokes. And for all he knew, I could be that guy. As we shook hands, I looked into his eyes and could almost hear him thinking, "Oh great, a guitar comedian. I hope he doesn't do parodies about his dick."

(Another thing that can fill a comedian with dread is following a prop comic. Y'know, guys like Carrot Top who would come onstage with Ryder truckloads of props and gadgets and things they use in their acts. It's not so much fear of following their acts as it is fear of having to clear the stage of the debris.)

I was playing a club in Philadelphia once and had to follow a prop comic who went by the name "The Legendary Wid." Wid used literally hundreds of props that he kept in huge cartons and which by the end of his act were strewn all over the stage. Since it would have taken hours to clean up after him, they instead introduced me immediately after Wid was done. I wound up doing my show amidst a huge heap of beach balls, plastic arms, and rubber chickens.

I also had to follow a guy once who ended his show juggling apples while taking huge bites of them. Unfortunately, everything wound up on the floor, so when I came out I spent the first ten minutes trying to avoid slipping on pits and apple slices.)

Showtime arrived. Out I went, and did my show. To my immense relief, it really went well. I certainly needed it to go well. This night and this show were like a job interview, with new people and a new organization, and the pressure to not suck was enormous. You always want the first show with a new headliner to go especially well, and this one did. I left the stage to a solid ovation. Then, as Joan had requested, I took an offstage microphone and introduced "my friend, Garry Shandling!," whom I had met about an hour before.

Garry went out and of course had a great show. Having been a fan of his for a long time, I relished this opportunity to watch his stage act. Great jokes, presented with that unique style of his. As everyone knows by now, not only did Garry write terrific material but his stage persona could reduce an audience to hysterics almost on its own. He was very much like Rodney in that what you see is what you get. Garry was basically that whiny, insecure guy he played onstage, and it was a perfect character for comedy. As a lifestyle however, I'm sure it could lead to large psychiatrist fees. I thoroughly enjoyed watching him, and was starting to feel that maybe accepting this engagement was the right choice to have made after all.

It was also interesting to watch the obviously close relationship between Joan and Garry. Even on this first night, it was clear how comfortable they were with each other. They made each other laugh constantly, sometimes with jokes and wisecracks, but often with a kind of verbal shorthand that was way too inside for me to figure out. They had some sort of chemistry that I couldn't completely fathom, but that kept them thoroughly entertained and glad to be in each other's company.

That chemistry often spilled out onto the stage. When Garry was on Joan would often watch at least a part of his show from the wings, and Garry would know it. Sometimes he'd do a joke that he knew might not register with the audience, but that would definitely crack her up. One night, right before he was to go on, Garry was complaining to Joan that his new pants were too tight and kept riding up his ass. She was in hysterics as he kept asking her to postpone the show till he could either get new pants on or pull these out of his crack. Joan insisted it was too late, he had already been introduced, and pushed him onstage.

He went out to the microphone and started doing his show, while intermittently grabbing at his ass and pulling on his pants, just so he could hear Joan cackling in the background. (By the way, the sight of Joan Rivers in a seven billion-dollar Bob Mackie gown doubled over in laughter watching a guy pulling pants out of his ass crack was pretty bizarre). Meanwhile, I kept watching the people in the audience as Garry was doing this. Some of them were chuckling, some of them were smiling, but most of them seemed to be wondering, "Why is Shandling picking his ass?"

When Joan went out after Garry, the place exploded. Joan's star was rising fast at this point in her career, and she would gather even more momentum as the months went on. This would ultimately culminate in her becoming the permanent guest host of "The Tonight Show" (until things got ugly and everything came crashing down later on.)

(By the way, I find it worth noting that destiny, or whatever you want to call it, seemed for some unknown reason to always hook me up with these stars just as their careers were about to sky-rocket. First with Rodney, then with Joan and Garry, then Lester Kornhauser.

Alright, two out of three.)

Still buzzed from my performance adrenaline at the Chateau de Ville, I took a break from watching Joan's show and went to my dressing room to get a drink. Alex, the backstage assistant and a friend since the Rodney days, approached me urgently with some news she thought I should know about. She said that Garry had watched my show and come away all bent out of shape, saying that this would never work, that my show didn't fit, it wasn't right for Joan and him. I asked Alex if she could be more specific - why didn't he like it, what didn't he like about it? The jokes? The song parodies? Me? All she could tell me was that Garry just didn't like my show and was pretty adamant about it. Alex seemed fairly upset herself. As I said, she was a friend and had known Peg and me from when we were with Rodney, and she thought I had a good act and didn't like the prospect of me being fired immediately by the Joan Rivers organization, especially after what I'd just been through.

I wasn't too thrilled with the prospect myself, but I didn't really have much of a say in the matter. I didn't know Garry well enough to ask him what the problem was. Maybe it was the age-old problem that so many monologists had with us so-called "prop" and "guitar" comics, and even if I'd wanted to confront him, he was nowhere to be found at the moment. I also assumed that even if Garry didn't like my show, the final decision whether to keep me or not would be made by Joan and Edgar, not by him. Of course, if they didn't like me, it was back to the comedy clubs and (shudder) the Catskills.

Maybe I could get my old job back at Fern's Harness Shop.

Then I thought, wait a minute; Joan must have seen a tape of me. She said I was funny. She had to know I'd just lost my Dangerfield gig, partly on account of taking this job. Surely she couldn't be cold and heartless enough to say, "Thanks kid, but it's not gonna work out." Then I remembered: Damn. This is show business. Of course she could.

So I hung around for that last hour or so, not knowing what to expect. It was a very long hour.

The show ended. Joan came off stage and hurried back to her dressing room followed closely by Annie, her official dresser. I heard them chatting behind Joan's dressing room door. Probably figuring out how best to let me go, I thought. After several minutes, Joan, Annie, and Edgar came out. They looked at me for a moment, then Joan said, "Come on, let's go eat!"

I looked at Peg, she looked at me. Edgar approached us, smiled thinly and said "You did good, Blair. Now come on, I'm hungry. And don't order anything too fucking expensive." We followed them out the door.

We were in.

I don't remember the exact details of that dinner or even much about the next batch of shows we did together. I do know that over the course of the engagement, Garry somehow went from supposedly hating my guitar-strummin' guts to becoming a friend of mine. He realized fairly quickly that I was as unbalanced and insecure as he was, and fairly quickly we just started getting along, cracking jokes, making each other laugh. I never did find out why he supposedly went berserk over my show, or even if he definitely ever did, for that matter. I can't remember a time that he was curt or rude or mean to me at all. Maybe Alex had imagined the whole thing, although that's probably a stretch. All I know is Garry never said a bad thing about my act to me or anyone else that I know of. He never had a problem with it as far as I could tell. He even went so far as to help me put my set together when I did my first Tonight Show, picking out the jokes and bits that he especially liked. We were living proof that yes, monologists and guitar comics can co-exist peacefully in this crazy, nutty world of ours. (Plate spinners and shadow-puppet performers however were another matter entirely. And don't get me started on mimes.)

I also found out that Joan had decided to keep me on indefinitely as her opener after the ten-show engagement ended. So less than a month after Rodney had cut me loose, I was back in the opening act business.

Chapter 21: Elvis Presley - sort of

That got your attention, didn't it?

Nope, I never opened for Elvis. But I did come in contact with him. Sort of. Allow me to explain.

Joan kept me gainfully employed over the next two and a half years. We did many one-nighters all across the country, with many laughs along the way. Also along the way were some particularly memorable gigs, in some particularly memorable cities.

Joan was a tourist at heart, and loved to go out exploring with her entourage in whatever town we found ourselves, seeing the sights, shopping, and whenever possible visiting famous landmarks. She usually dressed casually for this, in a Bob Mackie jogging outfit with sequins and Louie Vittón running shoes.

One night we played Memphis, which of course had been home to Elvis. Naturally, there was no way Joan was going to miss out on seeing Graceland, so in her uber-den-mother fashion she rounded us all up, piled us in the limo and took us out there. (Joan always seemed to have access to a limo. It must have been part of every contract at every venue she ever played. It got so I could never imagine or visualize her in a normal car. I always thought that if she ever owned a car herself, it would have to be a limo, and she would hire a limo to take her to the limo showroom so she could pick out the limo she wanted to buy.)

The trip to Graceland was very interesting, if for nothing else than we got to get a good look at Elvis' decorating ideas. The infamous jungle room, decked out in animal skins and huge potted plants and oversized furniture, in particular impressed me as the kind of look I would never allow in my own home.

Anyway, we took the standard tour and were about to head out when the Graceland curator or the custodian or the big cheese - whatever he was - approached Joan and told her what a huge fan he was and was there anything special he could do for her? She thought for a moment, then said actually yes, there was something he could do.

That night after the show, we all piled into limousines again (I always thought Joan should have "comedian/tour guide" on her business card) and made a return trip to Graceland. Joan had arranged with the big cheese of Graceland for us to come back after the regular tour was long over and be given a personal tour of ELVIS' PERSONAL UPSTAIRS QUARTERS. This is something which the general public never gets to see (but which certain celebrities do, if the big cheese happens to be a huge fan and if the celebrity drops a subtle hint along with free tickets to the show). I remember vividly that security guards and police actually held up traffic so that our little motorcade could enter the gates of Graceland. I kept wondering if the people in those cars were watching all this and wondering, "Is Elvis back? Better go get the camera."

So there we were. We went in to the mansion and were led quickly and quietly up the staircase into the hallowed upstairs inner- sanctum. The first thing I noticed was everyone began speaking in hushed tones, like we had just entered St. Patrick's Cathedral. Of course I realized the import of this event, but you have to remember, we were professional comedians. Our natural instinct is to make fun of solemn situations like this. It was very difficult for all of us to treat the occasion with the respect it deserved, but I must say that for the most part we did an excellent job of keeping our sick thoughts and wisecracks to ourselves. For the most part.

After an appropriate pause to take a deep breath and prepare our psyches, we were led into the King's bedroom. And there it was. Elvis' bed. It was large enough for a king but otherwise unremarkable from any other bed. Except that in the canopy above the headrest there were three TV screens facing straight down, so that Elvis could apparently watch three shows at the same time without ever having to lift his head off the pillow. Clearly, this was a man who knew how to make himself comfortable.

There was a huge prototype of one of the first videotape players ever made, connected to the TV setup, with a tape still in it of a wrestling match Elvis had been watching. I don't know if Elvis ever met Andy Kaufman, but I'm sure they would've had a lot of wrestling stories to swap.

As the others moved on, I lingered for a moment in the bedroom and wandered over to the dresser. There was his record player, with an old 45 rpm record still on the turntable, and I still kick myself for not memorizing what song it was. I'm sure it was one of the last songs he ever listened to. Also on the dresser was his I.D. bracelet, just as he had left it. I later learned that the housekeeping staff would only move the bracelet to dust underneath it, then replace it in the exact same place. I was surprised there wasn't a chalk outline around it.

Also - hold on to your hat - I looked over in the corner by the bed, and saw a guitar propped up against it. Elvis' guitar.

I've never been a huge Elvis fan, but I can certainly appreciate the role he had and his huge influence on the history of American music. And there was his guitar, a mere three feet away. I'll admit, I got a goosebump or two. Also, being the strange person that I am, weird, twisted fantasies began to occur to me:

-- of grabbing the guitar and playing "Stairway to Heaven" until security ran into the room and shot me.

-- of asking the big cheese if I could keep the guitar as a souvenir, since he was such a big fan of Joan's and all.

-- of wondering how long it would take the big cheese to stop laughing after I'd asked him that.

-- of stuffing the guitar under my shirt, then backing slowly out of the mansion, until security ran out after me and shot me.

---the ultimate sacrilege: lying down on the bed while strumming the guitar and turning on all three TV's, then yelling, "Hey Priscilla! Get me a cheeseburger!"

I chickened out of all of these and instead moved slowly out of the bedroom, to join the others in....The bathroom! You know, the bathroom. Where Elvis supposedly died.

The big cheese actually showed us the bathroom chair which he insisted Elvis had fallen out of on his final day. It was a black leather and chrome thing, propped against a wall facing the toilet. The seat itself sloped sharply backward, which made it seem

Touring with Legends

almost impossible to fall out of, even if you were an extremely heavy-set person who had nodded off. The big cheese insisted that indeed, this was the very chair. Elvis' final resting-place, so to speak.

Personally, Peg and I would have none of it. True, it might not sound right to say that the King of Rock and Roll died on the toilet, but we just couldn't buy the chair story. And to prove to ourselves that we were right, Peg and I waited til the group moved on and....TOOK TURNS SITTING IN AND TRYING TO FALL OUT OF ELVIS' CHAIR.

That's right. We are demented people, and maybe it wasn't the proper and respectful thing to do, seeing that we were guests in the forbidden upstairs sanctuary of the King. But let's face it... When you're old and gray and bouncing the grandkids on your knee, how many other grandparents will be able to say to those kids, "Let me tell you 'bout the time grandpa and grandma tried every which way to fall out of Elvis' chair."

The last thing we got to see was Elvis' hamburger bed. It was a bed custom-made by Elvis in the shape of a giant hamburger that he had bought as a present for his daughter. It was kept in storage in a spare room out of sight because the bed was so tacky, we were told, that Priscilla had refused to let her daughter sleep in it. The funny thing to me was Elvis had to actually order this thing from a store. I would've loved to have been a fly on the wall as Elvis made the call.

"Yeah, baby? Elvis. I need to order a bed for a girl's bedroom. You make 'em round?......Yeah, I need one that looks like a cheeseburger.....No, not White Castle, standard size. You by any chance got pickle-shaped pillow cases?....I'll also need a bun bedspread, lettuce comforter, and.....Oh, I dunno, I guess American cheese for the sheets. Medium well. When will that be ready? Cool. Thank you. Thank you very much."

I also imagined Elvis on the phone a month later, giving in to Priscilla, reluctantly having to cancel his order for tomato-shaped cushions and a ketchup-bottle nightstand.

That was the end of the tour. We said our thank you's and goodbyes and went back to our hotel. It had been an amazing evening.

Dennis Blair

Peg and I got into bed, and then turned out the light as I pulled the covers up over myself and Elvis' guitar.

Just kidding.

Chapter 22: Joan Rivers Part Two

Joan had a road manager named Kevin Jones. Kevin was a great guy with a good sense of humor and an "I don't give a crap" attitude that, believe me, comes in handy sometimes when you're dealing with show business bullshit and people. And we always had tons of laughs with him around.

One night we were on our way to Baltimore. I was driving from New York, and Kevin hadn't slept the night before. So, in his official role as road manager, he mapped out the route for us to take, then promptly fell asleep in the back seat while Peg and I did the driving. After about an hour and a half, we were closing in on the Baltimore area but needed help zeroing in on our hotel. No problem, we figured, Kevin's the road manager, he knows his way around. We'll just wake him up, he can tell us what route to take, and we'll be fine. We shook Kev awake.

"Huu—uuh?"

"Kevin, how do we get to the hotel?"

He poked his head up, looked out the window for a moment, then said,

"Beats the shit outta me."

And then promptly went right back to sleep.

Lake Tahoe

One of the places we played most frequently was Caesar's Palace in Lake Tahoe., the very place and on the very stage where Brian Wilson had asked my wife to get him five cups of coffee. We were booked there often, usually for a week at a time, so we really got to know each other there. And since Tahoe was a town devoted almost exclusively to resort activities, Joan got to play her den mother role to the hilt.

By far the most enjoyable of these activities was water-skiing. Joan would commandeer the luxurious Caesar's Yacht from the entertainment office and bring us all out on the lake - Peg, me, her manager Bill Sammeth, Edgar, her assistant (and future manager) Dorothy, Annie, her hairdresser Jason, and when she was in town her daughter Melissa. All of us would go out on the boat, and most of us would try to water-ski, our abilities ranging from "almost adequate" to "why-even-bother." You could always tell when I had gone water-skiing, because I was so exhausted by showtime that my delivery usually slowed to a near mumble. Steven Wright would've told me I needed more energy.

On one of these water-ski trips, Joan and her entourage had decided they were angry at Garry for some reason (sound vaguely familiar?), and had made up their minds to go out on the boat without telling him about it. This was one of those weird, quirky things that would happen with this group sometimes. I called it the "Cattiness Factor." Every so often, for some unforeseen reason, somebody in the organization would get a hair up their butt about somebody else in the organization and that person would be socially ostracized in some way for a few weeks until it was decided that person was okay after all and would once again be restored to the good graces of the powers that be. Show people....jeez!

It was Garry's turn at this time to be in the social doghouse. Peg and I (not being angry at Garry at all, but pressured to join the entourage all the same) went along with them. It was more than a little embarrassing when we ran into Garry in the parking lot and he said, "Hey, where are you guys going?" I forget exactly how we got out of that one, but I do remember feeling like a third-grader being pressured not to play with the new kid.

"Oooh, where are we going? Uuuummm...just out for a walk."
"With snorkels?"

We wound up letting Garry in on this "big secret" later on, and to tell the truth he couldn't really have cared less. We discussed it during a memorable telephone call I had with him when I got back home to New York.

First let me set this up by saying the following story is not politically correct. But many people in Joan's entourage were gay, I told them this story, and they laughed harder at it than anyone else. So here goes....

I was talking to Garry on the phone after the Tahoe gig, and he asked me what I had been doing that day when we met him in the parking lot. I said, "Oh you know, the usual; Water-skiing and getting fucked up the ass."

There was silence on the line. Then, Garry replied; "Wait a minute. I didn't know you water-skied."

Speaking of "the gays" *.... (*see chapter 18)

Joan was very popular in those days with many different segments of the population, and she had a pretty large gay following. They adored her, and were among her most rabid and loyal fans. I guess you could say that later on, Kathy Griffin and Joan Rivers were in a friendly, competitive death-match for the gay audience. So it came as no real shock when, after a show in Tulsa Oklahoma one night, Joan and her entourage were all invited to a drag show at a large gay bar downtown. And dag-nab it, we all went. I mean, we were with den mother Joan, for Chrissakes. You can't say no to den-mama Joan..

Admittedly, I don't remember much about that evening, except that I began drinking early and often and was pretty hammered by the time the female impersonators hit the stage. I do remember one of the performers in particular (it was either Marilyn Monroe or Julie Andrews) coming over to me constantly, singing to me, and trying to sit on my lap as I continued to down larger and larger quantities of beer. I was so out of it at one point that I vaguely remember taking out a ten-dollar bill and stuffing it in his/her bra strap, a fact that was confirmed by everyone the next morning as having actually happened. I also have a dim memory of Garry seeing me do the ten-dollar thing, looking at me in shock and mouthing the words, "What are you doing!?" and me shrugging and mouthing, "Having a great time!."

I also remember Jason, Joan's hairdresser, being despondent the next morning that the Marilyn/Dinah guy had been coming on to me and not to him. I mean, I was straight, for Chrissakes, why me?! I apologized to Jason and told him next time I would give him the ten-dollar bill. And besides, Marilyn Monroe was never my type anyway. Julie Andrews, however....

Touring with Legends

Rodney and me in a lighthearted moment backstage

Rodney and me moments later.

Caesar's Palace marquee, circa 1980.

One of my scenes with Rodney in "Easy Money." The moustache is fake.

Hanging at the Debbie Reynolds Hotel in Vegas with the great lady herself.

Dinner with Brad Grey and Garry Shandling, sitting across from Peggy Blair.

So proud to share this Bally's marquee with George.

I still have this poster from the Orleans Hotel in Vegas

The chartered jet crew, featuring the infamous pilot Cheater flipping the bird.

In the dugout at Shea Stadium with Mets' pitcher Sid Fernandez.

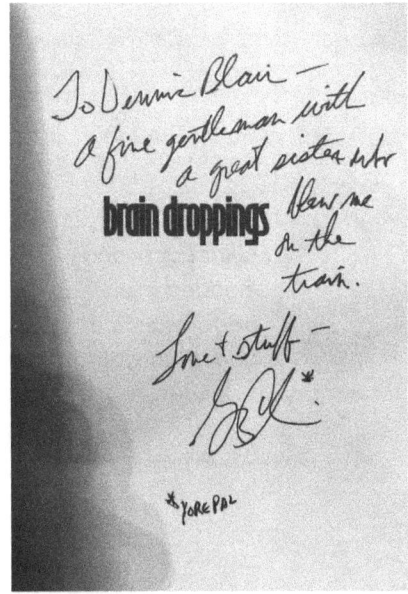

George Carlin graciously autographed my copy of his book.

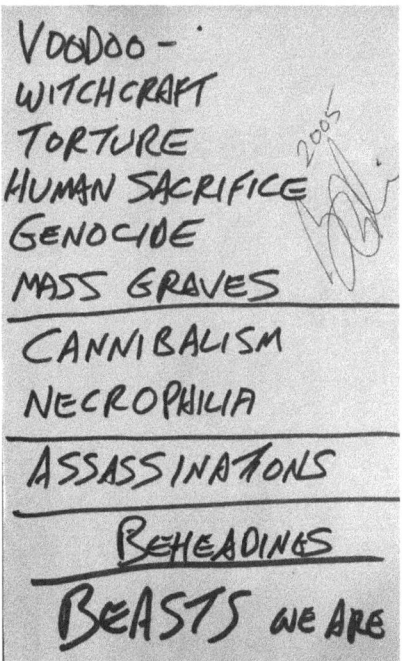

One of George's more upbeat set lists.

Backstage with GC at the Orleans in Vegas. One of his last shows.

Clint Eastwood enjoyed my performance at a benefit in California

With the great comedian Robert Klein at the Southpoint in Las Vegas.

Reunited in New York with old friend Jackie Mason.

After the show with Norm MacDonald.

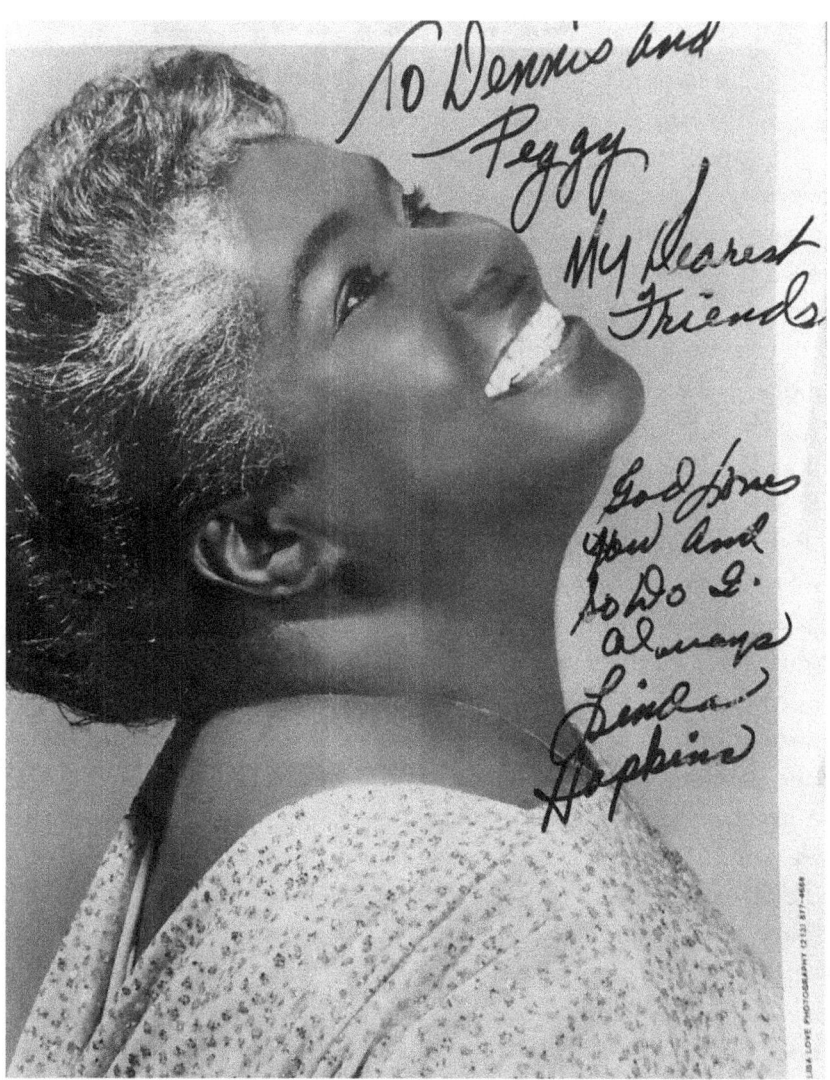

One of the sweetest persons in show business, Linda Hopkins.

Chapter 23: More Garry Shandling

I'd gotten to know Garry pretty well in the months we'd been working together, and we had good times on the road. His act really reflected his personality in many ways. For instance, he always had trouble making decisions about anything, especially women. If he met someone that he was interested in dating, he couldn't make the commitment without first polling everyone he met - "Did you meet her? What did you think? Do you like her? Do you think I'd like her? Do you think she likes me?" - on and on like that, sometimes for days. Once Garry was moaning about how he could never seem to meet women. "Why is that?," he wondered. "Because Garry," Peg said, "By the time you get the fifth opinion we're in the next town."

The paranoia and insecurity about his hair was a big part of his persona back then, and based completely on truth. Even before it became a staple of his act in the '80's, he would always be asking people before he went out on stage, "How's my hair?" I remember watching an appearance he made on the Tonight show. It was a great shot, every joke worked. I called him up to tell him I'd watched it and to congratulate him on a fine performance. He didn't care about that. The first thing he wanted to know was, "How did my hair look?"

There was a time when we were travelling late at night after all the stores had closed, and he was suffering acute anxiety because he was petrified that he would run out of hair mousse. When we got to our hotel we checked into adjacent rooms, and I could overhear him talking on the phone to his manager. He sounded stressed and upset, and the only word I could make out clearly was "hair," which he repeated at least twenty-five times. I could only assume that he had his manager were tracking down every all-night drugstore that carried mousse so that he would look okay by morning.

Peg was especially good at needling him, and he was equally good at taking it. As we've established, it's pretty much common knowledge that most performers have large egos and are fairly self-absorbed, and Garry, like all of us, was no exception to this rule. One night we were all hanging out in the lounge at Caesar's Tahoe. A woman who had seen the show was talking non-stop to Garry, who was wearing one of those pasted-on smiles that said, "Get me out of here, please." Finally, the woman gave Garry her number, then got up and left. Garry turned to us, tilted his head toward the woman, and asked us for our opinion.

"So? What do you think? Should I date her?"

Peg just smiled. "I don't think so, Garry. She was talking about *you* for an hour, and even *you* couldn't pay attention." He loved that.

Once there was a woman in the audience Garry wanted to impress. He was intent that everything be just right, down to the jacket and the pants he was wearing. He must have changed his clothes at least five different times in his dressing room, trying to make sure whatever ensemble he picked out was the one that made him look the best. Finally, he came out wearing what he thought looked good. He asked for an opinion. Peg looked at him for a few moments, then said, "The pants make your penis look small."

He changed into another outfit. With much tighter pants.

Garry was also intolerant of sugar, couldn't eat anything with sugar in it at all. So naturally, when we found this out, we would have a large slice of cake sent to his table, or his room, or wherever he was having dinner. We would do this every single day.

I never said we weren't jerks. It's clearly implied throughout the book.

These were the kind of inane and pointless pranks that would keep you from going insane on the road. Fortunately, Garry took it all well.

I called him up once to ask him something, an opinion about a joke or a bit I was writing. I left the message on his answering machine. A mere three minutes later I called him back with another message: "Yeah Garry, it's Dennis again. Listen, I don't know what the problem is, but I left a message for you and you haven't returned my call. Is it the money? Because if it is, don't worry, feel free to call me collect."

About a half hour later the phone rang. The operator said, "I have a collect call from a Garry Shandling......."

Cell phones were invented soon after, and none of this would have been funny.

Garry wasn't beyond playing a trick himself every once in a while. I remember Peg, Garry Joan and I were out riding around in a limousine (surprised?) after a show somewhere. Garry and Joan were really on each other's cases that night for some reason, half in fun but half seriously too. It was obvious that Garry was more than a little pissed off at her. At some point Joan had the driver stop at a particular hotel to see if the restaurant was open. Joan and the driver got out of the car and walked toward the hotel lobby. At which point Garry locked the doors, jumped in the drivers' seat and drove away, leaving them both stranded there. I can still remember the look of shock on Joan's face out the back window as we sped off.

We were gone for a good ten minutes. Peg and I were in hysterics as Garry drove, badly, recklessly, and anyplace but where Joan was. I think we hit about four convenience stores and bought a bag of pine nuts at each one, just to keep the car out. We kept asking him if he was ever going back, and he kept saying "I haven't decided yet." When he finally headed back and turned into the hotel driveway, they were there waiting. The driver was carrying Joan in his arms like a bride over a threshold, and both of them were laughing. I have no idea what they did for the ten minutes we were gone. Garry unlocked the doors and let them in, and from then on, the tension in the car was broken.

Which was a relief, because without his glasses, Garry was a road hazard.

* * * * *

The last time I saw Garry Shandling was in 2008 in the green room backstage at a great comedy club in Hermosa Beach California called the Comedy and Magic Club. To give you a brief background on this club, it's one of the prime hangouts for comedians, and often famous ones, who like to try out material when they're in the Los Angeles area, because the audiences at this club are uniformly fantastic and can be counted on to give the comedians a pure jolt of adrenaline almost every time they hit the stage. Jay Leno used it to test his Tonight Show monologues every Sunday night and still drops in to try out new stuff for when he goes on the road. It's one of those places where you never know who might stop by.

I was hanging out backstage one night talking with the other comics when Garry popped in. He said hi and I was very glad to see him, but he seemed extremely distracted that night. He was carrying reams of legal-sized note paper on which was scrawled what I only could assume were jokes he was intending to try out that evening, and he kept his head buried in those pages, not once looking up. Although it would have been great to catch up on what he'd been doing all these years since his great "The Larry Sanders Show" had finished its run on cable, and maybe talk over old times a little bit, I could see that he clearly was here to concentrate on whatever he had on those pages that he was clutching in his hands. So I left him alone, went up and did a brief set onstage, and came back to the green room where Garry still sat, buried in his notes. I did notice that he had lost some of his hair, which I considered to be a cruel and ironic tragedy.

I hung around for a while, talking with the other comics backstage, glancing every now and then towards Garry to see if he had any inclination at all towards having a conversation with me, but his notes held sway, so I decided to call it a night. I packed up my guitar and as I headed out the door I said, a bit sarcastically, "Okay Garry, talk to you next time." Garry for the first time looked up from his pages and gave me a big smile.

"Hey. So how are you doing? How've you been? How's Peggy?" I had miraculously somehow broken the spell, and we chatted for a few minutes before he said, "Well, really good to see you, take care." And he once again buried his face in his pages as I walked out down the hall.

Sometimes I remember that night and wonder if I should have stayed to watch Garry's set and see what was so damn important about hose notes in his hand. Maybe I should have. But I had taped an episode of "Family Guy" that I really wanted to see, so I missed out.

I was doing a weekend of shows outside of Seattle at the Chinook Winds Casino in 2016 when I got the news that Garry had died of an apparent heart attack. He was 66. I hadn't seen him since that green room encounter in California 8 years earlier, so the time and distance made the news a little easier to swallow, I guess. I got through the first show okay, but it was weird. The whole weekend was weird. A lot of reminiscing, melancholy, and poring over some great memories in my little hotel room.

Chapter 24: The Tonight Show

The period of time when I toured with Joan was also the period when she became the permanent guest host of the Tonight Show. The one thing for which I will be eternally grateful to her is getting me on that show against all odds.

I say against all odds because getting on the Tonight Show, even when you know and work with the guest host, was not as simple as you might think. I don't know how things go these days so much, but back then most of the difficulty I had stemmed from the nature of my act, which at the time was heavily laden with parodies of well-known songs by popular artists. The problem with T.V. appearances for a guy like me is that normally, especially with a high-profile program like the Tonight Show, I'd have to get clearance and permission from the artist's publisher to do the song on the air. This not only involves time and inconvenience but also payment for use of the songs, and many T.V. shows don't want to be hassled with that.

I had gathered enough material, both original song styles and traditional standup, to do these shows with no problems, but there also seemed to be a tendency for them to shy away from what they consider "novelty" or "specialty" acts in general. I never really understood this, since it would seem that if someone is funny and entertaining, no matter what they do, there should be a place for them on television. Granted, I was able to do the smaller shows at the time, like "Comedy Tonight," "Comic Strip Live," and "Evening at the Improv." But Letterman? Forget it. I think he had an aversion to guitar comics anyway, and he had seen me perform at Dangerfield's when I was just starting out and using a lot of blue material, so I could kiss my Letterman hopes goodbye. The Tonight Show was also a very remote possibility, because Johnny Carson had definite ideas about what he liked and wanted on his show, and novelty acts were not high on the list.

The talent coordinator for the Tonight Show with Johnny Carson was a guy named Jim McCawley. Rodney had asked Jim to watch me perform at the Comedy Store in LA in 1980 and consider me for an appearance on the show. When I came offstage that night, Jim came over to me and said, "Rodney's right. You're very funny. But you can't do parodies on the Tonight Show." It was to be my first lesson in what a tough path I'd chosen in terms of getting my act on television. I didn't have a problem with people thinking I was funny, just with the legalities of the musical parts.

Tom Snyder was a well-known broadcaster in the seventies and eighties who hosted a show that came on after the Tonight Show which was called, appropriately enough, "The Tomorrow Show." Tom happened to catch me at Dangerfield's in 1980 and booked me for his show on NBC. Being young and naïve, and having been doing the comedy thing for a short period of time, I thought I could show up at the studio that day and come up with my five-minute set right before the show. (This is just not done. Traditionally, when you were booked for a TV show, you'd prepare your set, work on it, and try it out at the comedy clubs for as much as a month before your appearance.) I threw together my set and handed it to Bob Morton, the producer (who later went on to produce David Letterman's show. I knew the producer of the Letterman show, and I still couldn't get on. I'm still taking self-esteem classes). Bob looked over my material, then came back a minute later and said, "Uh...Dennis, have you by any chance gotten clearance for these parodies?"

Uh...gotten what for which?.

They let me get away with it that time, but things would not be that easy in the coming years. I could not make a dent on getting on the big shows, the ones that would look great on your résumé and give a real boost to your career. So when Joan Rivers was red hot and hosting the Tonight Show, and went to Jim McCawley to tell him she wanted to have me on, Jim resisted. It was nothing personal, it was just that I was a guitar comic, who did parodies of published songs, etc. etc. yada yada. I was yada yada'd long before "Seinfeld" made it popular.

Meanwhile people who knew I was working with Joan kept asking me, "So? When is Joan gonna put you on the Tonight Show?" And I didn't know what to say to them. "She's working on it.," I'd reply. "Working on it?" They'd say. "She's the damn host! You tell her to put you on!"

Okay, yeah, I'll do that.

We were playing a theatre in St. Louis one night. I remember this night particularly because the entourage was buzzing, like they had some secret that involved me in some way but that they were trying to keep from me. Finally, they couldn't contain themselves any longer. Jason the hairdresser started chatting loudly with Bill Sammeth within earshot, for the express purpose of having me overhear them.

"So Bill, what's this I hear about Dennis Blair and the Tonight Show?"

"Oh, you mean that Joan finally got him on? It's true."

"What's true, Bill? That Dennis got the Tonight Show?"

"Yes, Jason. Dennis got the TONIGHT SHOW."

I kept getting the feeling they were trying to tell me something, in a REALLY SUBTLE WAY.

It wasn't exactly the same as having your agent call you with the news, but it was great news anyway. And I'm sure I'm the only comic that was ever informed he'd gotten the Tonight Show by means of a short, one-act backstage play.

I went to Joan and thanked her. I don't remember if it took the form of a simple handshake or if I threw myself weeping with joy at her feet, because at that exact moment, Robert Ludlum called to ask for his book back. No, I'm kidding, I was actually in a daze. This impossible wish had finally come true. God bless 'er, she came through for me.

I never found out what kind of strings she had to pull, or what lengths she had to go to in order to get me that shot. But the fact remains that without Joan Rivers, I would probably never have gotten the Tonight Show, and I couldn't thank her enough.

Chapter 25: Uh…I've Made It?

First of all, let me quickly say that I realize I've been talking about myself a lot in these last few pages, and I apologize. I know most of you don't know me, and that you bought this book to hear stories about famous people. But I also know a lot of people are fascinated with show business, and what it was like in the comedy world of the 80's, '90's and beyond, with people who were at the top of their games during that period of time, and what it must have been like to do the Tonight Show when there were so many fewer channels and outlets and platforms and the world was so different etc. etc. So bear with me a little longer as I describe what it was like to be in the belly of that beast. We'll get back to the celebrities soon, I promise.

I'd gotten my TV spot together the right way this time, rehearsing it, rearranging it, testing it out. Garry helped me, suggesting bits that might work better than others, giving me a lot of encouragement. It really meant a great deal to have his input. I was ready.

The day of my Tonight Show appearance arrived, December 6, 1984. I assumed I would be extremely nervous, but I wasn't. I was amazingly calm for a person who was about to tape a show that would be seen by, oh I don't know, about twenty million people. I showed up at NBC studios in Burbank. It was a sprawling complex on grounds which included the infamous commissary, a multitude of TV and movie sets and the Tonight studio itself, a cavernous, hangar-like building. They had just finished a taping of "Wheel of Fortune" next door to "Tonight." I thought of going in there and buying some vowels for a cab driver friend of mine who needed some for his name, but decided against it.

I was shown to my dressing room and told to be onstage in ten minutes for a run-through of my spot. I was out there in five.

I can't really describe the feeling of being a comedian and standing on that iconic stage, right on the spot where Johnny and Joan did their monologues every night. There was a little star set into the floor where Johnny stood, and I planted both feet right on it there for a while. Jeez. First Elvis' bedroom, and now this. As I did my run-through, looking up at the 500 empty seats where the audience would be in about an hour, at the lights, the cameras, the stagehands, I couldn't believe I was about to fulfill a fantasy I'd dreamed about for so long and had just about given up on.

After my run-through, Ed Shaugnessy, the legendary drummer for the Tonight Show band, came up to me and said, "Funny stuff, man. You're gonna have a great show."

Okay. If you say so.

The show began. I wandered into the green room to watch Joan's monologue. She announced the guests - Jane Seymour, Rita Moreno, Dennis Blair. I was the last guest, in the traditional "new comic" spot . Jim McCawley came to get me, wished me luck, and led me down the hallway. A priest joined me, reading my last rites as the door to the gas chamber swung open and they led me inside....

Excuse me. Wrong fantasy. Although oddly appropriate. I hoped the end result would be different.

I was brought backstage and led behind that famous curtain, where I waited until the band stopped playing and Joan began to introduce me. I was very calm, and I didn't know why. Shell shock? Ignorance? The fact that all the blood had left my head twelve minutes ago?

".....Please welcome....Dennis Blair!"

Music, curtain parting, Jim slapping me on the back. I remember the lights were incredibly hot and blinding, and I couldn't see the audience at all, but I could hear them. They were unbelievably pumped and enthusiastic, and they laughed at everything. When I was done, the band played me over to the couch as the audience cheered and applauded. We had planned a brief interview section, but Joan explained "We have to go to commercial. We went long, the audience was laughing so much."

They cut to commercial, came back. They did the end of show intros, where I got a nice hand again. And that was that.

I drove home after the show, and I truly don't remember how I got there. I was in such a dream state, a trance, like I was hypnotized. I'll never forget doing that show.

Okay mom, you can wake me up now. I'm ready to go to school. You won't believe the dream I just had!....

The shot had gone well enough to ensure I would do a second one. As a matter of fact, Jim McCawley, who had been so resistant before the shot, now began talking to me about preparing one for an appearance with Johnny himself. This was unbelievably tempting and a real honor, but Joan wanted me to do my second shot with her, and I felt I owed her that. And since Jim didn't bring up the subject again after our initial talk, I went ahead and made my second appearance on the Tonight Show.

I did this one about four months after the first, on April 12, 1985, and it went well also. I continued working with Joan on the road and when the time came, began setting my sights on preparing a set for my third shot, hoping maybe this one would be with Johnny Carson. At which time my life would have achieved complete critical mass and I would march into the sea like a contented lemming.

I never got to do that third show. I vividly recall Peg going into a store in Manhattan to buy a newspaper on our way home one night. When she came out, she looked pale. I asked her what was wrong. "Read this," she said.

She showed me the paper, with the headline "Joan Rivers Canned" across the front of it. (It was the New York Post, of course. "Joan Rivers Canned" just didn't have that sophisticated New York Times ring to it.) Joan had been fired as guest host of the Tonight Show when Johnny Carson found out she was negotiating to get her own show on Fox.

And there went my chances of doing the Tonight Show with Johnny. I was considered a "Joan Rivers" act by the Tonight Show people. (I never understood that thinking. It wasn't like I'd been branded, with a big "JR" burned into my ass.) I called Jim McCawley just to see if they would still consider using me, but I was a goner.

I did do several appearances On "The Late Show," Joan's new show on Fox. But when that was cancelled, my big time TV career dried up for a while. No matter. At least I'd done it.

(A few years later I appeared on Jay Leno's Tonight Show. Well, more accurately, my voice appeared. I was the off-screen voice of Bob Dylan for two telephone sketches that Jay did during his monologue. So I was still getting on the show, just less of me than I used to.)

* * * * *

Garry Shandling's own career began to take off in the mid-eighties, and he became too big a name and too busy with other projects to continue working with Joan in an opening capacity. So Joan looked elsewhere for performers to fill his slot while keeping me on as her utility man. One performer Joan used frequently was Linda Hopkins, a great blues singer and a truly nice person. She had a great innocence about her, and a complete honesty that made her say and do some extremely funny things. One night we were working at a theatre in Warwick, Rhode Island. Linda's dressing room was right next to mine, and both rooms opened onto a sort of shared greenroom area. Peg and I were in this greenroom, just hanging out and watching TV. Linda had gone into her dressing room and was getting ready for the show. Suddenly, Linda's door opened and she stepped out into the greenroom. Her eyes were wide, and she seemed very troubled.

"Oh No!," she said.

We turned to her. "Linda? What's wrong?"

"There's a wedding at my house today, and I forgot to go!" Then, after a brief pause, she turned to us and said, "D'ya think I should call?"

Another time Linda came out of her dressing room clutching several rolls of toilet paper in her arms. What the....?

"Linda? What are you doing?"

"They got all this toilet paper around here," she exclaimed. "And it's free!"

Peg and I watched in amazement as Linda walked from room to room, gathering up every roll she could find while mumbling things like, "It's not like they're gonna miss it or nothin'. And man, you can never have enough toilet paper. I'm gonna bring this right on the plane with me!"

We had visions of Linda sitting in first class with ten rolls of toilet paper on her lap, getting icy stares from Martha Stewart.

(This was, of course, long before the pandemic / toilet paper shortage of 2020. I hope she held onto that stash.)

Another performer Joan used to fill the Shandling void was Don Novello, alias Father Guido Sarducci (Don's iconic character on Saturday Night Live). He didn't work with us a lot, but it was always fun when he did. Don is another really nice person, with a good attitude and a friendly disposition. I had met and spoken briefly with him before the show at Caesar's Tahoe, when he went into his dressing room to get changed. I went out first and did my spot. When I came offstage, Don was standing there, dressed as Father Guido. I said, "Hey, that's what *I* was gonna wear!"

We also worked with actor/ singer Nell Carter and singer Clint Holmes, who had a big hit in 1975 with a song called "Playground In My Mind" (and who remains one of my best friends today). These four people - Linda, Don, Clint and Nell - were our rotating stable of Joan Rivers Show Openers for that year or so after Garry left. It was great to be working so much, with such good friends.

Then suddenly, Joan just stopped using me.

This Is Getting Monotonous

Let's see; I hadn't brought my dog anywhere near Joan, let alone swimming in her pool, so that couldn't be it. I was pretty sure her manager didn't hate me, and I didn't remember doing anything that got her upset. So imagine my surprise when not only did I stop getting booked on Joan's dates, but also found out that she was using another guitar comic who was basically doing my act!

That's what everyone was telling me, anyway. "Hey Dennis, Joan's using some guy who's doing almost all the same stuff you do. Did you sell your jokes to this guy? What happened?" I had no idea. All I knew was that for some reason, Joan stopped using me. I learned later on that Joan's agent was also the agent for this other guitar guy, so maybe he'd been pressuring her to use him until she finally gave in. I can only guess at this, because neither Joan nor her manager ever gave me a reason. They weren't obliged to, but I would've thought we were close enough to at least offer me an explanation.

This agent had pretended he was my friend. ("Wha-a-a-t!!? Do you mean to tell me there are unscrupulous people in show business? Ohh, let me slit my wrists!")

I left phone messages at Bill Sammeth's office which were never returned, so I finally resorted to writing Joan a letter, simply asking her why she would replace me with some clone who was stealing my material. The only answer I got was from her assistant, Dorothy, who helped throw a few more Joan gigs my way. I did the gigs, but it was never the same. Essentially, I was out.

I didn't let my second ejection from headliner orbit get me very down this time. I chalked it up to another adventure in celebrityville and let it go at that.

So, did I ever find out the truth? Did I anger Joan in some way? Did an agent who held a deep, dark secret about her that he would reveal to the world coerce her into using another guitar guy if she didn't comply? Or did she just figure it was time for a change?

As my old friend Kevin Jones would say, "Beats the shit outta me."

Chapter 26: Back to the Drawing Board

I was not traumatized this time. Really. I had grown, matured, become grounded in the harsh realities of show business and acquired a deep sense of confidence in myself and my abilities. And now that I was on Joan's "A" list, I could stop worrying about minor distractions like paying rent and eating.

First thing I did, I got me a good agent.

Fred Suss was a young, ambitious guy who worked at the William Morris Agency in New York and who was actually able to keep me working quite a ton during these traumatic times. As a supplement to my ongoing gigs at the comedy clubs around the country, Fred got me some interesting work both on my own and opening for a spate of headliners over the ensuing years.

The work on my own was, of course, always interesting, though not always great. I remember getting booked on a Mexican cruise once. This particular job went well, but it led to a similar experience later which proved disastrous at the time, and of course hilarious when I think of it now.

The worst thing about doing cruises, especially for a comic, was that if you bombed on land, you could sneak out a back door somewhere, get into your car, and drive off, never to be seen again. But if you bombed on a ship, you were stuck on the damn ship until the cruise was over. Which meant that for days on end, you would be forced to eat breakfast lunch and dinner and constantly come in contact with PEOPLE WHO THOUGHT YOU SUCKED.

I did this cruise to Mexico, and the audience enjoyed the show. So everywhere I went on the ship for the next couple of days, people would come up to me, say hello, buy me a drink, shake hands, etc. Not only that, but the pay was excellent and of course it was very enjoyable for Peg and I to be soaking up the sun on deck all day and eating gourmet meals from morning till night.

So William Morris booked me three months later on an Alaskan cruise, and I eagerly accepted. Of course, what I didn't realize was that the average age of a typical passenger on one of these Alaskan cruises was "dead four years." I've actually heard that in the mid-eighties on Alaskan cruises there were three refrigerators on the ship; one to keep meat, one to keep vegetables, and one to keep passengers who died on board.

I did my show, and they watched it. And that's all they did. Watch it. Not one laugh. They didn't understand any of my jokes or any of my references, probably because many of the references dealt with events that happened after the Spanish/American war. I was on for forty-five grueling minutes, and all I got was the sound of several hacking coughs and flashbacks of Catskills audiences coming at me with serving forks in their hands.

I remained in my cabin for the next three days. Peg came and brought me my meals, and when I did walk out on deck I was sure to always be wearing sunglasses, lipstick and a large blond wig. I did not do cruises again for another twenty years. (I do, however, put on the blond wig every once in a while. It's a look that works for me.)

(Cruise horror story #2: My story is not the worst by far. There's a true story about a comic whose show went so badly on a cruise ship that the entertainment director came up to him the next morning and said, "You're going to have to leave the ship." The comic was shaken, but understood, and said, "Okay, I'll get off as soon as we get back to L.A." The director shook his head. "No, you don't understand. These people hate you. You're gonna have to get off at our next port-of-call." The comic was actually forced to get off the ship at some tiny island and be airlifted by helicopter back to L.A. This is what I would call having a bad show)

I was booked to do some conventions too. Most of them went well, although not all...

I did some sort of award presentation/dance event where none other than Cher was one of the guests and everyone was in tuxedoes and there was a big thirty-piece orchestra and nobody had been informed, or apparently even cared, that there was a comedian on the bill this evening.

At one point the orchestra stopped playing, and the MC stepped up to the microphone. Actually, it would be more accurate to say the MC stepped up to the kazoo, because that's about how good the sound quality was. Anyway, he didn't get anyone's attention. He didn't ask for the house lights to be brought down. He merely said, "Ladies and gentlemen, Dennis Blair." Peg was in the crowd, and told me that what she heard the guy say over the loudspeaker was "Mumphig un suddlgum, Beggis Toor." I think it was for this reason that no one's attention was riveted to the stage. Also, everyone was half-plastered by then and kept talking and hooting and wondering why the band had stopped playing "The Theme from Fame." Through it all, I just kept hammering away, trying to tell jokes to loud hooligans in tuxes who weren't aware of my presence. Peg told me that Cher, who was sitting at her table and found out she was my wife, turned to her in the middle of all this and said, "So he really wants to be in show business?"

After a few minutes I just started asking the audience for requests, to no avail. Finally, I turned to a security guard who was looking at me with genuine pity in his eyes and said, "Sir, do you have any requests?"

He thought for a moment, then smiled and said, "Lionel Richie."

I did the song, and basically the whole show, for him.

Fortunately, Fred Suss did get me a lot of nice and successful gigs opening for headliners in Atlantic City.

Chapter 27: The Four Tops

I opened fairly frequently for The Four Tops at Caesar's hotel. They of course were renowned for their string of hits in the 'sixties such as "I Can't Help Myself," "Standing in the Shadow of Love," "Bernadette" and many others. "The Tops" were usually booked to do a week at a time at Caesar's, which was good, except for the fact that they had a large number of fans who would come to see every single show they did. For a comedian of course, this is not the best situation, because what often happened is these people would wind up seeing me do pretty much the same material night after night. And although they were nice and polite about it, I definitely noticed the laughs getting weaker and weaker as the days went on and they found it progressively harder to laugh at punchlines they had heard six times already. By the end of the run, I believe the Four Tops Fan Club was reciting each of my jokes along with me. If I'd forgotten a punchline, they probably could've shouted it out. It was around this time that I decided I should write some more material.

The Four Tops were nice people, and one of them, Laurence, had two adorable seven and eight-year-old daughters who came backstage one night and walked into my dressing room. They were a little nervous and very shy and respectful (I guess they figured I must've been famous or something). They never quite made eye contact and fidgeted constantly as they murmured things like, "Um, hi Mr. Blair ("Mr. Blair"!!?), umm, we just wanted to tell you we really like your show and we think you're really funny." I very gently thanked them and shook their darling little hands.

Now I don't know what it is about me exactly. But when kids are in a room with me for more than five minutes, they begin to realize that I in fact am not really an adult at all, but am in reality geekier than that classmate of theirs with the pocket protector. It was no different with these kids. Within minutes, these two quiet, charming little angels became loud and boisterous and started whacking me and kicking me and generally treating me like one of their school chums. Laurence at one point heard the commotion down the hall and yelled out sternly, "Girls, you stop bothering Dennis and Peggy. You leave them alone now, you hear?"

One of the girls yelled back, "But daddy, they looove us!"

It was true. We did. I still have the black and blue marks on my shins to prove it.

One night during the engagement Peg and I were trying to get some sleep in our room. It was three A.M., the loud party in the room next door was still going strong, and we'd finally had enough. We called security and asked if they could please tell the noisy people next door to quiet down so we could get some sleep. We watched through the peephole as a guard came up and knocked on the offending party's door. The person who answered was Obie Benson, who of course was one of the Four Tops, who didn't look at all happy that some idiot had told him to quiet down, which is why Peg and I quickly tiptoed back to our bed and dove back under the covers.

I kept envisioning running into Obie the next day;

"Hey Obie, how ya doing?"

"Not too good. Some idiot in the room next door called up and complained my room was too noisy last night. Racist sonofabitch probably."

"Uh...yeah, that's too bad. So anyway I wrote a song for you guys. You want me to play it for you now?"

"Nah, I'll come by and hear it later. What room you in?"

(By the way...Obie did jot down his address and phone number one evening after a show and told me if I ever wrote any songs they could use, I should send them to him. This thrilled me to no end, of course. Songwriting had always been my avocation, and I had stockpiled a large number of original tunes over the years, so an opportunity to place one of them with the Four Tops would be quite an honor. The only problem was, when Obie asked me this, he was pretty drunk (sound familiar?). So three weeks later, when I called him up, he didn't know who I was or what he'd told me (sound familiar?). When I reminded him of his offer, he kind of grunted and mumbled something like, "yeah, send it, what the hell." And of course, I never heard from him again. (SOUND FAMILIAR!?) I never saw Obie after that, but I've heard he and the Ludlums were talking about making a musical out of one of his books.

* * * * *

One of the duties of a good agent or manager is to get his or her artists the best deals possible. Among the perks Fred Suss would always get me in Las Vegas or Atlantic City were meal privileges, which meant I could eat for free in any of the hotel restaurants (usually known as an "RFB" - room, food, and beverage allowance). This is not something that the hotels always offer, by the way, so the agent or manager has to be sharp and make sure the artist gets whatever he can.

I'm not gonna come right out and say that whoever did the deal for the Four Tops at Caesar's had dropped the ball, but....well, let's put it this way. While Peggy and I were feasting in Caesar's restaurants every night, The legendary Four Tops - who were American Music Icons and who had a string of hit songs and who were headlining to packed houses at Caesar's - were eating in the employee cafeteria....All because their manager hadn't thought to ask for an RFB. I'm not lying, I know this for a fact. Because Herb Wolf, the entertainment director at Caesar's, told us so.

"Herb," we asked, "Why are the Four Tops eating in the employee's cafeteria?"

"Because their manager forgot to ask for an RFB. By the way, how's your filet mignon?"

"It's excellent. Look Herb, they're the Four Tops. You can't allow this to continue."

"My hands are tied. I'm not allowed by my supervisors to let them eat for free in the restaurants unless their manager specifically requests it. Do you want more caviar?"

"No, thanks. Listen, this is terrible. What if we called up their manager anonymously and told him to ask for an RFB?"

"Can't do it. Has to be his idea."

"Herb, please. This is killing us. We're here eating steak while Levi Stubbs is shooing flies away from his sloppy joe. Please let us..."

"No! It's corporate policy. I could get fired. Sorry. Are you gonna finish your bananas foster?"

So that was that. We were actually forbidden to leak this secret to the Tops' manager, because Herb was afraid it would end up like some big Monica Lewinsky scandal and he'd be drummed out of the entertainment industry. I suppose he had visions of being homeless on the boardwalk, pushing his belongings in a shopping cart while casino employees pointed and whispered, "See that guy? He gave the Four Tops an unrequested RFB. Dumb bastard." No, the Four Tops would be relegated to the employee's cafeteria until they changed management, and that was all there was to it.

Peg and I didn't really enjoy our meals all that much at Caesar's that week. We just couldn't shake the image of Obie Benson at a chipped Formica table yelling out for more home fries and corn beef hash.

Chapter 28: Gladys Knight and the Pips

I opened for Gladys Knight and the Pips for one weekend at Resorts International. There's nothing particularly noteworthy to report about the engagement itself. It went well, the audiences were good, and as far as I knew Gladys and the Pips had an RFB, so I suffered no guilt. My humorous story about Gladys Knight and the Pips involves a softball game.

Gladys' manager at the time was her son. A young man in his twenties and a real nice guy, he liked me enough to invite me to participate in a softball game they were all having the next day with friends and relatives at a nearby ballpark.

What I found out that day, as I boarded the bus with Gladys and the Pips and their various people, was that Gladys' son was apparently about the only one of the group who liked or even knew me. Unfortunately, her son was not along for this ride, and I neither knew nor was introduced to anyone else in the entourage, and no one asked who I was. For the entire ride to the field I was pretty much ignored and avoided. Occasionally someone would glance in my direction, but instead of a wave or a hello or a friendly nod, I usually got a wary look that seemed to say, "Who is this and what is he doing on our bus?" I don't know what prompted this. Maybe they'd found out I was the bastard that had called security on The Four Tops. I don't know. What I do know is that I started feeling a little awkward and began to think it wasn't such a good idea to have accepted this offer.

My feelings were reinforced once we got to the ballpark. When they chose up sides, I couldn't help noticing that I was conspicuously absent from the lineup. It wouldn't have been so bad sitting on the sidelines and supporting the team, except for the fact that basically, the team and their support group seemed to be wishing I would just go away. How could I cheer? What would I yell? "Go, people who wish me dead, Go!"

The game progressed for five innings. Fun was had. Cheers were shouted. High fives were given. And me? I had traced a hopscotch board on the sand to entertain myself.

Around the sixth inning, someone who had obviously taken pity on me came over and asked if I'd like to join the game.

"Sure!," I said, and asked if I could borrow a glove from someone. The man just looked at me.

"Uhh.....not to play. We just need a first base coach. Do you wanna do that?"

Happy to be given any sort of softball-related activity at all, I jumped at the offer and trotted out toward first base. I went through some jock-type motions, planting my feet, spitting out the side of my mouth and going into an athletic-looking squat, when I suddenly realized I had no idea what a first base coach was supposed to do. I also realized this was my big chance to be accepted by the Gladys Knight Softball Team, and I was determined to be the best gosh darn first base coach they had ever seen. So I turned toward the first baseman, got his attention and said, "Excuse me?"

He turned to me and said, "Yeah?"

"I was just wondering, I've never done this before. What is a first base coach supposed to do?"

He stared at me for a moment, looking as confused as I was. Apparently he didn't know the answer either. Finally, he said,

"Well - I guess when the runner gets here, you say 'Hi. Welcome to first base.'"

This seemed odd, but since I had no idea what to do, I decided, why not? So yes, every time a runner walked or got a single, I'd say, "Hi. Welcome to first base." I got the weirdest looks I've ever gotten from people in my life, including the time I showed up in college on Halloween dressed in a Spiderman costume.

They decided to play a second game, and believe it or not, the spell had somehow been broken and they put me in the lineup this time. Maybe they started warming up to me, or maybe they just felt bad that I hadn't really been included. Or more likely, maybe they wanted to get me away from first base. Whatever the reason, I was in. I was to bat right after Bubba, one of the Pips. I waited on deck as Bubba slapped a ground ball through the hole past third, rounded first base, slid into second.....and broke his wrist.

The game was called off. I was never to bat in a Gladys Knight Softball Event again. We just all got on the bus and headed back to the hotel. That night, Gladys and the Pips performed, with Bubba and his heavily bandaged wrist. I have to admit, it was kind of humorous watching those patented Pip hand-and-arm moves with Bubba thrusting this cumbersome cast in the air at every moment.

That was the only time I opened for them. Like I said, the shows went well, and the engagement was fairly uneventful. And look on the bright side. At least now, if there's ever a team that needs a first base coach, I'm ready.

Chapter 29:
Julie Budd, Three Dog Night, Gloria Estefan and Elayne Boosler

Julie Budd may not be a familiar name to many. But in the sixties she was well-known as a child prodigy, a teenaged singer with a voice mature and beautiful beyond her years, sort of like a latter-day LeAnn Rimes. She appeared frequently on the Mike Douglas and Ed Sullivan shows, among many, and was generally regarded as "the next big thing." She probably would have been a huge star if people like Barbra Streisand (to whom she's often unfairly compared) hadn't come along, and of course if Beatlemania and rock & roll hadn't rendered her style of singing out-of-synch with the times. But Julie had little trouble getting work, with a solid foundation of fans and a great deal of talent to buoy her. I was booked to open for her for two weeks at Caesar's in Atlantic City, in the lounge.

My manager at the time had been reluctant to have me perform in a casino lounge. First of all, I had by this time hooked up with George Carlin as his opening act, and had been playing in two thousand seat theatres. So a noisy, smoke-filled lounge was considered a step down for me. Casino lounges are not generally known for their classy surroundings. They are usually not sealed off from the surrounding casino area, so the performers are treated to the ear-piercing sound of slot machines constantly going off. This is especially horrifying for singers. It's not uncommon for a songstress in a sequined gown to be in the middle of a tender ballad like "Embraceable You" when suddenly a woman at the slots is heard screaming, "Jeez, Vinnie, I got the three lemons!"

Nevertheless, since they were offering to pay me very nicely, and since George was not working for that two-week period, the booking was accepted. Also, Caesar's had told us, assured us, *promised* us, that "Cleopatra's Barge" (the name of the room I'd be working) was not a lounge, but a sophisticated, elegant, intimate showroom. So I showed up for sound check at Cleopatra's Barge.

It was a lounge.

Not only was it a lounge, with slot machines erupting all around it, it was also a uniquely tacky one...not so much the show area, but the outside of it. As you entered, the bow of the "barge" was prominently displayed. It featured a life-sized sculpture of Cleopatra with a long, flowing gown, a tuft of brown hair, and big wooden tits. Seriously. They were the biggest wooden tits I'd ever seen. And let me tell you, I've seen big wooden tits before. In fact, I'm certain they were used more than once to direct patrons to the lounge.

"Excuse me, we're looking for Cleopatra's Barge?"

"Yes, ma'am, straight ahead past the food court. You see those big, wooden tits over there? That's it. We have Julie Budd and Dennis Blair tonight."

I kept wondering what the instructions to the builders must've been like. "Okay guys, what we need is seating for two hundred people, the bar area set back, and the look of a barge. Who's in charge of making the tits for Cleopatra? Eddie? Okay Eddie, we got a request from the contractor to make 'em really big. You got that? And make the nipples out of oak. We don't want none 'o those cheap, balsa wood nipples. Not for a classy dump like this."

Anyway, tits and all, we did the engagement. It went as well as any gig in a lounge could be expected to go. By the second week I had gotten quite used to the sound of the slots, and had begun to incorporate the annoyance into my act, which any comedian worth his salt would have done. And usually, people in the audience would realize halfway into my show that there was, in fact, a show going on, and maybe they should pay attention.

Comedians are lucky in that their occupation and temperament usually allows them and encourages them to deal with situations like this. This is not the case with singers. They are usually locked into an arrangement with the band, and since they are often not comedians by nature they are burdened with the task of trying to stay focused, and ignoring the bad stuff going on around them.

Lounges are conducive to conversation, to chatting, to socializing. Julie Budd was used to rapt audiences with high standards paying strict attention. Cleopatra's Barge and Julie were not a good mix. There were numerous occasions when Julie, unable to tolerate the rudeness anymore, would interrupt a ballad so that she could calmly yet firmly tell a loud audience member to shut up or get out. I always enjoyed this. There's something about a petite, willowy female singer wearing an elegant dress and expensive jewelry going at it with a guy wearing a bad toupeé and a polyester leisure suit that just gives me the jollies.

And oh, the clientele!

One night before my show was about to start, Herb Bernstein, Julie's manager and musical director, told me to "be careful what I say out there." When I asked him why, he pointed through the curtain at two big, beefy, sinister-looking guys seated front and center. "Those two.," Herb said. "They're with the St. Louis family. Y'know what I mean?"

One of the rules I have always tried to follow in life is "Never piss off a Mafia guy." It's embroidered into my socks.

I went out and carefully avoided saying anything offensive to these two fine, upstanding gentlemen. I also apparently avoided saying anything that made them laugh. During my entire show, all they did was stare at the floor, occasionally glance at their watches and try to decide if they should whack me or order the cheese plate. They were obviously here just to see Julie, and I was once again, in my perennial role as the opening act, an inconsequential obstruction to them. But they didn't kill me, which I took as a supreme compliment, suitable for inclusion in my resume:

(Dennis Blair Reviews: "Hilarious!" – Chicago Tribune. "Side-splittingly funny!" – Washington Post. "We let him live." – St. Louis Mafia dons)

The two "gentlemen" came to visit Julie backstage in her dressing room after the show. As I passed by, I overheard one of them talking to her in a deep, gruff voice, saying how much they liked her and how (I'm not making this up) they saw her "a few years ago, when you were opening for Don Wrinkle."

(I always love a good malaprop. While we were all having dinner one night, some guy with a thick New York accent came over to Julie and said, "Hey Jules, I remember seeing you a coupla years back when you were in that French show, "Less Miserabulls."

(My mom had one of the all-time great malaprops when I was twelve years old. I had been bitten slightly by a dog and had neglected to tell her about it. When she found out, she came to me all upset and blurted, "Why didn't you tell me you got bitten by a dog? Don't you know you could get rabbis?")

Julie and Herb have kept in touch with us over the years, but since our Caesar's experience we've never worked together. Couldn't find a lounge with tits big enough.

Three Dog Night

I worked a one-nighter with Three Dog Night in 1985 at a small theatre in the Midwest. The first thing I noticed was how young these guys were, making me think that maybe, just maybe, these were not the original guys. Especially since one of them didn't speak English.

I don't have much to say about this engagement or the group, because I never actually met them. I was booked, got to the theatre in time for the show, did the show and came off. That was it. No introductions, no bonding, no "You're on the A list, kid!," nothing. Just one of those quick "wham, bam, thank you, band" things where apparently the regular opening act couldn't make it that night, so they got me at the last minute to fill in. I'm pretty sure they had a guy who opened for them regularly, because I hung around long enough to watch from backstage as they did their first song. After the song, the lead singer grabbed the microphone and said, "Hey, how about that Michael Winslow? Wasn't he funny?" I looked out at the confused faces in the audience, applauding politely, looking at one another as if to say "Michael Winslow? Isn't he the black guy that was in those 'Police Academy' movies?"

Yes, he is. He'll be back tomorrow night.

Gloria Estefan

Back when the act was known as "Gloria Estefan and the Miami Sound Machine," I was their opening act for a few months' worth of shows in 1986. Not much to tell here. Gloria and the band were fine people and the gigs were good. But there were two memorable things about this series of engagements.

Number one was the routing. I have no idea who was responsible for mapping out the cities and venues we wound up doing, but I do know that none of them were anywhere near each other. Instead of a sane and normal schedule of cities that were strung close together, it was not unusual for us to do Cleveland Ohio, then Amarillo Texas, then Phoenix Arizona, then New York, etc., etc. If I remember correctly, within two months I racked up enough frequent flier miles to earn a free trip to Pluto.

The bad news was that I was tired all the time. Traveling thousands of miles almost every day is not the best thing you can do for your sleep patterns. I distinctly remember looking into many hotel room mirrors at the end of the day and yelping in fear at the haggard gargoyle that had snuck into my room, until I realized it was, in fact, me. I also remember that staying awake for an entire performance was considered a major accomplishment. The tour should have been sponsored by "No-Doz." I asked one of the equipment guys who had been with the group for a long time (and who had to travel by bus) if this routing was unusual. "Nah.," he said. "We usually don't play a city until we've driven past it at least five times."

The second memorable thing about the engagement was that Gloria actually kept pleading with me to do parodies of Miami Sound Machine songs.

It's true that a major portion of my act consists of song parodies of famous groups and singers, but usually as a common courtesy (and a survival tactic) I don't skewer the songs of the person I'm opening for. For instance, I used to do a joke about how I felt the Beach Boys had gotten a little too old to be referred to as "Boys" anymore. However, I never did my "Help me Rhonda, help me get up outta my chair" or "Round Round, Get Around, Can't

Get Around" parodies when I opened for them. First of all, they performed those songs every evening, and why ruin them for the fans? And second of all, what if they didn't like the parodies and they fired me? I may be dumb, but I'm not stupid.

I kept trying to explain this to Gloria, but she'd have none of it. "Come on, do it! Do 'Goys Will Be Goys" instead of 'Boys Will Be Boys'!"

"Uh....gee, Gloria, I don't think..."

"How about 'The Turds Get In The Way'" for "Words Get In The Way?"

"Would you stop? They're your fans, they'll kill me!"

"'Step On Your Feet' instead of "Get On Your Feet?"...

"Nooooooo!!!"

She was so insistent that I began thinking I might be fired for not making fun of her songs, which would have been a definite first in show business history. I mean, could you have imagined Sinatra coming up to his opener and begging him to change "These vagabond shoes" to "These vagabond Jews," or George Michael changing "I'm Never Gonna Dance Again" to "I'll Never Soil My Pants Again?" I think not, my good man.

Fortunately, Gloria eventually came to her senses and gave up trying to persuade me to trash her tunes. I have to admit though, it was refreshing to work with someone who didn't take herself as seriously as 98% of all the other performers in show business do. And I also have to admit that she almost wore me down to the point of actually doing a parody of one of her songs. Unfortunately, I was on No-Doz at the time, so I completely forgot to do it.

Elayne Boosler

Around this time I was booked to help open the new "Catch a Rising Star" comedy club at Bally's hotel in Las Vegas. For the first week of the new club's existence, I would be the opening act for Elayne Boosler.

Elayne had always been one of my favorite comedians, and we became friends quickly. I would do my show each night, then usually hang around to catch her performance, which consisted of approximately 45 minutes of smart, funny material that had the audiences howling.

One night after the show Elayne and I went out to dinner with some other comedian friends. Dinner invariably led to discussions about comedy and show business in general, which somehow led to each of us telling our favorite jokes. This was a windfall for me, because I had recently heard a joke that made me laugh harder than I had laughed in years. When my turn arrived, I told the joke to all assembled, including my new pal Elayne. The joke went like this:

"The Queen of England and the Queen of Spain are driving along in horse-drawn carriages. They both enter the forest from opposite sides, and wind up on a narrow path where the two carriages meet. The path is so narrow that neither one of the carriages can get past the other, but the egos of the monarchs makes it so neither one wants to be the first to get out of the way and let the other pass. So the two carriages just sit there for an hour, not moving. Darkness falls.

Finally, the driver of the Queen of England rises up, and with a loud voice (delivered with a proud, proper British accent), he says to the driver of the Queen of Spain:

'You there! I say, get out of our way and let us pass! I have in this carriage the Queen of England, the greatest monarch on the face of the earth, the proud ruler of all she surveys. As you must know, the sun never sets upon the British Empire, it shines like a beacon for all to see, and this grand Lady in this carriage is the leader, the ruler, the supreme arbiter of that proud and noble land, that vast and powerful Empire known as England. So, get out of our way!'

At which point the driver of the Queen of Spain rises up and says (in a thick New York accent),

'Hey, whaddya think I got <u>here, a bag of shit?</u>'

All my comic friends laughed. I turned to see what Elayne's reaction was.

She wasn't there.

I couldn't find her anywhere for at least thirty seconds. I looked up, down, all around. Nothing. Until I heard some faint, muffled squeals from...Underneath the table.

That's where she was. Underneath the table, Elayne had laughed so hard at the joke that she had fallen underneath the table. When she was finally able to rejoin us above the table, her eyes were stained with tears from the laughter. Her mascara was running down her cheeks. Her intestines were hanging limply from the hole she had burst in her abdomen. I assumed I had made a friend for life.

From then on, for the rest of the week's engagement, Elayne could not look at me without bursting into hysterics. It was just one of those jokes that either killed people or left them completely cold, and it had really scored with her. So, being the true friend and decent human being that I was, I made her life total hell for the rest of the week.

Every night at the club, I would come offstage and the middle act would go on. Elayne would be innocently preparing for her show, blissfully unaware of my presence, lurking in the nearby hallway. The middle act would come off. Elayne would mentally prepare. She'd smooth out her dress, apply a bit of blush, primp one last time before the mirror as the MC proclaimed, "Ladies and gentlemen, please welcome…"

At which point I would pop out from my hiding place and yell, "Whaddya think I got here, a bag of *shit*?" Whereupon Elayne would completely lose it. Tears streaming down. Mascara a mess.

"…Elayne Boosler!"

And out onstage she would have to go.

In one of those many instances of life that I never seem to understand, one day, out of the blue, for no reason that I could think of, Elayne stopped answering my calls or responding to emails. I kept trying. And trying. I asked her if there was something wrong, if I had done or said something to offend her or get her angry. No reply. Nothing. Finally, she emailed me back in 2016 that she wasn't angry at all, that she was just extremely busy, that everything was okay. I let it go at that.

I've not heard a word from her since, and I've given up trying. I recently heard from a mutual acquaintance that he'd been told that he'd heard there was indeed some kind of a problem, but he couldn't tell me what it was. This is the kind of stuff that will drive you crazy if you let it, so whatever it is I can't dwell on it anymore. Life is too short to worry about things you can't fix. It's just always a shame when you lose a friend and they won't tell you why.

Maybe someday the ice will melt and she'll let me know.

Maybe she met the queen of Spain and decided I shouldn't joke about her like that?

Onward…

Chapter 30: Tom Jones

I opened for Tom Jones for the better part of 1987. This was another case where I was booked for a limited engagement, which was extended indefinitely because, I suppose, Tom liked my show and decided to keep me on. I say "I suppose" because to the best of my recollection, for the entire year or so that I toured with Tom, we exchanged maybe twelve words. I don't think it was anything personal, because if he disliked me I'm sure I wouldn't have lasted on the tour for more than a week. It's just that Tom either wasn't an avid conversationalist by nature, or he just wasn't the kind of guy who liked to hang out with the opening act. He always struck me as a throwback from a time when there was such a thing as true show-business royalty, where those in the upper echelons (i.e. Tom Jones, Lawrence Olivier, Shirley Bassey) would never think to mix and mingle with those in the lower strata (i.e., slugs, vermin, guitar comics). His dressing room was always stocked with the best of everything, from fine linens and tablecloths to Dom Perignon and caviar. I can well understand how he might find it difficult to hold an interesting conversation with someone like me. I mean, how long can you discuss the merits of Coke versus Pepsi?

The members of Tom's band and I struck up an immediate friendship, however, and actually used Tom's reticence toward conversation as a profit-making device. Customarily, I would come offstage after my show and cross Tom's path as he prepared to go out. The band guys and I would always make five or ten dollar bets on how many words Tom would say to me as I passed him. I always came up with numbers like "two" or "one," and they'd always laugh and say "No way. He's in a chatty mood tonight!," and come up with ridiculous guesses like "six" or "seven." I won approximately 98% of the time. Invariably I would come off, say something like "Hi, Tom" or "How ya doin', Tom," and he'd always say something extremely wordy like, "Hi!" or "Good!" God bless him. He made me a wealthy man.

One of the few times I lost one of these bets was when Tom was nervous about the crowd. As soon as I came off, Tom stepped up to me and said, "How's the audience tonight, lad?" I was so stunned I could hardly reply. Not only had Tom uttered a total of five words to me (which cost me plenty, I'll have you know), but I was shaken by the fact that, for the first time, I could actually tell what Tom's speaking voice sounded like.

I remember one particularly frightening incident when Lloyd Greenfield, Tom's road manager, approached me after a show and said "Don't go back to the hotel just yet, Tom wants to talk to you." Talk to me? Tom wanted to talk to me? I broke into a cold sweat. Tom had never wanted to talk to me before. What was the occasion for this sudden change of heart? What was the catalyst for this strange turn of events? And most importantly, would it be a complete sentence?

Of course, by now, if you've stuck with the book this far, you know that one of my most notable traits is the ability to be fired or ostracized by celebrities for doing nothing wrong. So naturally, this was the first notion that crossed my mind. I realized that ever since I had been on the Tom Jones tour, I had shown up every night, done my allotted stage time, gotten my laughs and left. I had caused hardly a ripple. I had caused no problems whatsoever. I had been a model citizen. How could I have been so stupid?

As my mind continued to churn, I started hallucinating. Seriously, what could it be that would make Tom want to talk to me? I figured I must have done something truly hideous. I shuffled frantically through my mind to try to find the answer, but none was forthcoming. I had had all my pets put to death in anticipation of just such a moment. I had made sure that I steered clear of Tom so as never to risk being put on the "A" list. Baffled, I waited anxiously outside the dressing room door to be summoned. Finally, I was motioned inside.

All I could think was, naturally, that I was about to be canned. My heart was pounding. My mouth was dry. As I entered the dressing room, words of apology began forming on my lips, made all the more difficult by virtue of the fact that I HAD NO IDEA WHAT I HAD DONE. As I stood there, he looked me up and down. He nodded slightly. Then he reached into his bag, pulled out a gift-wrapped box and said, "Merry Christmas."

"Wh...wh...whaaat?"

Dazed but relieved, I said thank you, shook his hand, and went back to my room to check out the gift. It was a Tag-Heuer watch, not exactly a piece of junk. Tom had given everybody one - the band members, his road people, and me. Everything had turned out fine after all. I kept my job, and I had received a gracious, expensive Christmas gift from Mr. Jones. Also, I had won twenty bucks from the band betting that Tom would once again utter only two words to me (although the words I expected were "Get out!")

Tom was not one to break with tradition for any reason. When the year was over and I knew I wasn't going to work with him again, I approached him for the final time and said, "Tom, thanks for all the gigs. It was nice working with you." He shook my hand and said, "All the best!"

Three words! Doesn't this guy ever shut up?

For those of you who may not know, especially in those heady days (and maybe even today), fans of Tom Jones considered him akin to the Second Coming of Elvis. Audiences were rabid from the moment he hit the stage till he ran off into his waiting limousine. And yes, women did throw keys and underwear onstage when he performed. I also got underwear thrown at me, but usually with a note that said "Please give this to Tom."

The "Tom Is Elvis" analogy was never made clearer to me than at a place called "Mudd Island" just outside of Memphis Tennessee, a stone's throw from Graceland. We performed there at an outdoor theatre on Elvis Presley's birthday. The place was filled with fans who couldn't wait to see Tom Jones, who was the next best thing to Elvis as far as they were concerned, and who was well worth waiting and sweltering in the midday sun for, as long as they wouldn't have to put up with one of those god-damned annoying opening acts.

Guess how this show went for me?

The audience literally gasped and groaned when my name was announced. I might as well have been OJ's publicist with the way I was received. Fortunately, there was an orchestra pit separating the stage from the crowd, or else today I'd be writing this book while still wearing a permanent neck brace.

The orchestra pit was also the arbiter of one of my simultaneously most horrifying and most hilarious showbiz experiences to date. The doors to the orchestra pit were twenty feet away and faced the stage, and as I muddled through my act (thus the name "Mudd" Island?), the doors suddenly opened. Out stepped the members of Tom's band. They smiled at me. They waved. Then, in the middle of a song parody, they stripped naked and mooned me. They were no more than twenty feet from the stage, and yet they were completely unseen by the crowd, who were busy loading skeet-shooting guns in an attempt to frighten me off. I assure you, there is nothing more difficult than doing your act in front of a bloodthirsty mob while also trying to keep a straight face staring at sixteen hairy, flabby, milky-white butts.

By the way, the noises from some of those asses were the loudest reactions I got the entire night.

Tom happened to give one of the best performances I'd ever seen that night. The audience adored him, and he was in great form and greater voice. They gave him the kind of "Elvis in Vegas," "Beatles at Shea Stadium" ovations that performers dream of.

Yeah, but he didn't get mooned the whole night. That moment was mine and mine alone.

Back to the Concord

A quick story about a show I did opening for Tom at the Concord.

As soon as I learned we were booked into the infamous hotel, I began to warn my friends in the band that they could expect me to bomb that night. They didn't believe me. "No way, you're funny, you can play anywhere Denny, audiences love you!," etc. etc. "Earth audiences maybe," I told them. The audiences at the Concord, however, were often shipped in from the planet Kwanguno.

And so the band decided to make a concerted effort to watch my entire show that evening from the wings, to show their support and to see firsthand how wrong I was.

I was introduced. I did my jokes. You know the rest. In an eerie repetition of history, once again the only people I heard laughing were the guys in the band. When I came off, they had to admit they were wrong. I really wished I'd put money on it.

The amazing part of this story is what happened to me after the show. I headed down to the bar to clear my mind, forget the show and order about fifteen beers. As I entered, a middle-aged woman with a deep, froggy voice grabbed me and told me how much she'd enjoyed my show.

Huh?

"Let me tell you something about the Catskills, young man," she rasped. "You should consider the fact that you were able to stay onstage the whole time as a compliment. We had a British comedian here opening for Johnny Mathis last week, and we booed him off the stage. He left the hotel in tears. So the fact that you were able to get through your entire show without being shouted down is a testament to your talent!"

So apparently, not being booed off the stage in the Catskills was equivalent to having a real good show. Imagine if you were to actually get laughs and applause? They'd probably name the theatre after you.

* * * * *

In January of 1988, after a full year of successful tours, the Tom Jones people stopped calling. Again, like it was becoming a pattern, I had no idea why. All I knew was I was on my final week of shows and I had no future bookings with him.

My opening gigs for major headliners were starting to feel like Mafia hits. Everyone's real friendly, slapping you on the back, telling jokes. Everything seems to be going fine. Then suddenly, without warning, bang, you're gone. That's the way it was here. The only difference was there was no chalk outline, and the cleanup was a lot less messy.

Chapter 31: George Carlin

"Hey Dennis, where the fuck are ya?!"

Those were the first words I ever heard from the mouth of George Carlin as I paced nervously in my dressing room at the Orpheum Theater in Omaha In February of 1988. I had never met the man before. I had only idolized him from afar, as did so many of my fellow comedians and people of earth. He was a legend, and a well-deserved one, not only for his prolific output and his fearlessness on stage, but also for the fact that he was one of the funniest people who ever lived. And here I was, about to open for the first time ever for this comedy genius in front of a live audience of about two-thousand people. For a comedian, this was the equivalent of being a musical act and opening for someone like Bob Dylan.

It all came out of the blue, as I sat in my den at home in Studio City California. Peggy and I had loaded up the truck and moved out to the West Coast in 1987 to pursue the common comedic dream of landing a sitcom or a movie, most of which were filmed in Los Angeles. So here we were, recent New York transplants, with a house and a mortgage and once again no work on the horizon. On this particular day I was staring blankly at the Tag-Heuer watch I had gotten from Tom Jones as a Christmas present and wondering how many more celebrities would wind up hiring and then firing me before I admitted my career was finally over and I should open a taco stand. Just then, the phone rang.

It was my agent, Fred Suss, with some interesting news. This is basically how the conversation went:

> FRED: "Hey Dennis, we just got an offer...Do you want to open for George Carlin for 3 months? He's doing a bunch of one-nighters..."

ME: "Did you just say George Carlin wants me to open for him?"
FRED: "Right. He's doing a bunch of one-nighters..."
ME: "Yes."
FRED: "...and he needs an opening act. The pay is..."
ME: "Yes!"
FRED: "...pretty good. You'd have to book your own travel, but they would pay for..."
ME: "Fred, I said yes, stop talking."
FRED: "...your hotel and meals. The only thing is he needs to know..."
ME: "Yes! Yes! I'll do it! It's George Carlin, for Chrissakes, I said yes!"
FRED: "...right away. So whaddya think? Do you wanna do it?....hello?....Dennis?....Are you there?"
PEGGY: "Hi Fred, it's me, Peggy. Dennis handed me the phone. He's upstairs packing"

And so it was that I hooked up with George Carlin for an ongoing tour that I was slated to join for three months. Yes, I know, this could turn out to be another disaster in the Rodney Dangerfield / Joan Rivers / Tom Jones / Every Other Celebrity I've Ever Toured With mold, but it was only for three months. I could probably hold out for three months without something going terribly wrong. And besides...IT WAS GEORGE CARLIN! I hadn't been this over-the-top thrilled about working with someone since the Rodney days. Even though I was not one of those guys, like Jerry Seinfeld or Chris Rock, who had idolized comedians since they were kids and had wanted desperately to become one themselves, I still was, like so many other ordinary citizens, a big fan of George Carlin. A flood of memories washed over me in the days before I was to join the tour. I remembered all those great Tonight Show appearances when he would fill in for Johnny Carson, how his monologues on that show would floor me, not only because they were funny but because he was so unyielding in choosing the subject matter for his routines. Here's one that sticks with me to this day:

"What happens if you're picking your nose and someone comes over to shake your hand? You're holding a huge snot. What do you do? You can't put it back."

Who else would come up with that line of thought? Jack Benny? David Brenner? Barney the Dinosaur? I don't think so.

And even though I was not a fervent student of comedy, and my album purchases tilted heavily toward rock bands and singer-songwriters, I had occasionally over the years gone out and bought a comedy album if the comedian made me laugh so hard I couldn't in all good conscience do without it. Steve Martin was one of those guys. I owned several Monty Python albums as well as Firesign Theater releases. And when I was in college I went out and spent my money on Carlin's FM / AM and Class Clown. George's stuff was always brilliant, hilarious, and unlike anything else that was out there. And now that I was an actual comedian and understood how difficult it was to come up with a good bit or a funny joke, I respected him even more and marveled, as everyone did, at how much material he had in his arsenal, all of it top-notch and double-me-over funny.

So it was with complete joy and a little trepidation that I accepted this tour with one of my non-music-related show-business heroes. The joyful part was obvious. The trepidation part was because, if and when you ever meet one of your true heroes, there's always that nagging little voice in the back of your head that says, "Man, when I meet him, I hope he's not an asshole." Or even worse, 'Man, when I meet him, I hope I'm not an asshole." I had gotten lucky with Paul Newman, not so much with Billy Joel. What would my meeting with George be like?

The first stop on my leg of the George Carlin tour began at the aforementioned Orpheum Theater. I arrived my hotel the day of the engagement, went up to the front desk, gave them my name and was promptly told that I wasn't in the register. "Ummmm," I said, asserting myself like the true dork that I was. "Ummm... there has to be a mistake, I'm opening for George Carlin at the Orpheum Theater." The clerk looked again, clicked a few keys, search a few screens, then shook his head. "Sorry, we don't have your name. We have a Mr. Glenn Super registered, I think he's Mr. Carlin's opening act." I shook my head. "Ummmm..." (There was that take-charge attitude of mine creeping in again) "Uummm...no, I'm pretty sure it's me who's opening for Mr. Carlin.

I had heard of Glenn Super. I had actually met Glenn Super a few times. Nice guy, funny comedian, known as "Mister Bullhorn" because he used a bullhorn on stage to tell the bulk of his jokes. Was "Mister Bullhorn" playing a trick on me? Had Glenn Super impersonated my agent just to get me to fly all the way to Omaha to be the butt of a practical joke? Was I going to start weeping right here in the hotel lobby?

"Oh, here you are!" said the suddenly relieved desk clerk. He had found my name at last. "I guess the wires got crossed, so sorry." He handed me my room key with a cheery "Enjoy your stay, Mr. Blair. Is there anything else we can do for you?"

"Uummmm....no, you've done enough for one day, thank you."

I went to my room and looked out the window which faced the theater we would be playing that evening. Right there on the marquis was the announcement that made my heart leap to my throat; "Appearing Tonight - George Carlin - with Special Guest Glenn Super."

No, it wasn't a practical joke, it was just a mistake. The theater hadn't gotten the news that I was on the tour and so they hadn't received the new contract with me on it. But for a few moments, I feared that my agent had either gotten the information wrong or that I had dreamed the whole thing and would need to change my medications to prevent any more hallucinations in the future. Or even worse, that Marvin Hamlisch and Melissa Manchester had called George's agent and said, "Don't hire this guy. You'll give him false hope."

In any case, I made my way over to the theater 90 minutes before show time, did my sound check, went downstairs to the dressing room, and waited to meet my new boss. I was nervous about meeting George for the first time, hoping naturally that he would not be a jerk or a smartass, the kind of guy who would invite you into the bathroom to watch him take a shit. I paced around my dressing room (or, more accurately, my musty hellhole), munching on the grapes and carrot sticks that had apparently been left over from a production of "Vegetarian Jamboree." About a half-hour before show time, I heard from somewhere above me the stage door to the theater creak open, a flurry of footsteps, and then that familiar rasp of a voice that I had heard on "Class Clown" and "AM/FM" and numerous TV programs like the Ed Sullivan Show and the Tonight Show:

"Hey Dennis, where the fuck are ya?!" I somehow managed a weak, stunned reply;

"Ummm...down here?"

After another flurry of footsteps that got louder as they came closer, George Carlin came barreling into my room with his manager, Jerry Hamza, and proceeded to act as if he and I had been friends since high school. He was rail-thin and brimming with energy, with longish grey hair and the ever-present beard he was known for ever since his hippie-dippie days. With a quick handshake and a gruff "How ya doin' man?," he wandered around the room, raided my deli tray ("Hey, Dennis, what's with the carrot sticks? What are you, a goat? I'm takin' about a hundred, okay?") and pretty much allayed my fears and made me feel comfortable in approximately seven seconds. Then with a hasty "Good to meet you, have a good show, I'll be watchin' ya, you prick, so you'd better be good.," he blew out of the room, his manager trailing behind him.

Didn't seem like a jerk at all.

His manager, Jerry, had also shaken my hand, but had been distant, aloof. I found out later on that they'd had a series of mishaps and bad experiences with former opening acts they'd tried in the past, so I suppose Jerry was naturally on guard. Many of the agent-manager types I've met in the past are like this...protective of their clients, naturally, wary of being too friendly in case they have to perform the frequent duty of saying to the opening act, "This isn't working out. You're fired."

As show time approached I found myself getting more and more nervous. Visions of past-shows-gone-wrong danced in my head, naturally superseding the 95% of my shows that had gone well over all the years I had been doing comedy. It's a known truism that among the neurotic traits that performers in general, and comedians in particular, seem to share is the fact that we rarely remember the shows that go well and ALWAYS remember the ones that sucked.

One of my favorite showbiz stories is one that Bob Newhart told in his autobiography. He was visiting Harpo Marx at home, and Harpo was showing Bob his scrapbook with all the Marx Brothers paraphernalia, flyers, reviews, etc. By far the largest and most notable entry in the scrapbook was a full article in the local newspaper about a particular show the Marx Brothers had done. Bob asked Harpo why this particular entry dwarfed all the others. Harpo replied, "We didn't get one laugh that night. That's the one we always remembered."

It was with this near-crippling fear that I went out on stage for my first show ever opening for George. It's bad enough when you bomb in front of any audience, but to bomb in front of this one would probably lead to me being cut from the tour, another opener on the scrap heap of ex-Carlin hopefuls. This time, my luck would hold. No deafening silences, no guy in the third row yelling out, 'Where's George!? You suck!" Thankfully, they liked me, they really, really liked me.

I had not seen George at all since our encounter in the dressing room where he stole all my carrots. He had disappeared completely, a habit I was to find was common with him. I had continued my pre-show pacing, had done my show to a blissfully enthusiastic crowd, and had come offstage hoping that I had done well enough to continue the tour. I assumed that maybe George and his manager were listening somewhere…maybe on a backstage intercom or from some undisclosed location in the theater.

Or maybe they hadn't listened at all. That was entirely possible. It had happened to me before with Shirley Bassey, so if George had not seen me or heard my show, it would have been disappointing but not unprecedented. But to me it would have been so great to know that George had seen, and maybe even approved of, the performance I had just completed.

As I did my post-show walk towards my downstairs dressing nook, I heard the sound of two hands clapping, followed by a forceful "Yeah!!" I glanced behind the curtain and saw George, who gave me the thumbs-up. He had been pacing back and forth behind the backdrop, listening to my show from behind me the whole time. He seemed pleased, telling me and Jerry, who I guess had been watching me from the wings, that "This was great, this is gonna work out." George gave me a pat on the back, and even Jerry managed a slight smile in my direction. Then they both disappeared, as quickly as they had come. Slightly bewildered but happy that things had apparently gone well, I packed up my guitar and headed to my dressing room, where a hologram of Shirley Bassey was waiting and said, 'See? What'd I tell you? You're the best!" And then I made my way up to the balcony to watch the man himself perform. I had not seen George Carlin perform live since the eighties, when I caught his show in Atlantic City with Rodney. I had been convulsed with laughter then, and expected nothing less now. I would not be disappointed.

The lights went down, the crowd went nuts, and then George walked out, no introduction, no fanfare. He just wandered onto the stage to the sounds of whooping and hollering and thunderous applause. Seemingly unaffected, he arranged his notes and postcards containing the points he wanted to get to on the table that had been placed onstage, then grabbed the microphone and started in. There was no "Good evening ladies and gentlemen," no "How ya doing," none of that common show-business banter most comedians engage in to greet the audience. He got right to the point.

"I'd like to begin with a list of people I can do without."

The crowd laughed and cheered as he went through each item one by one, like a shopping list of things he detested... "Guys in their fifties named Skip....A dentist with blood in his hair....People with big gums and small teeth...any woman who buys vaginal jelly with a gold American Express card..." The list went on and on, the audience loving it. This opening piece lasted about three or four minutes, at which point he put that list to bed and went on to something else, and then something else, and then something else, for about an hour and a half.

One of the things that impressed me most about the show, besides the fact that it was so funny and smart and unique, is that there was not one thing I had ever heard him say before. It was all new, or at least new to me. I had heard George on many occasions, from the Tonight Show to Merv Griffin to Mike Douglas and on many of his albums like Class Clown, AM/FM, and Occupation Foole, and this was all brand spanking new. I was floored by the fact that one man could write so much without repeating a word, and that it was all so good. No wonder people paid the big bucks just to come and see him. I had been doing comedy for 8 years, and I had about an hour, maybe an hour and fifteen minutes, if I stretched it, of material that I felt was good enough to use in my act. This guy had just done an hour and a half of stuff he had thought up in the last two years since his previous HBO special, which I believe at the time was HBO special number seven. So he had at least seven hours of stuff, not including this show I just saw, which meant George had eight hours of material to my one and change. And that wasn't counting the stuff he did on Merv Griffin and Johnny Carson and Mike Douglas.

The message for me was clear as I sat in that darkened balcony. If I was serious about doing this, I had to start writing more. That's a goal I set for myself that I still try to reach as often as possible.

After George's show was over, I walked back to my hotel. As soon as I arrived in my room, I got a call from Jerry, asking if I wanted to have dinner in the hotel restaurant with George and him. I thought about it for less than one eight of a hundredth of a millisecond and said yes.

I don't remember much about that dinner, mainly due to the fact that, ohh, I don't know, I was having DINNER WITH GEORGE CARLIN. I was still in a sort of hazy, altered state of disbelief, caused both by the fact that I had been asked to share the stage with this legendary guy, and that I had done well enough to be included in their intimate circle. I do remember wandering down to the lobby, looking around for the restaurant, and hearing George's voice form within yelling out, 'Hey, Pricko! Over here!" One of the reasons I remember this particular greeting was because the restaurant was a pretty high-class place, and the thought of George yelling out "Hey Pricko!" surrounded by tables of people in their expensive clothes smoking their expensive cigars and sipping their vintage wines filled me with glee. I could almost imagine Margaret Dumont sitting at the next table, turning to her distinguished tuxedoed dinner partner and whispering, in her high-toned cultured voice, "Did he just say 'Hey. Pricko'? (Pricko actually sounded to me like the sixth Marx Brother, the one who only did porno movies.)

When I sat down, I remember saying how great I thought his show had been. George, never one to be full of himself, said, 'Oh yeah, that was a good one, I'm having the chicken, what are you having, Prick-o? It's on me and Jerry, so don't hold back." I also remember that at one point during this little "get-acquainted" dinner, we started telling each other some of our favorite jokes. I told one of my favorites that I reserve only for special occasions and for people I think might be depraved enough to get it...Yes indeed, it was the infamous Queen of England / Queen of Spain joke. They laughed hysterically. George said, "Good one, Dennis." Dennis! He called me Dennis, not Prick-o! I was in! (Although, admittedly and to my complete surprise, I kind of missed being called Prick-o.)

I also remember that I went to bed that night thinking that if things continued like this, it would be a very pleasant three months.

Little did I know that three months would turn into almost twenty years.

* * * * *

Over the three months that I was contracted to do the tour, I found out some things about George that I didn't know but wasn't particularly surprised to learn. For instance, I found out that the legendary drug use that we'd all heard about in the past was, at least to our eyes, pretty much over. Three heart attacks in the 'seventies had apparently put the kibosh on the illegal substance habits that were part of the George Carlin legend. It was amusing to me, when I hooked up with this counter-culture legendary guy, to witness him often ordering chicken with the skin cut off, pasta with no butter, and non-alcoholic beer.

I'll always remember Peggy and I going with Rodney, after our show was over, to see George perform one night in Atlantic City. This was in 1981, long before I'd met George of course, and I was really looking forward to seeing him perform live. Oddly enough, the show itself was one of those strange pairings that seem to make no sense. George was not the headliner this night. He was the opening act for Suzanne Somers, the actress from 'Three's Company." George Carlin and Suzanne Somers. That would be like going to a show where Lenny Bruce was opening for Julie Andrews, or Chris Rock was opening for Debbie Reynolds. I'd love to have met the agent that put this show together. I'm pretty sure he had poor motor skills.

I don't remember much about Suzanne's show that night. She was sweet and endearing and I know she sang some songs and told some stories, but what stood out for me was George's set. He came out to a smattering of applause...most of the people were there to see Suzanne...and launched immediately into his first no-holds-barred joke;

> "Hey, why is it that most of the people who are against abortion are people you wouldn't wanna fuck in the first place?"

The overriding response to that from the older Suzanne-primed crowd was gasping, followed by coughing and stunned murmuring...except from Rodney, Peggy and me, who were hysterically laughing.

George then went on to talk about his recent heart attacks, comparing them with Richard Pryor's recent troubles with both his own heart condition and his recent experiences with bursting into flames during a freebasing accident:

> "Well, Richard Pryor and I have been neck and neck lately. He had a heart attack, so I had a heart attack. Then he had another heart attack, so I had another heart attack. Then he burned himself up, and I said, 'fuck that, I'm gonna have another heart attack!'"

After the show, Rodney took us backstage to say hello to George. The backstage door opened, and there with her husband was

Suzanne Somers, who greeted us warmly, followed close behind by George, who saw only Rodney. As Suzanne and her husband chatted with Peggy and me, George quickly took Rodney aside, whispered something in his ear, and within seconds both of them disappeared into the bathroom. As Suzanne and her husband offered Peggy and me drinks and peanuts and exchanged small talk, I became discreetly aware of a series of intermittent sniffing and snorting sounds emanating from the bathroom, followed by occasional giggles. To say the scene was a bit surreal would be a cliché and an understatement, even though it was entirely true… my wife and I sitting casually on the dressing room sofa, chatting amiably with America's girl-next-door Suzanne Somers while trying to ignore the obvious facts that there were two comedians inhaling and/or snorting copious amounts of illegal contraband less than ten feet away.

After what seemed like an eternity later, Rodney came out of the bathroom, his shirt loosened and his eyes glazed over, a stupefied smirk plastered on his face. He was followed out by George, who in contrast seemed strangely unaffected by what had gone on in that bathroom. No glassy eyes, no silly grin…it was almost as if he had done this so many times before he was unaffected by any of it and only did it for the pleasure of watching his friends get high. I half-expected him to look around the room and holler, 'Next!" Doctor Carlin at your service.

It was the memory of this night in particular that caused me to smile knowingly to myself every time, when I had become George's friend and tour mate, he would order that skinless chicken and that non-alcoholic beer. How things had changed.

There was only one time that I can remember seeing George resort at least partially to what must have been his old ways. It was in the mid-nineties, when George's career was doing so well he was chartering private planes to get him, me and Jerry to his gigs (not a bad way at all to travel, and the source of several funny stories…more on that later). We had landed at an airstrip in the Midwest so that the plane could re-fuel. I had gone to the bathroom and was now heading back out to re-board the plane and continue on our way. The only problem was, George was nowhere in sight. Since it would be very uncool to leave without him, we started searching for him. After a few minutes, we heard his harshly-whispered voice from behind the terminal building... 'Yeah...over here. I'll be there in a minute." I turned toward the building in time to see George take one last hit of a joint and toss it to the ground. As he passed me on the way to the plane, he said, "Damn. I haven't done THAT in a while."...and got on the plane.

Another thing I found out during this three-month period (and beyond) was that, although George was a great guy to hang out with when the opportunities presented themselves, he wasn't an especially social, "hanging out" sort of a guy to begin with. He wasn't against human contact, but he wasn't a person who would seek it out either. George was basically a pretty private person who was okay with social interaction but was just as comfortable, and probably even more so, sequestering himself in his room and working, working, working on his next standup piece or HBO special. Once we hit a town on the tour we pretty much would go to our separate rooms and double-bolt the doors.

Here's a good example of how much of a "hermit" George could be...

At one point in his career, George signed on to do an extended engagement at Bally's hotel and casino in Las Vegas, a relationship that would last almost ten years. Usually, George would be booked to do a series of three-week runs, and I was aboard to do these runs with him. I was a youngish father with two children by this time, and of course staying in a hotel room for three weeks with two hyperactive children was out of the question. Every day I'd be up and out of the hotel by 10 AM or so, on my way to bring my little youngsters to the local petting zoo or playground or theme park or Chuck E. Cheese. Meanwhile, George, who had driven to Vegas and had his car parked in a convenient spot so that he could hop in and drive whenever the spirit moved him, was nowhere to be seen. Ever. Except for those times when he'd be required to appear, such as performing in the show, no one ever saw him for the three weeks he was at the hotel. He was a ghost, a cypher. People started doubting that there was an actual

George Carlin, thinking that maybe he was a hologram. His car was there, parked in the same spot, every day. It never moved.

I'd made friends among the valet parking staff at Bally's, and every day when my kids and I would come out for one of our typical runs to the mall or the batting cage or the go-cart races, I'd ask one of the valet people...

"So? Did you see him today?"
And they'd answer, 'See who?'
"George. Did he come out?"
"No. He doesn't come out. He never comes out."
"But his car is here," I'd say. "He obviously drove it here, thinking he'd be using it every now and then."
'Well, maybe he drives it before we get here. We haven't seen him. No one sees him. Maybe he's in the trunk."
"Nah. If he was in the trunk, he would've had to come out. He never comes out."

All any of us could figure out was he stayed in his room, getting room service, morning noon and night, typing away on his computer, writing constantly, writing, writing, writing. He probably had enough for his next HBO special already. He probably had enough for his next three, or four, or five HBO specials. Maybe he'd finished all his HBO specials and was now working on writing other comedians' HBO specials. He was a workaholic, that George Carlin guy.

And then, one day, it happened. I was coming out of the hotel at 10 AM one morning, with my kids, on our way to a children's museum or a Discovery Zone or a toy store, when Frank, one of the valet guys, came running up to me, his eyes glowing, a big smile plastered on his face, dying to tell me something.

'Dennis!," he said, out of breath. "We saw him."
"Who?"
"George. We saw him, early this morning. He came out. We couldn't believe it. None of us had cameras, we were so pissed."
'George came out!?" I couldn't believe it. "Did he see his shadow? Will we have three more weeks of winter?"

"Huh?"

"Never mind. Where did he go?"

No one knew. Frank asked the other valet people, but no one had the answer. Till finally one of the valet women spoke up.

"I know where he went.," she said, puffing on a cigarette. We surrounded her.

"Where? Where did he go?"

She took another drag on her cigarette.

"He went to buy some plums.

"Plums?"

"Plums. Or maybe peaches? No, it was definitely plums. Then he came right back."

Plums. That was George's big adventure. That's why he'd driven the car to Vegas. Not to go driving in the mountains or to check out the casinos or the action on the strip. Not to visit other celebrities in town, maybe hobnob with Wayne Newton or Tom Jones or Celine Dion. No. He took his car to buy plums. And then he came right back, no time for dawdling. He had to get started on his 47th HBO special.

He was a workaholic, that George Carlin.

This headliner-as-hermit experience threw me for a loop at first, especially after my experiences with Rodney and Joan. But as time went on, I began to see it as a positive. I'd been very close to Rodney, and it had led to the "poodle in the pool" incident and me being fired. I had been relatively close to Joan Rivers, and that hadn't saved me either. So it came as something of a relief when I realized that George, unlike Rodney and Joan, stayed very much to himself. In the many instances that we found ourselves together, either travelling in rental cars or wandering around backstage before a show and bumping into each other, we would have some real belly-laughs and cut up and do bits and impressions for each other and have a good time. But 98% of the time, after we had arrived in a town and were hunkered down between shows, we would all stay in our rooms or go our separate ways. That was, as you can imagine, fine by me. There is much less of a chance that anything can go wrong with your employer when you hardly even see the guy to begin with. Which is what makes the following story all the more interesting…

I had been working with George for a few weeks when we did our first run at Bally's in Las Vegas. It was to be a three-week engagement, and Peggy and I were all set to relax and soak up some sun by the pool in the typical 378-degree Las Vegas summer. As it turned out, one of the weeks at Bally's included my birthday. I had invited some comedian friends to join Peg and me for a little birthday celebration dinner before the show. We were given a semi-private room in one of the restaurants in the hotel and gathered there at about 6 PM for the get-together. I had put in a call to George's room on the off-chance that maybe he and his wife Brenda would like to join us. Naturally it was a complete shot in the dark, and I had told my friends that even though I had invited George, the chance of him stopping by was minimal at best.. By now I was familiar with George's proclivity for privacy and aversion to social events, and I wasn't expecting a reply.

As Peg and I and our comic pals sat and ordered, I was shocked to see Brenda Carlin heading our way followed close behind by her reclusive husband. I got the distinct feeling that Brenda, who was naturally warm and outgoing and actually receptive to human contact, had talked George into coming down for my birthday dinner. I was touched by the fact that he had broken his vow of social celibacy to hang out with his opening guy and his group of weirdos.

George was quieter than usual at the dinner. Maybe it was natural for him to recede a bit into the background and let Brenda take the focus. Or maybe he had truly been forced into this situation against his will and was only doing it to make Brenda happy. I don't know. What I do know is that I couldn't help noticing my two comedian friends seemed to be auditioning for George. Not just auditioning, but *intensely* auditioning, as if they were trying to get a part in the George Carlin Traveling Show. They were literally climbing over each other to top each other, spitting out jokes and gags, doing impressions, comedy bits, attempting to make George laugh at every opportunity. It was really over the top, like a contest to see who could get the biggest response from George. It was suddenly as if I, the birthday boy, didn't even exist. I thought for a moment that I was imagining it...maybe they were just trying to be funny out of nervousness. It was like the Pope of Comedy had arrived at our little gathering and the courtiers were trying to please him in any and every way possible.

At one point, one of the comedians took out a notebook and started reading from a prepared monologue that he had composed in case George decided to make an appearance. When he pulled out the notebook, at first I thought it was a joke, but as his presentation continued ad infinitum, I realized that something weird was going on here. Peggy and I kept exchanging glances as if to say, "Is he trying to get Dennis' job away from him?" George was indeed laughing at this presentation, and I noticed that every time he laughed, my friend would make eye contact with him and get even more energized in his reading. Eventually, thankfully, the reading ended, the dinner came to a close, and George and Brenda went back to their rooms.

Peg and I continued hanging with our friends for a while, then walked with them towards the parking lot to say so long before I went up to do my show. I tried to shake the bad taste of that dinner (the "audition," not the food, which was delicious) out of my mouth. Something inside me hoped that I was just being paranoid, that such a blatant attempt at undermining me and my new gig was just in my imagination. As we walked, oddly enough the talk got around to a story we had heard about someone trying to get someone's opening-act gig away from him. I chimed in and said, "I hope that never happens to me." At that point, my friend, my pal, my buddy, notebook boy, turned to me and said, "Hey, it's dog eat dog out there. If you ever lost your gig with Carlin, I'd send him my tape immediately."

At least he was honest. And at least I wasn't paranoid.

From then on, I vowed that if I ever had another birthday dinner with George, I'd only invite accountants, street sweepers or furtrappers. Anything but comedians. Or if I did invite comedians, I would check for notebooks before entering the restaurant.

Even with all that disappearing and keeping to himself that he did so well, we did spend enough time together during this trial run for George to realize that I was indeed weird and depraved and would therefore fit in nicely with him and his select circle of lunatics. So after the three months was up, I was invited to stay on as George's permanent opening act. Jerry called me over near the end of the tour and said he wanted to talk to me. Naturally, being the confident and self-assured person that I was, I immediately assumed I was going to be let go. Or at least put on the 'A" list.

On the contrary. Jerry said he had spoken to George, that both of them had agreed they liked me personally and that my act fit in well with George's show and warmed up the audience to a perfect pitch so that George went out onstage to an already-fired-up crowd. So he asked me if I'd like to stay on as the permanent opener.

Uh oh.

I began to hallucinate. I heard weird conflicting voices in my head, saw strange, warring images swimming around me..."Not again....Not gonna do it...But he's a Legend...Remember Rodney... He's a Comedy Genius...Remember Joan....He seems almost normal...So did Marvin Hamlisch...." Was I going to do this to myself again?

After I was dropped from the Tom Jones tour, I had told Fred Suss: "Next time I decide to go on one of these extended runs, do me a favor...shoot me in the leg." I had promised myself that I would never again put myself in a position where I would be tied down professionally to one celebrity. After all the crap I'd been through, I would much rather give up the obvious benefits of job security than become involved with the kind of craziness and turmoil and agony that accompanies an association with a typical headline performer. I thought too much of myself for that, and I certainly wasn't going to put myself through it ever again.

So of course, I accepted the job with George Carlin immediately.

Chapter 32: A Steady Job in Show Business?

I was sound asleep in my room at Bally's Hotel in Las Vegas when the phone rang, jerking me awake. I answered it sleepily and recognized the voice of Linda Skelly, the entertainment director at the hotel.

>LINDA: Dennis?
>ME: Hmmgb?
>LINDA: Did I wake you?
>ME: Mmm mmm. Grbbghh.
>LINDA: Listen, I hate to tell you this, but the engagement's been cancelled. It looks like George had a heart attack."
>I sat bolt upright in bed.
>ME: Shit, really? Is he alright?
>LINDA: "Too soon to tell. He had chest pains and drove himself to the hospital. He's under observation."

I was dimly aware that Linda was continuing to speak as I tried to take this all in. I'd been working with George for about a year now. This was to be our second run at Bally's Las Vegas, a three-week engagement that hadn't even begun yet. I had driven to Vegas the night before with Peggy so that we could settle in to our hotel room. As it turned out, the long engagement was to be suddenly cut short. George had been driving to Las Vegas with his wife, Brenda, when he apparently started having a series of sharp, stabbing chest pains. He pulled off the main drag and checked himself into a hospital. I looked at Peg who had been sleeping beside me and continued talking into the receiver.

>ME: Well, tell him to rest and get better. We'll see you next time, I guess. I hope.
>LINDA: Sure. Sorry.

George would make a full recovery and go on to have many more years of touring and writing and performing and brilliant success. But on that afternoon in Las Vegas, I couldn't help feeling that this did not bode well for any of us. It had been a long time since George's last heart attack, which he had apparently suffered while attending a Dodgers game in the seventies. He had changed his habits, eating better, cutting out all the illicit activities (as far as we knew) that had probably contributed to his condition which was at least partially hereditary but very likely exacerbated by his excesses as a younger man. When I hooked up with him in 1988, he seemed to be the picture of health. I remember vividly watching him perform on stage and thinking to myself, "Where does he get all that energy?" He was 51 years old then, not really old by any means, not really young either, but still much more vibrant than many people that I knew who were that age or even younger. I had uncles and aunts in their fifties who liked nothing better than to sit down at the slightest opportunity and have a donut. I remembered teachers in high school and college who were in their forties who would do anything not to exert themselves beyond walking to a vending machine. I even knew a few people in their thirties who acted like they were ready to retire. And here was a guy who had suffered several heart attacks and yet could travel across the country on a plane, do a 90-minute energetic, animated, "in-your-face" show that same night, and then go back to his hotel and write all night and day until it was time to repeat the process.

So on this day that George had to cancel his Las Vegas run, I was concerned for him both as a friend and, I'll admit, a little bit out of selfishness. I had grown to like this gig...a lot. George's audiences were generally smart and receptive and, happily, mostly in tune to my comedy as well because, as I had grown to realize, George and I seemed to be in synch on a lot of levels. We both loved to work, we both liked touring and, as evidenced by the occasional times we would spend together, our politics were basically similar. I'm not, and never had been, a particularly political comedian, but there are opinions and a belief system that inform the attitude of my (and every performer's) shows and that naturally come out in the material I present. And there was never really a time that I could see my perspective ever conflicting with George's. Of course, George inhabited a solar system where only geniuses lived and that I could only dream of approaching, but at least I felt we were on the same basic plane, if nowhere near the same level. The difference was that his plane was a supersonic transport, and I was in a propeller craft. But I was definitely enjoying the ride.

What I am saying is this; I believe I was a good opener for George because I created the correct mood for the hurricane he would unleash every night in a darkened theater. And so I had come to like this gig a lot. I had come to like it so much that I had become territorial with it, predatory, to the point where I had become protective of it.

So when his manager offered to become my manager, I literally jumped at the chance. Not so much because I was enthused at having a manager at all, but because Jerry was George's right-hand man and this would be, or so I thought, a means for me to cement the relationship with George even further. Plus, who knew...maybe something would actually come of it.

I have never, in my entire career, had what I would consider good management. I have had agents along the way, good, fair and indifferent, but I can honestly say that every single experience I have had with "personal managers" has not panned out. All of my encounters with management types have been, pretty much, disastrous. I've already related the story of my unfortunate contractual hell with Rodney's business partner, and, having been fairly well traumatized by that situation, I would avoid offers of management like the plague. I ran the other way from offers by the likes of the Scotti Brothers (who handled Weird Al Yankovic) and several others who I was convinced would just put me in their large stables of artists and just let me get lost.

It was with these visions dancing in my head that I went to lunch at the Ivy Restaurant in Los Angeles with Jerry. Jerry told me that he thought I was going to be a huge star and that, with George's considerable clout behind us, good things would come my way if I agreed to let him manage my career. I felt it would be a good move for two reasons. Firstly, as I said before, I felt that saying yes would strengthen my hold on this gig that I had come to enjoy so much. And secondly, I felt that if I said no, I would be off the tour. It was as simple as that.

Yes, it's true that, in the back of my head, I half-entertained the notion that maybe my career would be placed into high gear by making this move. But deep down I really didn't have much faith that something like that would ever happen. I had become cynical enough to believe, at least partially, that there were only a handful of true powerhouse managers in show business who had enough clout to get big things done for their clients. I also had come to believe, rightly or wrongly, that my ship had sailed some time ago...that I was perhaps too old (mid-thirties) or too problematic (a guitar comic who did song parodies that were subject to possible lawsuits) to make it really big as a mainstream comedian. I had begun to believe that hooking up with a tour like this for as long as possible would be the best way for me to ensure that I made a living and that I could care for my family (I had a child on the way). Sure, I'd been fired from gigs like this many times in the past, but maybe this time...especially if the guy in charge of this tour was my "manager" and I paid him a portion of my earnings...I could stay on board this train for a long, long time.

So in the summer of 1989, Jerry Hamza became my manager. And I decided to go for the security of what I hoped, finally, would be a steady job in show business.

* * * * *

Even though George was basically a hermit and kept to himself, there were times on the road when we would end up together, either travelling to and from gigs or hanging out backstage. One of the greatest things that happened was baseball-related.

Since George and I were both native New Yorkers, even though we both lived in California, we still had an affinity for our original hometown teams. In our case, we shared a passion for the New York Mets. Whenever we would find ourselves in a rental car going to a venue in the New York area, we'd tune in the game on the radio and yell at the players, just like any self-respecting New York sports fan who happens to choose the perennial underdog team as their go-to franchise. We were travelling back from a gig in 1989 when George casually asked me if I'd like to go to Shea Stadium and hang out with the Mets.

"What?...Really?...Sure."

I had grown up a rabid Mets fan. 1986 was one of my favorite years because the Mets won the World Series, and I loved the team lineup from that era, especially Keith Hernandez, who seemed like a high-tension wire that could snap at any second. I like guys like that. I'm surprised I'm not friends with more skydivers.

George had a passing friendship with some of the guys on that late-eighties team - Sid Fernandez, Roger McDowell - and he had been invited to hang out at batting practice before the game. Knowing my affinity for the team, he invited me to come along to watch batting practice before a game. As it turned out, it was too rainy to hold batting practice that day, so we wound up hanging out in the dugout, with what were essentially the 1986 World Champion New York Mets. The Mets and George and Me. Y'know, just shootin' the breeze.

I STILL HAVEN'T GOTTEN OVER IT.

I shook Keith Hernandez's and Darryl Strawberry's hands. I said hi to Ron Darling. And here's an interesting aside....George introduced me to relief pitcher Sid Fernandez, and while George busied himself talking to the other guys on the team, Sid showed me how to throw a split-fingered fastball. That's right! I can now throw a split-fingered fastball (it's been clocked at 4 miles-per-hour). Sid – who had pitched in the 1986 World Series, mind you - asked me what it was like to work with George, if it was fun, if it was cool to play for his audiences – it was another Paul Newman moment.

It was after this visit with my hometown heroes that I realized even if George were to fire me tomorrow, it would be okay because HE'D INTRODUCED ME TO THE NEW YORK METS.

As it turned out, our little threesome (Jerry, George and I) spent a fair amount of time in rental cars. Often what would happen was, we would fly into a city like Chicago or Detroit or St. Louis and would be booked in the same hotel together near the airport the night before a gig. Usually the theater would be within driving distance of that hotel, and George and Jerry would invite me to drive with them to the theater. This worked out well all-around. For one thing, it would save me the expense of having to rent a car myself, which was greatly appreciated; and it would help George and Jerry to expedite the end-of-show practice known as the "Zippo Bango."

The What-o Which-o?

The Zippo Bango. Here's how it went...

George did not like to hang around the theater after his show was over. He was not very big on after-show schmoozing, preferring to get off the stage and into a car as quickly as possible so we could all get back to the hotel and collapse in an exhausted heap. So the procedure that developed was...about five minutes before the end of the show, I would start up the car, bring it around to the backstage door and keep it running. As soon as George was done, he would "zip" off the stage, out the door, and into the waiting car with Jerry right behind him. I'd gun the gas pedal and "bang-o!"... we'd be out of there, before the crowds even had a chance to exit the theater. We were on the highway and buying Almond Joys and pretzels at the local 7-11 before the theater announcer had even said "Thanks for coming, hope you enjoyed the show."

That was the "Zippo Bango."

Sometimes we didn't have a rental car. Sometimes there was an actual limo driver who was instructed to be at the wheel ready to go as soon as George and Jerry got in the car. This was understandably frustrating for many of these limo drivers, who had been trained to hold the door open so their clients could get in, then calmly close the door and be on their way. This wasn't George's thing at all. He would zip into the car, and as the driver pulled away and people started coming out of the theater, he'd say "Okay, driver, go as fast as you can, we don't wanna get stuck. If you wanna run over a couple of these cocksuckers that's fine by me!"

You never knew what was going to happen on those car rides to and from the venue. Occasionally George, Jerry and I would have these impromptu brain-teaser "contests" where we would invent a premise and then try to come up with the funniest answer.

George would usually win. One example of this was the premise, "Restaurants you never want to eat in." We all tried valiantly, and came up with some good answers, ("Any restaurant where truckers are vomiting as they leave" for instance) but George won easily with two entries in quick succession; "Any restaurant with the name 'Moldy's'," and "Any restaurant where the waiter is taking a shit in the soup."

There was only one time that I walked away as the winner. The premise was "What Was The last thing JFK Said." I forgot what the other submissions were, but mine was "Hey, why is my head whistling?" (Yes, I know, sick and depraved to be sure, but George and Jerry declared me the winner, and damn it, I'll take that proudly to my grave!)

On several occasions while riding in the car together, George would burst out into an improvised song that he would make up on the spot completely unprompted and for no reason at all. One of my favorites was a particularly lighthearted ditty which went like this:

"When your sister takes a piss in the moonlight
I'll be watching from the highest tree"
Cole Porter would have been proud.

As you can imagine when riding in a car with George Carlin, decorum and political correctness never entered into anything that was said or discussed. The adrenaline rush created by being on stage led to some very strange versions of these impromptu "contests." I remember spending an entire 45-minute drive with the three of us coming up with names of famous people who were alive but should be dead. Another hour-long drive produced a list of actresses who we thought must have the bushiest pubic hair. And of course, there were numerous "dead pools" where we each came up with the names of famous people we thought would die that year, arranged them in order of highest to lowest probability, and then put money in the pool. Whoever scored the most points at the end of the year would win all the money in the pool. I remember that one year I actually won the pool (a substantial sum...fifteen hundred dollars) and George actually got pissed off at me because he was sure I had somehow gotten an "inside track" on celebrities who had cancer. I had no such track, but it didn't matter. That was the last year we ever did the dead pool.

Yet another fond rental-car memory came as I waited behind the wheel for George to show up so we could drive out to Connecticut for a show. The back door opened, and in came George, but instead of saying "how are ya" or any of that crap, he simply presented me with a thought he'd obviously been recently toying with;

"Hey, Dennis," he said. 'I was thinking...They got yardage, right? And they got footage, right? How come they don't got inchage?"

Good point. And who else could have come up with something like that, before breakfast, on a Sunday?

I've really never encountered a mind as amazing and unique as George's, and as you now know I've worked with some pretty amazing minds. Not only could he come up with the goods, in quality and in volume, but his self-confidence astounded me. Even the most confident comedians I've known occasionally display at least a trace of self-doubt every now and then. Even if they come up with a joke or a bit that they are sure is going to work onstage, there is always that little voice gnawing at them that says "unless of course it doesn't." George never seemed to have that. I can remember one time before a show when he came into my dressing room at a theater somewhere and told me he was going to insert a new bit into his act that night. Naturally I was curious, so I decided to watch.

You have to understand one thing; in my experience, when most comedians say they're going to drop in a new bit, it generally means they're going to try out a new joke or two, or at the most a one or two-minute hunk of material. The thought of going much farther than that into untested waters is usually too frightening to even consider.

That night, George did fifteen new minutes. And it was all funny.

I remember that night clearly, because I was feeling fairly satisfied with some of the new bits I had "dropped in" to my own act in recent weeks. After watching George do his new fifteen-minute "bit," I thought maybe it was time for me to stop feeling smug and start working a little harder. Like maybe twenty-three hours a day, with a small break for lunch and a trip to the therapist.

(One of the "bits" that he did for the first time that night was one that came to be known as "Modern Man." Before a show one night he just came over to my dressing room and said, 'Hey, Dentist (this was one of his more frequent nicknames for me), I've got this thing I'm gonna do tonight, whaddya think?"...and then he launched into "Modern man," a private recitation of it just for me, wanting my opinion.

GEORGE: "Whaddya think?"
ME: (to myself) "I think I hate you."

The piece was basically a list of phrases that had become almost clichéd in our society, woven in to a pastiche that came out sounding like a spoken-word symphony. It was brilliant.

He not only put that piece in that night, he opened the show with it. He opened the show with a new five minute piece. I was stunned. I'm still stunned.)

Usually George, Jerry and I would ride in the rental car to gigs, but one time Jerry couldn't make the gig and I was commissioned to get the car and drive George and myself to the theater in New Jersey. I remember the drive taking about an hour, with George and I talking about nothing in particular until the conversation turned to the Copacabana in New York in the sixties and how he hated playing there. This was about the time he was starting to grow the hair and the beard and was making the transition from being a mainstream comic "for all the squares" to being the edgier performer he would eventually become. I asked him to expound on that performance and what happened to him.

He told me the story of that last show at the Copacabana. He knew he wasn't enjoying himself on stage. He wanted to perform for college kids and young people and people who understood what he wanted to really say, not the morons in suits that were just staring up at him with stony faces. He trudged his way through most of the show, and finally near the end he couldn't take it anymore.

GEORGE: "I finally just sunk down on my knees, and then I laid down and crawled under the piano, which I knew would piss off the club owner. And I just laid there with the microphone, just moaning into the microphone, just saying over and over..."Fire me...Fire me...Fire me..." And slowly, the spotlight started fading out until I was on the stage in complete darkness. And that was it. I was out of there." And from then on, he never went back to his old mainstream ways. He was the counterculture guy from there on in.

* * * * *

Whenever George was backstage before a show, he was usually in "serious" mode. He would be mentally preparing for the show, especially if he was working on new stuff. I would often pass his dressing room door and hear him talking out loud, at almost performance-level, trying to memorize the new piece he was working on. In later years he would actually bring his new bits onstage with him, reading from printed notes, so that he could get the piece exactly right. Every word had to be exact and in its place, and George didn't want to take the chance that he would blow it. So he came out, told the audience point blank "I'm gonna read this shit because I wanna get it right," and then put on his glasses and perform it.

Sometimes though, when George was in a good mood, he wouldn't be so serious backstage and we'd joke and kid around. George loved impressions of famous stars, and I could always get him to belly laugh by doing impressions of certain personalities that we had particular fondness's for...Sometimes I would do Woody Allen, or James Mason singing "The Sound of Music," or Humphrey Bogart ordering groceries, or classic old-time late-night New York talk show host Joe Franklin introducing his guests - "On the show tonight we have Fred Astaire and a man who makes model airplanes out of tortilla chips" - and George would double over. It was always incredibly satisfying to me whenever I could make George laugh like that.

You never knew when the backstage hijinks would crop up. George would occasionally write me a horrifying note and leave it in my dressing room for me to discover when I came offstage. These notes would usually contain quick, terse messages such as "Your Sister's Legs!" or "Jerry Lewis' Ballbag!" I always enjoyed getting them and sharing them with friends and clergy members, but I must admit my all-time favorite of these was a note he left me in St. Louis. It read simply;

> "Dennis – Some of us were talking, and we feel you should blow more people. Thanking you in advance, I remain, George Carlin."

My other favorite was this one, an autograph for my copy of his book, "Brain Droppings":

> "To Dennis Blair – a fine gentleman with a great sister who blew me on the train. Love & Stuff – George Carlin"

The fun times were fast and furious with George. And besides being funny and goofy and fun to be around, he had a very generous side as well.

Thinking Fast....

One time there was a blizzard on the East Coast and our connecting flight from Chicago was cancelled. George was able to get on another flight, but I had to take a flight that would get me in after the show had already started. It seemed certain that I would miss doing my portion of the show, but George came up with an unusual and creative plan. Instead of me opening, George went on for the first forty-five minutes, which gave me time enough to get to the theatre. He had explained the situation to the audience and told them that his opening act would be coming on, oddly enough, in the middle of the show. As soon as I got there, George broke for an intermission. After the intermission, I went on, then George came on immediately after and did his last forty-five minutes. For the first time in my career, I was a middling act.

What impressed me most was that he obviously had said enough complimentary things about me to the audience that, instead of being bummed out when George left the stage and brought me on, they were responsive and supportive and laughed throughout my whole show. I think it's safe to say there aren't many performers who would have done that.

Another time we were all driving to a gig in the rental car and the discussion got around to Christmas and what gifts we were hoping to get. I happened to mention that I was thinking about splurging on a big-screen TV (Hey kids, that's what we used to watch before we had plasma screens and HD and the interwebs. C'mere, let me show you my eight-track tape player...) George turned to Jerry and, out of the blue, said, "Hey Jerry, let's you and I get that for him. He deserves it, don't you think?" I chuckled at the joke. Oh that George.

Two weeks later, about three days before Christmas, there was a knock on the door, and I opened it to see two burly delivery guys and a huge cardboard box on my stoop. It was a Sony 40-inch TV, courtesy of George and Jerry. I called and thanked them profusely. I really couldn't believe it, I had thought they were kidding. I also thought that I should have mentioned in that rental car that I was thinking of paying off my mortgage for Christmas, but this Sony would do very nicely.

Chapter 33: Rodney Returns

I had been working with George Carlin for about four years when I ran into Rodney at the Improv in L.A. We hadn't seen each other in about ten years. I had my two-year-old son Ian with me that night, and Rodney seemed to soften a little bit when he realized I was a father. He also seemed a little conflicted and disoriented, as if he was struggling to remember, "Gee, why am I mad at Dennis again?" We exchanged small talk, pleasantries, "How ya been?," that sort of stuff. Then we said our good-byes, and I figured that was the end of it.

A few weeks later, I got a call from Eddie Shine, an old friend of Rodney who had taken over as his transitional manager in recent years. Eddie told me that Rodney was doing a gig in an amphitheater in Phoenix and wondered if I'd like to open for him for old time's sake, along with his regular opening act Harry Basil. I was stunned. Eddie was one of the friends whom Rodney had called that fateful morning after the infamous Doggy Jacuzzi Disaster and bitched about what hideous humans Peggy and I were. I asked Eddie why the sudden change of heart.

"Rodney still likes you.," he said, then started to laugh. "And to tell you the truth, I think he forgot why he's pissed off at you."

It so happened I was free on the weekend in question, so I accepted Rodney's offer. Maybe we could put all that stupidity behind us after all.

It was strange to say the least, to be reunited after ten years with the guy who gave me my biggest start in comedy and who dropped me three years later over a wet poodle. What would be my first words to him after all this time? "Hey, Rodney. You ever get all that dog hair out of your drain?"

The big day arrived, and it was eerie. Rodney was living at the Beverly Wilshire hotel in L.A. at the time, and I met him and Harry there. As we drove to the airport, I became uncomfortably aware that Rodney was hanging on my every word and action, sizing me up after all these years. He also seemed to be trying to make it clear to me how chummy he was with Harry, laughing at all of Harry's jokes and not nearly as much at mine. If I didn't know better, I would have thought he was trying to make me jealous.

All this aside though, he was still the same old Rodney; funny, angry, warm and cranky all at the same time. We had some laughs and even reminisced a bit, although the fateful Jacuzzi Tragedy was never mentioned.

The show itself went all right, though not as well as the ones I had been doing with George. I don't know if I was a little out of synch with Rodney's audience, or if I was just nervous and off-kilter because of the circumstances and the history. All I know is that it took me awhile to grab them, and when I did it was just okay. On a scale of 1-10, I gave my show a 6.

Harry Basil had a good, solid show. And Rodney of course killed the room. He was really on that night, and I remembered once again why he was considered one of the greats.

We caught a late-night flight back home, which Rodney utilized to have a few drinks and carry on with the stewardesses. Unfortunately for me at one point in the flight the meaner part of his personality overtook him. Rodney leaned over to Harry and said, "Harry, you were great tonight!" Then he turned to me and said, "Dennis, you were.... okay."

Suddenly, I couldn't wait to get the hell home.

About a month later Eddie Shine offered me another weekend in Detroit with Rodney and Harry. I thanked him, but told him I couldn't because I was working with George that weekend, and to please keep me in mind for some other date in the future. I was never offered a gig with Rodney again. I could almost imagine him getting offended because I didn't blow off the Carlin weekend to work with him. I envisioned him calling up his friends..."I offered Dennis a weekend, and he turned me down because he was busy. See what I mean? Definitely shows a lack of character..."

An Amusing Corollary...

About two weeks after the Phoenix show, I got a call from a person named Sally who said she'd seen the show and was so impressed she wanted to hire me for a function she was holding in Arizona two months from now. The pay was excellent and I happened to be available, and so Jerry (who by now had become my manager) arranged for me to do the date.

A day later, I had a horrifying thought. What if Sally had mixed our names up and thought I was Harry Basil?

In my estimation, the response for my show that night had been mediocre at best, while Harry had done considerably better. What if Sally had gotten hold of my number thinking I was Harry? What if Harry was the person she really wanted to hire? What if I showed up at her function and she said, "You? I didn't want you. You sucked."

To fill you in briefly, Harry Basil does a great show which involves takeoffs on popular movies. He uses taped music, film clips on a screen backdrop, and a plethora of props such as a Superman suit, Darth Vader masks, and my personal favorite, underpants on his head. The crowds eat it up. My act is decidedly different from Harry's. Would Sally kill me if I showed up with my little guitar and nothing else? Would she say, "Where's the underpants?" I didn't know what to do, because there was a chance that I was indeed the one she wanted for her show, and I was just being paranoid. But I just couldn't shake the feeling that maybe, just maybe, she'd gotten the two of us confused.

George Carlin to the rescue!

Sally called me to say her supervisor, the guy who would be actually paying me, had not been in Phoenix that night and, although he trusted Sally's instincts completely, would still like to see my show to make sure I was right for the event. I told her I was playing Vegas with George in two weeks, and she said, "Perfect! I'll bring him to the show, and we'll come backstage afterwards. See you then."

Every night for those two weeks, I kept imagining Sally and this guy in the audience as I was introduced in the Bally's Las Vegas

Showroom. I could envision their faces as I walked out, guitar in hand, clearly not the guy they were expecting to see. I could see Sally's face dropping as her supervisor turned to her and said, "Does he keep his Darth Vader mask inside the guitar?"

The night arrived. I did my show, then waited backstage. The security guard knocked on my door..."There's a Sally here to see you?" "Send her up.," I said, bracing myself against the dressing room table. Sally and Bill, her supervisor, entered the room. She crossed over and extended her hand. I examined her smiling expression carefully. It didn't change to one of abject disappointment as I'd half expected. "Great show!," she said. "Looking forward to having you at our party," said Bill. "Whew," said my relaxing neck and shoulder muscles.

After ten minutes of conversation, I confided in them about my unfounded fears. "Y'know," I said, "because Harry had such a great show that night, I was wondering for a while if you actually wanted him instead of me."

"You mean the guy after you?," she replied. "No, we want you." Bill laughed and said jokingly to Sally, "I dunno, maybe I should see him too."

Sally turned to him. "You wouldn't want him for our crowd, Bill. He puts underpants on his head."

A Reconciliation?

Halfway through the year 2000, I ran into Rodney again, at a club called "The Laugh Factory" in Los Angeles. I'd run into him on occasion over the years, and he'd always been courteous enough, but you could always tell he still harbored resentment and anger toward me (I guess he'd remembered why he was pissed). But this time was different.

He had gotten married several years earlier, and I don't know if marriage or just time in general had helped to mellow him. All I know is, he was doing a set onstage, and when he came off I said hi and offered my hand, not knowing for sure if he'd take it or slap it away. To my delight, he was extremely friendly, asking how Peggy and my kids were (I had two now), remembering some of our old times together, kidding around with me like he used to. Not a great deal was said, and he didn't hang around long, but I got the feeling he was genuinely pleased to see me, or at least had made some kind of peace with the past. It was almost as if he'd put all of the "bad" stuff behind him.

More chance meetings between us at the Laugh Factory would occur, with the same results...a warm handshake, a quick joke or two, a few minutes of good-natured kidding and conversation. I would almost find myself wishing for a phone call from him out of the blue someday, inviting Peg and I and the kids over for a cup of coffee, to relive old times and revitalize an old friendship. I even fantasized how it would go. We would laugh, we would tell jokes, maybe even discuss some half-hearted projects we could collaborate on in the future.

We would, however, decline any invitation to take a quick dip in the pool.

* * * * *

When Rodney died in 2004, I was on the road with George Carlin in Florida, so I couldn't attend the funeral. I heard a lot of great people were there like Jim Carrey and Dom Irrera and people I hadn't seen in a long time. I sent my condolences to Rodney's wife, but I do admit to suffering a twinge of regret for not being able to be there in person. I always will feel that I owe Rodney a great deal. Without him, it's entirely possible my career would never have happened. I owe him that, as do many of us "young comedians of the '80's."

I still find it hard to let my disappointment at what happened between us go sometimes, for all those wasted years. In that way I guess I'm not unlike him. Where he held a grudge, I similarly hold resentment and regret. The fact that the friendship was destroyed for such a variety of unfair, unfounded, and just plain stupid reasons still hangs on me to this day. I think we could have actually written some good movies together. But more importantly it would've been nice to have maintained some friendly contact over those years. The truth is he was a good friend for a long time, and underneath it all he had a good soul and a big heart.

Chapter 34: "The George Carlin Show" and My Own Personal Hell

There was one brief period in which my association with George Carlin resembled a form of Chinese water torture. In 1993, George was offered his own sitcom called "The George Carlin Show" (talented Hollywood executives came up with that name after a grueling seven-hour meeting at The Polo Lounge). It was to air on the Fox Network Sunday nights after "Married with Children."

I was initially pleased to hear that George was getting his own T.V. show. In addition to being happy for him to be getting this kind of a break, I also thought it might help my career. Surely I would be offered some kind of a role on the show. Surely I would be given the opportunity to display my considerable acting chops. Surely I would be appreciated for the fine comedic talent I was and be well on my way to my long-delayed rendezvous with celebrity.

I reveled in this illusion, until I was informed by the producer of the show that I was well on my way to being the warmup guy for the studio audiences.

And I thought the Concord was bad.

Let me tell you a little bit about what it was like warming up audiences for TV shows in the '90's. First of all, although the occasions are rare these days, if you ever get an opportunity to go to the taping of a live TV sitcom, and there is a comedian doing the warmup, please give this person your undivided attention and your utmost respect. In my opinion, it was and still may be the hardest job in show business. Even the most difficult show you can have as an opening act for a celebrity will be over within thirty or forty minutes at the most. Tapings for a TV sitcom last far longer than that. There are scene changes, and set changes, and actors flubbing lines, and re-takes, and re-takes on the re-takes. As the warmup person, it is your duty to entertain the people between scenes during these times. You need to perform, keep the audience interested, and be funny for as long as the taping lasts, which was three or four hours during the time span when I was forced to supplement my road income by being "warm up boy." That was not a misprint, let me repeat that: YOU NEEDED TO PERFORM FOR A SITCOM AUDIENCE FOR THREE OR FOUR HOURS. Even if the audience sucked, even if the audience hated you, even if audience members were hiring hit-men on their cell phones to have you whacked in the studio cafeteria after the show, YOU NEEDED TO PERFORM FOR THREE OR FOUR HOURS. That would be like going to a dentist and having him say, "You know, the bad news is we're gonna have to do root canal on that tooth of yours, but at least it'll only take THREE OR FOUR HOURS.

Now, I'm not saying the audiences for George's TV show were bad. They were often pretty good, and I usually did well with them. And even though doing the three and sometimes four-hour tapings were hard on me physically, having the audience on my side did a lot to help get me through the evening. Occasionally though, you would get certain audiences that were, for all intents and purposes, demon spawn.

I don't know where these hideous groups of people that sometimes arrived at the tapings came from, but by the looks of them, prisons and sanitariums would not be a bad guess. One night I counted seven hundred forty-three piercings and tattoos. Seven hundred forty-four, if you count the guy during the show who added a tattoo with my name attached to a hangman's noose. Some of them wore apparel that read "Mom and Dad Killed the Warmup Guy and All I Got was this Lousy T-Shirt." Nights like this made me long for the good old days in the Catskills where the audience only hated you for twenty minutes. A typical taping with this kind of crowd would usually go something like this:

Me: "Hey, welcome to the George Carlin Show!"
Satanist: "Hey, you suck!."
Me: "Okay, before we begin, I need everyone to laugh as loud as you can."
Hooligan: "Your sister was great last night."

Me: "We're gonna have a lot of fun, let me introduce you to the members of the cast."

Demon Spawn: "Let me introduce you to my fist if you don't shut up."

And naturally, you couldn't merely do your act. At a four-hour taping, if you relied on just your act you would run out of material in the first hour or two. So you would have to fill the time with other things. Many warm-up acts would be great at this. They would do crowd work with audience members, get them involved in games, magic tricks, mindreading, anything that worked. Me? I gave away free crap.

Before I was to arrive at the studio, I would go over to the 99-cent store and buy the tackiest, cheesiest items I could find – back-scratchers, pot-holders, plastic religious figures, carrot-graters, anything I could get my hands on. Then I would hold joke-telling contests at the taping, and the person who told the best joke would get to choose a gift from my vast stash. The most popular item by far was the Regis and Kathie Lee Wall Calendar. Often the audiences would be completely won over by the end, but even on the best nights, I wound up feeling less like a comedian and more like Bob Barker on a busman's holiday.

On the really bad nights, you would just have to ignore all the rudeness and hostility and somehow get through it, which I did. After four hours, half the audience would have left and the other half had just given up and decided to ignore me. It left me with a real bad taste in my mouth and a longing to go back on the road and do what I do best. But I did comfort myself at least with the knowledge that as nasty as these people had been, at least when I went to bed that night the last thing I heard would not be "Lights out!"

One of the few good things that came out of the run of George's TV show for me was that I got to meet some fun and interesting characters who were associated with the production. My favorite cast member was Alex Rocco, who is probably best-known for playing the role of Moe Greene in "The Godfather." Alex was one of the most down-to-earth, sweet people I've ever met. My most vivid memory of Alex is of a conversation we had while driving from the studio one day. I figured that probably eighteen thousand people had asked him this question, but I needed to know and so I posed it anyway. "Alex," I said. "I know you're probably tired of answering this question, but I was wondering..."

Without missing he beat he nodded and replied, "The gunshot through the eyeball, right?"

As all you Godfather fans surely know, in the movie Moe Greene meets his violent end by getting shot in the eye. He's lying on a table getting a massage, and as he puts on his glasses a bullet shatters the glass and blows his eyeball out.

"Yeah," I said. "How did they do that?"

He explained it this way: There was a thin hollow tube that ran from a hydraulic machine up the side of his eyeglasses and attached to the Plexiglas lens. A tiny metal pellet was inserted into the tube, and when the blank in the gun went off, they activated the hydraulic pump, which shot the pellet up the tube and out the lens, shattering it, while fake blood was pumped out of another tube. If you look closely, Alex told me, you can see him closing his eye because he could hear the hissing of the pump and the pellet travelling through it a split second before it broke the lens. Pretty cool.

The other good memory I have of the show was that once a month or so, George would hold an informal lunch at a restaurant in Los Angeles with Jerry, me, a few of the cast members plus the director, Sam Simon, and the legendary Pat McCormack, who had been the head writer for the Tonight Show during the Johnny Carson era and was always hysterical and completely off-the-wall. Sometimes all I could do was sit and watch Pat McCormick do improvised bits at the table with the salt and pepper shakers, the tablecloth, the candles, anything he could get his hands on. He was amazing.

After one of these lunches (which George had named "A Gathering of Turds"), we walked out of the restaurant just in time to see Arnold Schwarzenegger pulling up in a gigantic Hummer. This was before Hummers became a fairly common sight on the streets of Los Angeles, and we had never seen a car as gigantic or gaudy as this. George and Pat started hurling taunts at Arnold, "Hey Arnold, what the fuck is that a tank?!," "Jesus Arnold, is that thing big enough for your ego?!," etc. etc. Arnold laughed and took it all in stride. And then he suddenly scowled at all of us and said, "I'll be back!"

"The George Carlin Show" was cancelled after the second season. The ratings had been respectable, but I guess not good enough to keep the show going. I was secretly elated. No more four-hour marathons. No more embarrassing joke-telling contests and prize giveaways. No more trips down to the police station to identify felons. I felt badly for George though, until I actually spoke with him. I went up to him at the last taping and said, "Sorry about the show getting cancelled." He turned to me and said, "I'm glad. I can't wait to get outta here."

I never got the full story, but apparently as the show went on the network execs and honchos had begun to intrude more and more. Young studio types in their twenties and thirties were weighing in on the creative process, actually suggesting to George ways to be funnier. TV executives suggesting ways for George Carlin to be funnier. That would be like suggesting ways for Ozzie Osbourne to be more incoherent. You just don't do that sort of thing. From then on George returned to what he loved best, doing standup comedy on the road for packed theaters around the country. And he took me with him. However, he would not allow me to bring the Regis and Kathie Lee calendars along.

I remember one conversation with him shortly after the sitcom was cancelled and he was back in the mode he knew so well, doing standup in front of live audiences. He had just agreed to do another HBO TV Special, and was really looking forward to it because, to put it in his words, "This is what I was born to do. My goal is to be the only 65-year-old comedian to say 'cocksucker' on television!"

George was back!

The Hall of Fame

In 1994 George was inducted into the Comedy Hall of Fame. He invited Peggy and me to accompany him to the ceremony in Los Angeles and we gladly accepted. We sat at George's table behind a dais that included the other honorees such as Mary Tyler Moore, Kelsey Grammer, Shirley MacLaine and Bob Hope.

Several things stand out in my memory of that evening. The first is that I got to see some of my favorite comedians do short sets that were very funny...Richard Belzer, Paula Poundstone and John Lovitz gave good performances.

The second thing that stood out was that even though those comics that were from my generation did an admirable job, when the old school (or more accurately, the OLD old school guys) guys started to get up, the guys from the "Golden Age" of comedy such as Jonathan Winters, Sid Caesar and Red Buttons, there was just no comparison. They absolutely ruled the night. No one matched the level and intensity of the laughs they got. Red Buttons did his infamous "Never Got a Dinner" routine, Sid Caesar did his Professor character, Jonathan Winters just ad-libbed frequently and noisily from his table and the audience reaction was thunderous all around. I also remember that George got to deliver one of my favorite lines of his that night:

> "Some say the glass is half-empty. Some say the glass is half-full. I say the glass is too big."

Bob Hope was at this time closing in on being 100 years old. For the entire time he sat on the dais he seemed frail, old and out of sorts. Near the end of the ceremony, when he was called up to give his speech, he arose and walked slowly toward the stage assisted by Mary Tyler Moore. I felt badly for him and braced myself to hear what I was sure would be a weak and rambling speech. As soon as he hit the stage and the spotlight found him, if it was as if 40 years had melted away. He was sharp and focused and funny, and that is coming from someone who was never exactly a huge Bob Hope fan. He was on for about five minutes and I laughed loudly and frequently as did the audience, who of course gave him a standing ovation.

It was a great night and a proud one for George, as well as a well-deserved one.

Love and Airplanes

On May 11, 1997, at 9:00 in the morning in my bedroom in North Hollywood, I got a call from Jerry giving me the news that George's wife of thirty-five years, Brenda, had died the previous night of complications from liver disease. Brenda had been sick for a long time, but somehow we never thought her illness was serious enough to be life-threatening. I called George immediately and got his daughter Kelly on the phone, who told us to come right over to the house. We immediately drove over to George's place in Brentwood. Kelly was in a daze, and George was just sort of drifting aimlessly about the house, lost. Kelly told Peg and me that George had spent the night curled up in bed and had placed stuffed animals in the place where Brenda had always slept.

There was a memorial at the house a few days later, and it was sad and poignant and great. Friends and relatives of Brenda spoke, and when George finally got up to speak, he said;

"Well, I don't believe in an afterlife. But if there is a God, he'd better be on his toes, because Brenda's on her way and she doesn't take shit from anybody."

Several years later George and I were driving to a gig somewhere and he said to me, "You're going to be hearing me talk a lot about a woman named Sally Wade. She's the greatest thing that's happened to me in years." George had met Sally in a bookstore in Los Angeles and had made an immediate connection. He was head over heels. After every show we did on the road, immediately after the zippo bango and as soon as he was in the car, the first thing he did was call Sally and tell her how the show went. It was good to see him back with someone who could make him happy again.

George had always done well on the road and toured consistently for many years. But when he did a special for HBO called "Jammin' In New York," his popularity started to soar off the charts. His TV specials had always been great and frequently groundbreaking, but he seemed to reach a creative pinnacle with "Jammin' In New York." Critics and audiences loved it and subsequently his live performances were consistently sold out. And in addition to the specials, George was writing books that repeatedly landed on the New York Times best-seller lists. So in 1997, George was doing so well financially that Jerry was able to start chartering airplanes to get to our gigs.

George had always hated travelling on commercial airlines anyway, and he especially hated dealing with airline security. We all of course detest having to go through metal detectors and having to virtually disrobe to do so, but for some reason George set off more alarms than most and was often commanded to empty his pockets and carry-on luggage, which would send him into a rage. I have clear memories of getting through security only to wait for George as he was probed, prodded and searched while cursing out the airport personnel the whole time.

> SECURITY PERSON: Is this your bag, sir? We need to run a check on it.
> GEORGE: There's nothing in the damn bag.
> SECURITY PERSON: Sir, we just have to check..
> GEORGE: This is bullshit. I'm not carrying a bomb in my carry-on. What do you think I am, stupid?
> SECURITY PERSON: ...And could you raise your arms, we need to do a pat-down.
> GEORGE: Are you kidding me?! What is this, Russia?!

Then he would have to watch helplessly as the security person opened his roll-away bag and go through his personal items. There are few things worse than a helpless George Carlin, watching from a distance and blurting out phrases like, "Hey watch it, those are my pain pills" or "Jeez, are you gonna search my fucking underwear?!"

I was amazed that he never got detained or arrested for those outbursts. I do know that he started putting a lot of material about airline security in his act soon after that, and I remember it was reeeeeeeeally edgy. So naturally chartering private planes would go a long way towards soothing George's frayed nerves.

George had done a movie with Robert Duvall several years earlier where they had hired a private pilot nicknamed "Cheater" to bring the actors to the remote location where filming took place.

We found out later on that he had gotten the nickname "Cheater" because he had "cheated death" so many times before as a pilot. This knowledge set me slightly on edge, but not enough to say "no thanks" when George and Jerry invited me to go with them to our gigs on Cheater's private jet.

Cheater was one of those guys who looked like he had fallen out of a 'seventies TV series; Longish 'seventies hair, big ol' walrus porn moustache, shirt and vest cowboy boots. He looked like a sheriff in a Coen Borthers movie. He was a real nice guy, and funny too. And he got us to the gigs on time and, thankfully, in one piece. We flew with Cheater for a few years until one fateful flight caused George and Jerry to re-think the association.

We were coming in for a landing at a small airport on Montauk, Long Island. The weather was dreary and there was a low-lying fog that lay near to the ground. No one could even see the runway, and Cheater was flying on instruments. We were all a little nervous to begin with. We had been approaching the airport for what seemed an eternity when suddenly we broke through the fog and saw the ground rushing up at us merely twenty or so feet below. "Shit!," exclaimed Cheater. "Fuck!," exclaimed his co-pilot Danny. "ShitFuck!," yelled I in my head.

George had remained eerily calm during all this. He just looked out the window and muttered resignedly, "Wow. This could be it."

We hit the ground with a loud thud and I was convinced we had crashed. I heard screeching tires and brakes thrown into overdrive and we finally, mercifully came to a halt before smashing in to a tree.

"Cocksucker!" yelled Cheater as he opened the door and rushed outside to see if there was any damage. Jerry and I just looked at each other with our eyes bulging. George continued looking out the window. The only thing I remember him saying was, "Look at that runway. There's grass and shit growing out of the cracks."

George Carlin..."The Man Who Didn't Fear Death"

I of course was never at the business meetings that were held between Jerry and George, but I do know that after that flight, we never saw Cheater again. They still chartered jets to get to the gigs, but from then on they hired them from a company in Los Angeles that used pilots with crisp white uniforms and modern, contemporary hair and that didn't, to my memory, yell expletives when they landed.

A Funny Airplane Story...

When we were still associated with Cheater there was a situation when one of the guys who sold merchandise at the show, whose name was Ralph, was stuck without a car and had to somehow make it quickly to the next town which was about 900 miles away. George took mercy on Ralph and invited him and the merchandise to come on the plane ride with all of us.

Ralph is a very big guy and had a little trouble squeezing onto the small airplane, but he did and he got to the gig in plenty of time. Of course, he did not arrive unscathed. Many jokes about his considerable bulk and his consequently uncomfortable seating posture were unleashed during the course of the flight. We were all friends and none of it was mean-spirited, and Ralph laughed along with the rest of us. But it was indeed brutal.

Ralph got his car back and never travelled on the plane again. A few weeks later, Ralph got a copy of George's book, "Braindroppings," and asked George to sign it for him, which he did. A few hours later, Ralph came up to me with a big grin on his face.

RALPH: Hey Dennis, George signed my book. You've got to read what he wrote. It's hilarious.

He gave me the book and I read what George had written on the front page:

"Hey Ralph...the plane flies higher when you're not on it!
- George"

Chapter 35:
Jackie Mason saves Vaudeville

The year was 2003. I had spent the last 15 years touring with George and had been living in Agoura Hills California with my family for some time. It was a beautiful spring day, and I was reading a magazine at my kitchen table when my phone rang. It was Jill Rosenberg, Jackie Mason's long-time manager and confidant, speaking to me in a state of near-panic. "Dennis! It's Jill," she blurted into the phone.

"Jill? What's wrong?"

The anxiety in her voice was so palpable and intense I was sure something terrible had happened to Jackie. I'll never forget what she said to me just then...

"Can you write sketches!?"

From the tone in her voice I had expected something different; "Heart attack," or "Hit by a taxi on 58th Street," or "Choking on a blintz."

"Sketches?," I said. "Uuummm...yes, I have written sketches. Why do you ask?"

Jill explained that over the last few years she and Jackie had been working on a project that Jackie had dreamed about for some time. He had decided he was going to single-handedly bring vaudeville back to Broadway. And the way he was going to do this was by starring in a musical revue. Now Jackie, of course, had enjoyed many years of success on the Broadway stage presenting himself in his hilariously funny one-man shows. He had done several of these over the years, and they were indeed great, but they were getting harder for him to do as he grew older. Writing an entire new act and then standing alone onstage for seven shows a week, including matinees, for a year or longer, each show lasting two hours or more, was a grueling pace for anyone, but especially for a man in his mid-seventies. Jackie still wanted to do Broadway, but not have to be on stage constantly. He wanted to parcel the time out to a cast of actors, maybe acting as a host or MC, doing his monologues in short bursts and then leaving the stage to the cast members, maybe appearing in a few sketches with them, but basically leaving most of the heavy lifting to the actors. He felt he had earned the right to slow down a little bit.

This was not news to me. Years earlier, in one of our typical New York Coffee Shop meetings, Jackie had asked me to write a movie for him. He was convinced he could do a movie on the cheap. He said:

"I could make a movie for a hundred thousand dollars. Who needs a million dollars to make a movie? Most of that is bullshit wasteful spending! You can eliminate the catering, hire one sound person, maybe a lighting person, maybe a director (maybe a director?), a camera, one of those slate board things with the clapper, and that's IT!. How much can that be? I can do it for a hundred thousand, tops."

In my youthful naïveté, I actually went ahead and began to write a low-budget (to say the least) movie for Jackie, based on a funny real-life incident that had happened to him years earlier involving a kidnapped woman and payoffs that kept disappearing. Jill and Jackie gave me the go-ahead, but Jill laid down two simple rules for the screenplay:

> NUMBER ONE: "I don't want Jackie working too hard, so put him in as few scenes as possible."
> NUMBER TWO: "Jackie likes to sit. So if you have to put him in a scene, try to have him sitting."

The result was "The Money Trail," starring an often-sitting and sometimes-missing Jackie Mason. Jackie and Jill loved the screenplay, and it got great reactions from both actor/director Joe Bologna and also Alan Metter who directed the Rodney Dangerfield movie, "Back To School." Unfortunately the project never got off the ground because, for some odd reason, everyone seemed to think they needed more than a hundred thousand dollars to make the movie. Even without the catering.

But enough about "The Money Trail." That would be for another time. Right now there were other mountains to climb. Right now, Jackie was going to be in a musical revue!

Jackie Mason in a musical revue. Very much like Fran Lebowitz playing shortstop for the Yankees. "How so?," you ask.

For one thing, Jackie Mason is not a singer. He can carry a tune, but only for a few feet, before it crashes to the floor. I think he would admit this today. But back in 2003, Jackie thought he could sing. Or Jill had convinced him he could sing. It doesn't matter. The fact is, Jackie Mason is a brilliant comedian, but he's not a singer. Yet somehow, unbeknownst to me, and without my permission, "The Jackie Mason Organization" had decided sometime near the turn of the century that vaudeville was due for a comeback and that he was just the man to do it. And so, also unbeknownst to me and without my permission, Jill and Jackie had booked the Brooks Atkinson Theater for a run that would begin in November of 2003, then had hired writers to come up with a script, and had hired a composer to come up with music and songs, and had set about the task of creating the Great American Yiddish-Flavored Musical.

But the first script they got from the writer was bad, so they fired that writer and got a new writer. And the script they got from the new writer was awful, so they fired that writer and hired a second writer. The script from that writer was terrible, so they hired a third writer, who was more horrible than both the terrible and the awful writer, which forced them to hire a fourth writer, whose script was hideous. By this time they were running out of money, time and adjectives, which led them in an act of sheer desperation to hire me, henceforth known as "writer number five."

Since Jill and Jackie knew that I had written a movie and TV specials for Rodney Dangerfield in the 1980's, they sent me a copy of one of the sketches from the most recent script and asked me to fix it. It was an old-timey doctor sketch, the kind that would have been at home in the 1920's or on the TV show "Laugh-In" from the 1970's. I worked on it, punching up the jokes, tightening the scene as best I could, and then sent it back to them. Within an hour, my phone rang. It was Jill and Jackie on a conference call., begging me to rewrite the whole script for them. Or better yet, could I come to New York for, say, six months and work on it from inception through rehearsals through out-of-town tryouts to opening night on Broadway?

Since I still loved and missed New York, and since it was an opportunity to write the book for a Broadway show, and not only a Broadway show but one starring my old pal Jackie Mason, I agreed to fly eastward and help to see this grand project to fruition. Was it the right decision?

Oy.

I moved into the Mayflower hotel on West 61st street and geared up for the job at hand. Meetings were held with the director and the choreographer and the composer and the five enthusiastic, fresh-faced cast members that had been chosen for the show, all talented Broadway professionals who had appeared in several musicals and plays already and were looking forward to working with the great Jackie Mason. Day after day I would turn in rewrites of old sketches and ideas for new sketches, and day after day Jackie and Jill and everyone involved would tell me how brilliant and funny my sketches were and what a big hit this show was going to be. We moved from the writing and talking stage to the rehearsal process. Watching the show begin to take shape was thrilling. There were gales of laughter as the actors ran through their lines and sang their songs. Jackie would rehearse his short bits of monologue and his parts in the sketches, which had everybody howling, and even started singing his songs, which at this early stage were a little out of key but which, we all figured, would improve with time. I even had written a musical sketch based on the fact that Jackie wanted to sit down as much as possible. It was a choreographed number with Jackie "dancing" while sitting on a swivel chair, joined by the other actors who were also on swivel chairs. We invited friends and co-workers to watch this early rehearsal, and they laughed loud and long and told us the scene, as well as the show, couldn't miss. After weeks and weeks of hard work, sometimes fourteen hours a day, we were exhausted but happy. Jill told me that I was destined to be "a real

Broadway writer!" I felt very, very good about the way things had turned out.

And then came the out-of-town tryouts in Nyack New York.

It was several months before the official opening on Broadway in November when we arrived at the theater in Nyack. The sets were built, the blocking was worked out, the lines were memorized and the songs were orchestrated. We had ourselves an honest-to-Betsy Musical Revue, entitled "Laughing Room Only," starring Jackie Mason, singing and dancing and sitting in a swivel chair, just the way his fans had always wanted to see him. Or not.

It certainly turned out that was not how his fans in Nyack wanted to see him. There was laughter for the first few minutes of the show as Jackie sat at the grand piano and placed a candelabra, which was actually a large menorah, on top. There was laughter as he started to sing the opening song...or, more accurately, as he began to talk the opening song. Then less laughter. Then a chuckle or two. Then nothing. For a long, long time. This show that couldn't miss was... missing.

We were stunned, quite frankly. We expected that there would be bumps and glitches and dead spots here and there. We expected that Jackie's singing abilities would cause some problems. But that's what tryouts were for. We would make note of the problems as they arose and fix them. But we didn't expect an audience reaction that was lifted from "Springtime for Hitler." Whenever Jackie would appear on stage, for a few minutes between the sketches doing his standup routines, everything would be fine and the laughs would come. And then Jackie would leave and another sketch would begin and people would sit in their seats, as if they were wondering, "Why are these five gentiles singing and jumping around and interrupting Jackie's monologues?" It was brutal. And what made it even worse was that Jill kept coming over to me every two minutes as I stood at the back of the theater and asked me what was going wrong, as if I would have an immediate answer, like a comedy doctor.

JILL: "Why aren't they laughing at the hospital sketch?"
ME: "Well, obviously the doctor's gown is the wrong color. It needs to be magenta. And we should change the nurse's

name to Blanche. Oh, and we should drop this sketch from the show entirely, but of course I won't know that for another agonizing five weeks. Instead I'll keep trying to save a sketch whose premise in 2003 would even be rejected by RIP TAYLOR."

I had no such answers. I hadn't a clue. Except for the hospital sketch, I felt that I should be able to make the comedy work. But these people weren't even laughing at the Swivel Chair sketch, which had been so "brilliant" in rehearsal. Everything, except for Jackie's masterful monologues, just laid there. After two hours of torture, about the only sounds that could be heard in the theater were silence and Jill's footsteps walking toward me to ask "Why isn't THIS funny?"

Mingling with the audience in the lobby and getting feedback during intermission was among one of my most depressing show business experiences. The comments were maddening; "Worst show I've ever seen," "It'll close by the second night," "He can't sing, why does he even try?," "Why isn't he doing more standup?," "I wish the writer were here so I could rip his heart out," etc, etc.

The following, grueling weeks were devoted to trying to suddenly insert laughter into "Laughing Room Only "so that it wouldn't have to be renamed "All Seats Available." Since you could always depend on Jackie's standup, he started adding more and more of his classic monologues into the show, which was exactly what he didn't want to do but was, under the circumstances, unavoidable. Meanwhile, I worked feverishly, day and night, with the director, the choreographer, the composer, forgoing sleep, hardly eating, trying to fix, patch, overhaul. Slowly, things started to get better. There was definitely more laughter weeks later than there was when we started, but it still wasn't where it needed to be. The applause at the end of each nightly show was good, sometimes even strong, but there was never a showstopper or a standing ovation. And when I did sleep, I would invariably have nightmares where I would be watching the show and would hear Jill's footsteps, louder and louder, coming closer, closer, until I'd hear her voice...

"It's not funny. Why isn't it funny? It needs to be funny. FUNNYFUNNYFUNNYFUNNYFUNNYMAKEITFUNNYMAKEITFUNNYMAKEIT FUNNYREDRUMREDRUMREDRUM!!!....."

I learned a few weeks later that, in order to encourage ticket sales for the Nyack performances, the box office at the theater had been instructed to tell everyone that the show they were about to see was Jackie Mason's latest one-man show, not the musical ensemble production that it actually was. So people in Nyack had come to the show expecting to see a two-hour stand-up performance, and what they got of course was Jackie trying to sing in tune and then disappearing for long stretches while a group of relative unknowns ran around in costumes warbling show tunes. Of course this contributed to the tough times in Nyack, but in a way it was too late. Word was already starting to leak out that the show was a dead herring.

Now you may be expecting me to say that by the time we got the show to its Broadway previews we had lost all hope. But I can honestly say that for the two weeks of Broadway previews, the audiences were laughing. Not uproariously or all the time, but they were laughing. It was not a classic by any means, but it was not a dud, and people were enjoying it. One night at the end of the show, I overheard a couple saying something I never thought I'd hear anybody say about the show. They said, "That was fun." I hadn't heard those words since my wedding night.

Through grit and sweat and force of will and the desire to not have Jill walk towards me anymore, we somehow got the show into decent enough shape that we thought maybe, just maybe, we had a shot. That given time, this show starring a Jewish Icon who couldn't sing or dance but had decided to star in a musical, would find its audience.

The critics disagreed.

We got absolutely hammered in the New York press. I can't remember one word of one review, but I do remember that none of them were good. And one week later, tired and worn out and sick of losing money for Jackie and his investors, Jill pulled the plug on the show. My career as a Broadway writer was over, and it was back to doing standup, which was fine by me.

I felt very bad for a long time after the show closed. Even though I tried my best, I really felt as if I'd let everybody down. Sometime in December I finally gathered up the nerve to call Jackie. I left a message on his voice mail about how sorry I was that it didn't work out.

He called me back a half-hour later, and said this;

"It's not your fault at all. It took me all this time to realize.... Nobody wants to see me in a musical. I don't know what I was thinking. When they come to my show, they want to see a Jew who talks for an hour, and that's IT!"

Throughout this entire experience of bringing vaudeville back to Broadway I had continued my touring with George, the only change being that I had based out of New York instead of California. Thankfully when "Laughing Room Only" came to an end I still had my touring schedule to rely on and happily resumed my opening act career.

Chapter 36: Trouble

In December of 2004, George and I finished up another year of successful shows on the road. After all these years, George still seemed energized and engaged and ready to do at least two more HBO Specials, if not more. And I remember being pretty content as I reflected on my life. Peg and I and my two kids (Ian and Madeline, who had arrived in 1993) had lived in a house in North Hollywood California for thirteen years, and it was a fairly nice house except for one annoying fact; it was thirty yards from where three noisy freeways intersected. When we bought the house in 1988, out of all the homes we'd looked at, this was the only one we could afford. The noise from the freeways had a lot to do with the affordability of the house. Even though we installed triple-paned windows which blocked out a lot of the noise, occasionally we would have to do things like open the door and go outside... and we would hear the constant "whhhooooshhh, rooowwwrrrr, beeeep beeeep!" of the freeway and be reminded once again that things were alright, but could be better. I tried to reconcile the situation in my mind by telling myself, "Hey, look at it this way... sure it's noisy, but it kind of sounds like the ocean in some ways. So basically, it's like we have a house on the ocean, except for the occasional police siren and yelled obscenity."

In 2001 we decided that we felt secure enough with my career with George that we could make a move to a quieter neighborhood. So we found a house about thirty miles outside of Los Angeles in Agoura Hills on a quiet street surrounded by trees and mountains and with a backyard that we could actually sit in without suffering hearing loss. Yes, life was very, very nice. All was well. Can you guess what's coming?

In January of 2005, I got a call from Jerry that George had gone into rehab.

"Huh? What? When? Why?" (I might have also said "Where" and "Who," but I had gone numb by that point)

I was told that George had voluntarily checked himself into a Rehab Center in Malibu to finally "sober up" after years of addiction to red wine and Vicodin. What was amazing and baffling to me and to others who had known George over the years was that he had always seemed, as I said before, absolutely fine. There was no outward indication whatsoever that something like this was in the cards. A few weeks later I read in a magazine interview that George had apparently been addicted to Vicodin for the last twenty years. This was complete news to me. But here it was. George's stint in rehab would take a month, followed by another month for recuperation and monitoring. Which meant that for the months of January and February, I was out of work.

When I had been thrown out of work in the past with Rodney and Joan and even Tom Jones, I had been able to rely on my agent to get me work at other venues and with other headliners. The scary thing about this situation with George was that, for approximately fifteen years, I hadn't had an agent. There had been no need for one, since I was working all the time and felt 100% secure that George would always work and would always use me. George had actually told me about three years previously that, as long as he did this, I would always be his opening act. I had no reason to doubt his word.

In March of 2005 George felt well enough to go back to work. I felt a little nervous about seeing him again, since I'd had no contact with him and didn't know what to expect. It was almost like a replay of that night in Omaha when I waited to meet him for the first time, wondering what he'd be like. What would he be like now that he was sober? Would he be dour? Would he be depressed? Or would he be chanting "Hare Krishna" and telling us all to love one another, and by the way, stay away from Vicodin?

I climbed onto the plane and found him sitting there with a slight smile on his face. He seemed fine, relaxed, and the first words out of his mouth were "Sorry to have disrupted everyone's lives for the last two months." Then we took off, on our way once again to another theater in another town. It seemed like life would get

Touring with Legends

back to normal again. Things did go well for a while. But then, slowly, things began to change. I've heard that when people who have been addicted to alcohol or drugs all their lives suddenly become sober, it transforms their thought processes, alters their minds gradually, can even turn them into a different person. It wasn't immediately apparent that this was happening to George, but there were changes taking place that were impossible to miss.

We had played Las Vegas together for over sixteen years, first Caesar's Palace, then Bally's for ten years, then the MGM Grand for four years. George had never been fond of Las Vegas audiences, but he had always sucked it up and done the shows without complaining. As early as 2004, that had all begun to go south. As his material had become more challenging and edgy, the generic Vegas crowds, who were usually not die-hard George Carlin fans to begin with, had become more easily shocked and offended. George was never the kind of comic who would tailor a performance to the audience, and as the crowd response became more reserved he began to berate and attack them. I can remember several occasions where I would be watching George from the wings as he did his show for a crowd that just sat there and stared at him. At some point, he would get frustrated and angry, then sigh deeply and start ranting…

"What the fuck is wrong with you people? This is good shit, this ain't Bill Cosby, y'know. You have to think a little bit to get with this shit. I've had a great fucking career, I've been on the road with audiences that appreciate what I do, I don't need to be up here while you assholes just sit there and look at me." And then, after he had gotten that out of his system, he would go back into his prepared show, which was something I always loved. George would tear into these people, tell them how stupid and imbecilic and unimaginative and worthless they were, and then go back into his routine as if nothing had happened.

This kind of thing, by the way, had occurred every so often even earlier in his career. George once played me a tape of a concert he did in New Haven Connecticut in the mid-1980's where his then-opening act bombed so badly she ran off the stage in tears.

George came on right afterwards and proceeded to tear the audience a new one, berating them for being so cruel to the opener. His comments, which went on and on and on, went something like this:

"You assholes! (Name of opening act) is in tears backstage because you morons really did a number on her. Fuck all of ya's!! What do you think I asked her to open for me for, so she could get booed by scumbags like you? Blow me!!"

...Whereupon he would launch into his regular show. I cannot stress strongly enough how the fact that George could berate an audience or a heckler with the most vile, vicious, disgusting language for five minutes and then just go into his show as if he was only kidding, thrilled me to no end. And it also thrilled and touched me that he had gone to bat so vociferously for his opening act. That's the George that I loved.

I remember another incident when I had already been working with him for a few years. George had been onstage for about ten minutes when I heard something that sounded a lot like yelling coming from his general direction. I came running from my dressing room and watched from the wings as George was in the middle of going off on a heckler who apparently would not stop talking.

"...Shut the fuck up, shut up! Will someone put a dick in this guy's mouth, please? God damn it, fuck you for ruining my show. You should die in a fiery plane crash, motherfucker! Someone should take a broom handle, break it in half and shove it up your grandmother's pie-hole! Security, grab this jagoff, throw him out... Is he gone? Good! See, ya gotta use psychology on these people!....(audience cheers)....and now, I would like to talk about the differences between dogs and cats..."

(there are other examples of George going off on a heckler. Here's one on YouTube...
https://youtu.be/N8gXUUtZogw)

As I mentioned, this sort of anger and hostility had surfaced every so often in his career, and was usually directed at either a heckler or an entire audience that he'd lost patience with. But now it was getting more frequent. The same act that was doing great with the fans that came to see him on the road was not doing so well with the more homogenous Las Vegas clientele, and he hated it more and more.

After one particularly venomous performance where he attacked the MGM audience for about five minutes, a reviewer for the local newspaper reported on it in the paper the following day. Whether it was because of this review or because of a number of other related factors, George's four-year engagement at the MGM Grand came to an end. In 2005, George and I would begin a one-year stint at the Stardust Hotel. (see? I'm not the only one in show business who keeps getting fired.)

After George got out of rehab, he did his first week of shows at the Stardust. I was fairly nervous about how these shows would go, knowing his feelings for the town in general coupled with his recent sobriety, but to my relief he seemed to enjoy these audiences much better than the ones at the MGM. The Stardust was a little farther removed from the heart of the Las Vegas strip, and it seemed that more of his die-hard fans were making the effort to seek him out at the Stardust than the more "touristy" crowds at the MGM. Maybe we had finally found a home in Vegas.

That warm, tingly glow lasted only a few months. As 2005 progressed, George was once again getting irritable with the Vegas audiences. He wasn't tearing into them as fiercely as he had at the MGM, but it was clear that he wasn't enjoying himself and was just going through the motions.

There was another change that was going on with George. Where once he had seemed to be one of the happiest and most energetic comedians I'd ever met, there was a definite pattern emerging where he had become more closed off, more aloof, less joyful. He seemed to tire more easily and not get as much as a charge out of performing. This was amazing to me. George had always reminded me more than a little bit of Johnny Carson, who seemed to get his vitality from the very act of doing the Tonight Show every night. When Carson retired, many comedians were sure he would take a little time off and then return to some form of show business vehicle, because he seemed to be the type who needed to perform. George always fit into that same class for me.

I would watch him typing on his computer, coming up with material, organizing it into bits, working on it, expanding it, chipping away until it he got it right, then working it out on stage and refining it some more. It gave him great pleasure, and watching him do it, you could imagine him keeping at it till his last breath.

We performed in Houston Texas that summer. George came offstage and into the car where he, as of late, collapsed into the back seat in a tired heap. Not so long ago he would have bounded offstage and into the car, excited about the audience, saying "Yeah, they were great, that new piece is working great!," etc. etc. and then called Sally. Now he just stared straight ahead. Jerry was next to him and said "Next time we play Houston, I'm gonna book a different theater." George turned to him and said, "When are we playing Houston again?," to which Jerry replied, "Three years." George shook his head and said, "I'm not gonna be on the road in three years."

That comment hit me like a thunderbolt. Could the indestructible, unstoppable George Carlin actually be thinking of retiring?

As the tour went on, things went from bad to worse and I figured that I should start looking around for other work, just in case things started getting really bad. I started to explore alternative avenues, but there were slim pickings out there in the comedy world. Things had changed since the '80's when the comedy clubs were thriving and I was sort of a name on the circuit. Now, even though I was known a bit from my association with George, I had been off the comedy club circuit for such a long time that it seemed an uphill battle to get back into it. I hoped desperately that George would pull out of this funk he was in and get back to his old self, but it wasn't happening. George did his 13th HBO Special in November while battling a problem with his throat that made speaking difficult. And then in December, I was informed that he had decided he would not do the Stardust in Las Vegas in 2006. That meant twelve weeks of work were down the drain just like that.

In December of 2005, I got another fateful call...George was canceling the remainder of the December tour because he had suffered from congestive heart failure and was in the hospital.

The doctors put a stent in his artery and he was on the road to recovery, but the writing by now was definitely on the wall. George would be canceling all of January's dates, and would be cutting his touring schedule by half for the rest of the year. That was bad enough, but the worst of it for me came soon afterward like a kick in the stomach.

George was going to start using other comedians to open for him. I was gone.

Enter Clear Channel...

In March of 2006 I got a phone call from Jerry Hamza. I remember how it began very clearly. It started like this:

> JERRY: "Dennis? Yeah, it's Jerry. Listen, I guess you know I've been dealing with Clear Channel lately and there's been some changes going on. We've decided to go another way with the opening act situation. I talked to George and he agrees we need to go another way."

That's the only part I remember clearly. I'm amazed at how deeply this affects me still as I write it many years later. Not only the fact that I was being fired after so many years and after having been recently told that I was "part of the family," but at the utter coldness of it. I do vaguely remember bits and pieces of phrases from that phone call..."you can finish out the tour till May," "Nothing we can do," "Yeah George knows, he's fine with it," etc. etc. George was fine with it? Really?

As I mentioned before, in a conversation I'd had with George at the MGM Grand in 2002, I had asked him point blank how secure my job was. The reason I felt the need to ask him this at the time was because Jerry and I had had an argument over something that I don't even remember anymore, but I do remember it made me fearful and paranoid about my future with the organization. When I approached George about my status, he had told me, "As long as I'm doing this, you will be my opening act." It gave me great comfort to hear that. George had never lied to me, and I knew he wouldn't, because I knew he was fond of me and cared about me and my family. I also believed he liked my comedy and felt I enhanced the show.

And yet, after eighteen years together, I was being replaced. Not completely, not immediately, but for at least half of whatever shows George would decide to do and possibly for more than that. The reason I was being replaced was Clear Channel, the monolithic radio network. The head honchos at Clear Channel had become so powerful in promoting George's shows and getting tickets sold that they had begun to flex their muscles, and demanded that George start using some of the comedians they favored to open the show. Apparently, since they were so instrumental in getting people in the seats, there was little George could do about it. He needed them.

Nevertheless, I was still devastated. After eighteen years of loyalty and friendship, I was being thrown overboard by, ironically, the very same kind of corporate entity that George railed about often in his performances. I had called and left him a voice mail, pleading with him to at least let me finish out the year with him before cutting me loose. I had reminded him about what he'd said about me "always being his opening act." I didn't even consider pleading with Jerry, because his tone had been so cold and bloodless on that horrible phone call that I could sense it would be useless.

Nothing. I heard nothing from George. For at least a week.

Finally, after what seemed like an eternity, he emailed me. He explained what was happening and how he needed to go along with Clear Channel for economic reasons, and that his days of touring would probably be ending soon anyway. He obviously felt bad, and reiterated that feeling when I saw him at our next gig in Eau Claire Wisconsin. He offered to help me out financially if and when he could and told me that our friendship meant a lot to him. But it was obvious...I had reached the end of the road with yet another in a long string of headliners. I did my show in Eau Claire, walked out of the theater, and didn't see or hear from George Carlin for a long time.

2006 and Beyond

I had somehow survived 2006 relatively intact. In times like these, it's true that you find out who your friends are, and I had some good ones. Elayne Boosler, who was always there for me when I needed someone to talk to and had a legendary reputation for helping out people in need, certainly came through for me here. Elayne was at the time a substitute host for Stephanie Miller on her radio show for the occasional weeks that Stephanie would take a vacation, and would bring me on as a co-host and pay me out of her own pocket. My pal Ron Shock, a great friend and a great guy and one of the best comedians out there, came to my rescue and hooked me up with all of his comedy club connections and got me back into the club scene. Another comedian friend, Chris Bliss, helped me sign on with his cruise ship agent, and so I started doing the cruise ships as well. It was gratifying to know that there were great people out there who were willing and able to help me out in a time of need. My income was less than half of what it used to be, but with some major belt-tightening I could still make ends meet and support my family. It looked like I would be okay.

In 2007 I got a call from Ashley Hamza, Jerry's daughter, who I guess was doing some work in the office and had been assigned to handle this phone call to me. She wanted to know if I was available to do some upcoming one-nighters with George. I was speechless.

Really? Of course, I'd be glad to!

I was offered a random collection of dates in California, Texas, and a few other places, about ten in all. Plus I was offered a string of dates at the Orleans Hotel in Las Vegas that George was now doing (I guess he had gotten over his Vegas hatred...I assumed they must have given him an offer he couldn't refuse). I was surprised, pleased, cautious, confused, and a bunch of other adjectives that don't immediately come to mind. I had no idea what was happening, and I wasn't sure how I felt about all this given the circumstances. But a gig was a gig, and my family still had a fondness for being housed and clothed and fed, so I accepted all the offers willingly.

The first date I had been offered was at the Grove Theater in Anaheim, California. Peggy drove up with me, for moral support as well as companionship. I was very nervous, not knowing what to expect. Would Jerry be there? Would he be friendly? Would he be cold? And how would George be? Would he even know I was on the date?

Peggy and I went backstage and ran smack into Jerry, who said hello and extended his hand. We talked for a while, and he asked how I was doing. Then he told me The Clear Channel deal would be expiring in a year or so and that I could expect to be put back on some dates, although I would no longer be George's exclusive guy. "Some dates" would be better than "No dates" I figured. And besides, it was beginning to look like I'd entered a phase where I was finally doing shows on my own. Even though the money was nowhere near as good, I was sort of enjoying this new era of being able to do full one-hour shows in clubs and other venues as a headliner. So I was pretty much okay with this arrangement.

And then I went over to the other side of the stage to say hi to George.

We hugged and he was glad to see me, but there was a reticence I had not noticed in the old days. There was none of the joking around, none of the in-jokes and the belly-laughs. He seemed quiet, almost pensive and withdrawn. But I could tell he was happy I was on the date and it was genuinely good to see him again.

As I slowly worked my way back into this partial reconciliation, I couldn't help noticing how different things seemed. The stints in rehab and the withdrawal from addictions I guess had been bad enough, but now George seemed to be suffering silently from something else which I could only assume was his heart condition. There was no possibility of visiting his dressing room unannounced like I used to. His door backstage was always closed, and his privacy was to be respected. Even when I started doing the dates in Las Vegas at the Orleans Hotel with him, he would show up backstage and quickly say hello, and then disappear into his dressing room. Occasionally he would show up in a good mood and display some of the old fire and mischievousness, but that was rare. He was sick, and he had aged, and I felt bad for him.

But even with all that, once he got on stage, the years dropped away, just like they had for Bob Hope at the Comedy Hall of Fame Awards, and he was as amazing as ever. He had done his 14th HBO Special and was already at work on his next show, and the new stuff was excellent. And the comparative lack of energy that was apparent backstage dissipated once he was in his element. The body language, the facial expressions, the power and flexibility in his voice, the passion for what he was saying, it was all there. And the material was as raw and unapologetic as ever. That was a great thing to see.

* * * * *

In April of 2008 I opened for George during his 4-day run at the Orleans hotel. It was a good run and I was looking forward to the next one which was to be in three months or so.

In June Peggy and the kids and I were driving home from attending a relatives' wedding in Grass Valley California when my cell phone rang. Peg answered it. It was Ira, the New York limo driver who had driven George whenever he had been in the New York area over the years and who had become a good friend during that time. He had just gotten a call from a hysterical Sally Wade that George had died.

I had hardly any reaction at all. I was numb for a long time. I'd have to say his death didn't come as a complete shock because I knew he was battling all sorts of ailments in his final years. But some part of me still didn't believe he was actually gone and still has trouble coping with it to this day. I still have dreams where George and I are doing a gig in a theater somewhere and hanging out before the show, and then wake up and realize that, even though it seemed unbelievably real, it had been a dream.

It was actually a good thing that Ira called because I never heard anything about his death from anyone else in George's inner circle.

Once again, as with Rodney, about a week later I was in Fort Worth Texas doing a club when Jerry's assistant called to tell me there would be a memorial service at Jerry's house the next day, and would I like to come. I couldn't cancel my club date on such late notice, and sent Peggy and my son Ian in my stead. They told me it was a nice service for about a hundred or so people. Bill Maher, Lewis Black and Garry Shandling were all there and each talked briefly about George and what he had meant to them.

I stared at the ceiling in a hotel room in Texas at two in the morning and thought about a guy who once stole my dressing room carrots and left me horrifying notes while I was on stage.

Chapter 37: Joan Rivers One More Time

In late 2008 I got an offer from Joan Rivers' agent to open for her for one night at the Tropicana Hotel in Las Vegas. Even though the money wasn't great, I decided to treat it like a paid vacation and accepted the offer. I took my two kids with me and we drove to Las Vegas together.

It was good to see Joan again. She of course by this time was enjoying a resurgence in popularity and was doing very well. We talked backstage and had some laughs, and then I introduced her to my two teenagers. She was very funny with them.

> JOAN: Do you get along with your father?
> KIDS: Yeah.
> JOAN: Do you like what he does for a living?
> KIDS: Yeah, it's pretty cool.
> JOAN: He doesn't embarrass you around the house?
> KIDS: No.
> JOAN: It's okay, you can tell me.
> KIDS: He doesn't.
> JOAN: Good. (to me) Great kids, you raised them right.

I did my show and then went out with my kids to watch her. Her show was dirtier and raunchier than I'd ever remembered, and the audience loved it. A normal father would never had let his kids see a show like that, but my kids had literally grown up in the shadow of Carlin, and Joan's show was mild by comparison.

The next year I did two nights in St. Louis with Joan. This time she was surrounded by her entourage (some things never change) so we didn't have time to socialize at all. She blew the roof off the theater that night.

The next day I rode with Joan and her assistants to the airport in her limousine. We talked and laughed and then she gave me a scarf from her personal QVC collection, saying "here, give this to

Peggy." The limo pulled up to the gate, we said our goodbyes, and she was gone.

Chapter 38: Skipping Ahead...

As of this writing, here I am in 2020, in the teeth of a global pandemic, trying to keep as active as I can, which these days means binge-watching "Ozark" and "Schitt's Creek" on Netflix, walking around the block fifteen times, and going to the MacDonald's drive-thru for my coffee fix and to just get out of the house occasionally. Work for so many performers is on hold, and as a result I'm left with a ton of free time to pause and reflect...

A lot had happened in the last 12 years. We lost Joan Rivers to a botched plastic surgery, the irony of which I'm sure she would have joked about mercilessly on stage had she survived it. Tom Jones was now one of the only remaining superstars I had been lucky enough to tour with extensively in this "accidental" journey of mine. During a showcase where I performed in Florida, the legendary comedian Dick Capri introduced me this way:

> "Our next performer has had an interesting career. He opened for Rodney Dangerfield. Rodney's dead. He opened for Joan Rivers. Joan is dead. He opened for George Carlin. Carlin is dead. (pause) I'm afraid to bring him out."

My agent Fred Suss had left show business years ago, so I was now booking myself, unable to bring myself to retire and hop off this addictive and still enjoyable comedy train, not so much as an opening act but as a headliner in comedy clubs and on cruise ships and for a time as "Joey Bishop" in the Las Vegas based production of "The Rat Pack Is Back." I was still making a decent living at it, and my kids were grown, out of the house and gainfully employed, so Peggy and I didn't have to worry about feeding, clothing, and housing them anymore.

Billy Davis/Marilyn McCoo, Melissa Manchester, Charo...

Every once in a while, I still got to open for some legendary stars. I would play what was known as the "condo" circuit in Florida, which entailed performing in a string of some really beautiful theaters that were set up inside communities of condominiums that catered to retirees. You might think that fact would terrify me, judging by the reaction I had gotten in the Catskills years ago, but there was one major difference...I was getting closer and closer to these audience's ages. They all knew who Mick Jagger was now!

I toured these condo theaters with Billy Davis and Marilyn McCoo in 2015, husband and wife singers who were members of "The Fifth Dimension" during their heyday, scoring such hits as "Up Up and Away," "One Less Bell to Answer" and "Aquarius." They were great performers and nice people, even when I mistook Marilyn's dressing room for my own on our first night, prompting her to sweetly say, "So nice to meet you, but could you not get undressed in here?"

And imagine my joy when I was booked in the condos two years later to open once again for the great Melissa Manchester. On the first night of the tour, I introduced myself and reminded her that I had once opened her show in the Catskills and had bombed terribly, and how nice she had been to me, and then waited for her to laugh heartily and say "Oh yes, I remember!," which of course, she didn't. Happily, this tour went much better than our previous pairing, and a splendid time was had by all involved.

My most recent opening foray in the condos was in the beginning of 2020, right before the world was attacked by the invisible Covid19 gremlins, opening for Charo. Charo is one of those celebrities I remembered from my childhood on shows like the Tonight Show and Merv Griffin and Mike Douglas, a Spanish "sexpot" as she was called back in the day, who sang and danced and played flamenco guitar astoundingly well, and who had a catch phrase, "coochy-coochy," which, as far as I could tell, meant "coochy-coochy." She was still an icon for these audiences, supremely energetic, talented, sweet and endearing and, no joke, really good on the guitar, which she played beautifully during the second half of her show. We got along well, to the point that as the tour progressed, she would request that I do more and more time up front. I was originally slated to do about 20 minutes, but after several days and a stubborn sore throat she was fighting, she asked that I stretch it to 30. And then 40. And then 45. I was half-expecting her to one day hand me a wig, a slinky dress and a guitar and say, in her thick accent, "Denis, you are an impressionist, yes? Do the whole show as me, I need a night off."

Norm MacDonald

During A Christmas party at the Southpoint Hotel in Las Vegas in 2018, Michael Libonati, the entertainment director for the hotel, asked me if I'd be interested in opening for Norm MacDonald for his upcoming weekend engagement at the beginning of 2019. I accepted, if I remember correctly, before the words "Hey, would you be interested..." left Michael's lips.

Like so many comedy fans, I just adored Norm's standup. From "Weekend Update" on SNL to his appearances on Letterman and Conan and everywhere in between, he was always one of those guys who could make me laugh out loud no matter where I was or what mood I was in. I had met him briefly several times at the Improv in L.A. during the '80's, but a lot of time had passed since then and, as I paced in my Southpoint dressing room that first night, I didn't even know if he'd remember me. Norm came into the green room area and from behind my closed door I heard Michael say, "Hey Norm, good to see you. Dennis Blair is here." I heard Norm respond, "Dennis Blair! That's great, Where is he?" Whereupon I stepped out and gave Norm a big hug, just like we'd been solid buddies for the last 35 years. .He had two young writers from his recent talk show with him, and I greeted them as well.

After some pleasantries and reminiscing, I asked Norm how long he wanted me to do, figuring he would want anywhere from 20 to 30 minutes. To my surprise, he pointed to the two writers and said, "I dunno, these guys will go on and two ten minutes each, and then you can do...how about 15?"

Aha. So I was about to be the 15-minute closing act for the trio of opening acts Norm had decided to use. Suddenly. Without warning. Hey, no problem, 15 minutes. I think I can probably squeeze that out.

The two guys he had brought along were nice guys, funny, personable. But the first guy on the stage that night had apparently not done standup very much, if at all. He walked out in front of the waiting-to-see-Norm crowd (none of us had any billing of course. Occupational hazard), and he had a tough time getting laughs. He struggled valiantly, but I could tell he was nervous and wanted to get this over with as quickly as possible. The audience went along with it for a while, probably figuring Norm was up next.

Norm was not up next.

Norm was in the green room backstage, watching a football game on TV and talking to me about the intricacies of the game and his love of gambling and how he really couldn't afford to lose the money he had bet on it and the nine other games he had placed bets on.

Meanwhile the second guy took the stage, and he was cooler and calmer and apparently a little more experienced than the first guy. He did fine, but the audience was getting a little fidgety. They reeeeally wanted to see Norm. So naturally, why not put on another barrier to the main attraction?

Norm was still chatting amiably with me when I got my one-minute call. I turned to Norm as he was trying to explain the over/under in words a sports nerd like me couldn't possibly understand...

"Norm, I'm on."

"Oh, you are? Okay."

The second guy introduced me, and since I only had fifteen minutes, and since I had years of experience working in front of hundreds of fidgety, anxious audiences as an opening act under my belt, I assessed the situation, threw up in my mouth a little, and decided to go out full bore, guns blazing, to get this crowd on my side quickly. It worked. They got into it, laughing, applauding, and yelling out requests until I said "Enjoy Norm!" and exited the stage, thinking Norm was coming right out.

Norm was not coming right out.

The first guy was forced to come again to do five minutes, because Norm was still glued to that TV screen, watching the game, and would not leave until he saw how it would end and if he would be on the winning end of the bet he'd made. Meanwhile, the first guy was out there battling an audience that was getting very antsy, even hostile. Some of them were yelling, "Where's Norm? We didn't come here to see you!" I think two of them were the guy's parents.

A stage hand came back and told Norm this guy was not doing well, but Norm would have none of it.

"Tell him to keep going."

I offered to go back onstage and help, but Norm was insistent... "No, he's gotta get through this on his own. I already told him to do his time. Besides, I gotta watch this next play. And then I have to take a crap."

The play ended. Badly. Norm cursed, then went into the bathroom and closed the door.

I went out to the side of the stage to watch the comic flailing, fighting for his life. He kept looking anxiously offstage, hoping Norm was coming to the rescue. We were all helpless.

Finally, after an eternity, Norm emerged, strode out onto the stage, and began his brilliant show as the comic happily scurried off.

All of us opening acts that night went out to dinner with Norm after his incredibly funny show. Everyone was in a good mood, including the hapless first guy, who had been subjected to so much torture but seemed okay with it and completely at ease. I came to realize that Norm wasn't being cruel or insensitive by exposing his friend to this ordeal. I really think that Norm wanted this guy to take a crash course on how to deal with a hostile audience, in case standup was something he was serious about and really wanted to pursue. And he had survived, after all.

On the final night of the engagement, I said a warm goodbye to Norm, secure in the knowledge that I would never, under any circumstances, bet on football.

AFTERWORD

As Jackie Mason would always say when nearing the end of a show, 'Well, that's it." At least for now. As I said, as of this writing we are in the midst of the Coronavirus pandemic that has stopped the world cold, and protests and unrest that have made this country and the rest of the world take a good, hard look at some changes that are desperately needed. Strange days indeed…

As for me, before the world came crashing down I was still on the road doing the club-comedy thing as well as the occasional opening act turn, and I had also revitalized my dormant music career, performing in bands and shows in and around Las Vegas, doing cover songs again and writing original tunes and putting them out on albums (a jazz one called "Hapless Romantic" and two country/pop/blues ones, "Music from Big Brick" and "Songs From Captivity." They're all on itunes and spotify and amazon and other streaming services…check 'em out if you can! I also have CD's which I can sell from the trunk of my car, as soon as I'm allowed to go outside again.)

As I sit here in isolation, no one knows how things are going to turn out, or even when entertainment will be coming back, and what form it will take when it does. All we can do is hope. We've gone through hard times before, and we've always gotten through them. Hopefully by the time you're reading this we'll have gotten back to some kind of normal and I'll be back on tour with my clown show and my music.

Speaking of hope, I hope you enjoyed this little memoir of my life on the road with some of the most legendary and gifted stars the world had the pleasure of getting to know. Even though there were some rough times along the way, they were also some of the best times of my life and I'm glad I got to take part in them. And now, if you'll excuse me, "Shawshank Redemption" is cued up on my watch list.

Onward!
Dennis

www.ingramcontent.com/pod-product-compliance
Lightning Source LLC
Chambersburg PA
CBHW071001160426
43193CB00012B/1871